SAME
PLACE,
MORE
SPACE

NOV   2011

SAME PLACE, MORE SPACE

50 PROJECTS TO MAXIMIZE EVERY ROOM IN THE HOUSE

By Karl Champley

with Karen Kelly

Illustrations by Arthur Mount

CHRONICLE BOOKS

SAN FRANCISCO

LIBRARY OF CONGRESS CATALOGING-IN-PUBLICATION DATA
CHAMPLEY, KARL.
  SAME PLACE, MORE SPACE : 50 PROJECTS TO MAXIMIZE EVERY ROOM
 IN THE HOUSE / KARL CHAMPLEY; ILLUSTRATIONS BY ARTHUR MOUNT.
   P. CM.
  ISBN 978-0-8118-7473-1
  1. DWELLINGS—REMODELING. I. TITLE.
 TH4816.C425 2011
 643'.7—DC22
 2010023731

MANUFACTURED IN CHINA
DESIGNED BY ANDREW SCHAPIRO
TYPESETTING BY JANIS REED AND HAPPENSTANCE TYPE-O-RAMA
TYPESET IN SWISS BT AND UNITED

10 9 8 7 6 5 4 3 2 1

CHRONICLE BOOKS LLC
680 SECOND STREET
SAN FRANCISCO, CALIFORNIA 94107
WWW.CHRONICLEBOOKS.COM

TABLE OF CONTENTS

INTRODUCTION

Do you feel cramped? Do your rooms seem too small? Is there too little storage in your house? Do you feel you've outgrown your home? I have good news: it's not that your house is too small; you simply haven't discovered its hidden assets—behind walls, under floorboards, and above your head, to name a few. *Same Place, More Space* demonstrates how to achieve the seemingly impossible—make the house or apartment you are living in larger, more functional, accommodating, and enjoyable *without adding on*.

How do I know where to find the overlooked areas in houses, condos, and apartments? For more than twenty-seven years, I have plied my skills as a master builder, building consultant, certified home inspector, certified environmental home inspector, author, carpenter, contractor, and as host on the DIY and HGTV network's *DIY to the Rescue* and *Wasted Spaces*, as well as many other how-to, home improvement and renovation programs, including shows for Habitat for Humanity and the popular *Home Live* national radio show.

Along with my on-air experience helping homeowners reclaim their domestic sanity, I have built, renovated, and remodeled hundreds of homes and commercial properties, squeezing out every available square inch in pied-à-terres and mansions;

spaces have room for everything you need. My wife and I built a house in Los Angeles, and while it was being constructed, we, along with our young son, lived on the construction site for three years in a 427-square-foot space that will eventually go back to being the home's garage.

Many of our friends felt sorry for us when we told them the size of the space we lived in, but after they saw it they felt very differently—some were even envious that we could have such a pleasant existence in such a cozy and compact space. There was room for a California king-size bed, a fully loaded kitchen (full-size fridge and stove, sink, island, seating), a bathroom, a sitting room, and a sleeping area for our son (if only he had slept in it!). That living experience really proved to me that it is possible to be happy, comfortable, and organized no matter how big (or small) your home. I want to inspire you to feel this way, too.

The majority of projects in *Same Place, More Space* are minimally disruptive, invading only unused space and not everyday life. Adding an office to the garage doesn't turn the house upside down; transforming one bedroom into two won't disrupt the household for weeks or days; making kitchen cupboards work harder cuts clutter and makes mealtimes more fun, and believe it or not

USING WHAT YOU ALREADY HAVE IS NOT JUST A PRACTICAL UNDERTAKING; IT'S AN INVENTIVE AND AESTHETIC ENTERPRISE.

fire stations and factories; colleges and restaurants. I can attest to the fact that big renovation, or "reno," projects can take a toll on families and relationships, with workmen coming and going and kitchens and bathrooms being out of commission for weeks or months on end. *Same Place, More Space* shows you how to make improving your home a pleasurable enterprise, with limited intrusion on your everyday life.

No matter how big our homes are, we rarely feel as if we have all the space we need. Yet everyone always has more room than they think they do, even those who live in tiny townhouses, modulars, or studios. I know firsthand that even the smallest

you can still cook dinner while the project is being completed. Using what you already have is not just a practical undertaking; it's an inventive and aesthetic enterprise. I'll show you how to customize any space and make it more handsome, too.

On many episodes of *DIY to the Rescue* and *Wasted Spaces*, and in my life as a professional builder, I meet creative, enthusiastic people who live in what I call Monopoly houses. Their homes have standard baseboards and trim, plain sheetrock walls, and predictable "footprints" (first floor: kitchen, gathering or family room, powder room, master suite; second floor: three bedrooms, one bath). Every project in *Same Place, More Space* has visual integrity as well as function and provides opportunity for you to customize your home to your own particular taste. Appearance is an important aspect of space-making projects. When you carve out spaces to suit both individual needs *and* tastes, your home will start to work for you.

Same Place, More Space shares more than three dozen ways to add more to and make more of every space in your home. The majority of the projects are do-it-yourself (DIY) friendly, but a few need advice and help from a professional or a handy friend (if you don't have one, make one!). Plus, there's advice on decluttering, quick fixes for storage woes, construction basics, and lots of tips on building smart.

Each project has separate tools and materials lists; has estimates for the approximate time required to complete the task or item (whether that's a few hours, a day, a weekend, or longer); and includes a skill-level rating of 1 to 5 hammers (see the Skill-Level Key box at right). Some projects have "subprojects" and "optional" steps that show how to add more detail or a particular finish.

Part 1, specifically in Chapters 1 and 2, has advice on getting started by examining your home and space/storage needs. Chapter 3 includes descriptions of all the major tools used in the book, a discussion of types of wood and other common building stock materials, and an easy-to-use metric conversion chart. Part 2 details instructions for all the DIY projects, with helpful drawings and illustrations of the finished product. Part 3 tackles larger space-saving and space-making issues that involve structural changes and the help of a few pros (or, again, skilled friends). A resources and suppliers section gives you the heads up on brands, manufacturers, and sources that I trust. Throughout the book, you'll find useful tips; these "secrets of the pros" make jobs run faster, cleaner, and safer—and end more successfully.

I hope that you find this book to be an inspiring and practical manual that you can use for your current home, holiday house, apartment, or condominium, as well as for planning future residences. So please join me on this journey to discover all of the hidden spaces in your place!

SKILL-LEVEL KEY
Each project in this book has a difficulty rating. Here's the simple key:

1 hammer: Simple; requires homeowner-level rudimentary DIY skills, including measuring, nailing and screwing, and sanding and painting.

2 hammers: Basic; requires tinkerer's-level DIY skills, such as using the full range of hand tools (handsaws, wrenches, pliers, clamps, combination squares, and so on) and constructing basic butt joints.

3 hammers: Moderate; requires carpenter's apprentice-level DIY skills, such as using small power tools (drills and jigsaws) and nail guns, accomplishing simple demolition, and constructing mitered corners.

4 hammers: Advanced; requires carpenter-level DIY skills, such as knowledge of and comfort with large power tools (circular, reciprocal, and table saws, etc.), and sometimes another pair of knowing hands to help assemble larger projects.

5 hammers: Challenging; requires carpenter-to master carpenter-level DIY skills, such as experience with house framing and construction, as well as another pair of skilled helping hands for complex demolition and construction and heavy-duty hauling and assembly.

PART

UNCOVER YOUR HOME'S HIDDEN ASSETS

Planning is essential. In my experience, homeowners who tackle home improvement projects without spending time preparing and planning often don't finish them or are unhappy with the results. This is especially true for space planning, which is probably the most complicated aspect of expanding your space. That's why the first three chapters of this book are devoted to getting you ready, willing, and able to discover and exploit the extra space in your home. In the next few chapters, you'll learn how to give up stuff and sort out your true storage needs. It's worth taking the extra time to get it right before you begin; this way, you're much more likely to successfully complete every project you take on.

01
A CLEAN SLATE

The *Same Place, More Space* process begins with thinking about what you truly want in your home. It's hard to honestly judge space when looking through a distorted lens of clutter and chaos. My goal is to help you streamline your belongings to only those that make your life easier and happier.

The cleaning-out process goes hand in hand with locating and exploiting every inch of space you have. A little soul searching and honesty is in order. Most homeowners whom I have helped through this process have shown me that getting rid of clutter can be a heart-wrenching task. Assessing your life through your possessions is deeply emotional. I've even had to stop the camera from rolling on a few occasions because people have become too distressed over having to part with their belongings. But, ultimately, even the most emotional homeowners tell me they felt liberated and less anxious after cleaning out the clutter. It's funny how that works; the more space you make for yourself, the more room you have for emotional and psychological abundance.

And one more thing—if the only things you undertake after reading this book are a good decluttering and one or two simple projects, you will have accomplished a lot. We all need to be more "energy efficient," and, as we become more organized, this will happen. You will have increased the value of your home also. So let's get cracking.

CLEAN OUT

I am not expecting that you will toss out family photographs, children's artwork, heirlooms, or keepsakes—at least not without considerable thought. The *Same Place, More Space* philosophy is not just about creating more room for everyday tasks and household obligations. I want you to find more ways to indulge your passions, have fun at home, and enjoy the possessions that mean the most to you. So, no, I'm not going to make you feel guilty about your personal shoe museum. I'd never make a woman toss out her collection of designer high heels or insist that a mate pitch his vintage bamboo fishing rods *if that's what is truly important to her or him*. It's a matter of choice: keep what you love and lose the rest.

You cannot get through clutter in two minutes. Start with a room that you know you can finish in a day or an afternoon and move on to the next room only when you are done. Smaller goals, especially when starting a clean out, result in greater satisfaction (completion!) and encourage you to keep going. For example, a bedroom, a bathroom, or the kitchen may be an easier place to begin than a family room, basement, or garage.

Choose a day or a weekend when you know you have time to devote to cleaning. Mark the date in your calendar as you would any other important appointment so you don't double book yourself. If you're serious about getting more space out of your place, you have to be serious about this stage! On the chosen day, designate an area of your room to separate items into categories. The organizational formula I like best is to create signs and bins for the following five groups:

+ Keep
+ Sell
+ Donate
+ Recycle
+ Trash

As you sift through items, go with your gut and think about this: Home economists have found that people use 20 percent of the things they own about 80 percent of the time. Ask yourself: "Am I really using this item?" Then, don't agonize over every decision. Make a quick first choice, remembering that after your initial sort, you'll have time to circle back later and reassess items and switch them around (mainly out of the Keep pile and into a Donate or Recycle pile!). This makes the initial sorting go much faster.

KEEP

In my experience, the Keep pile tends to be the biggest heap of the lot, simply because we have so much trouble getting rid of things, including stuff we don't like and never use! At this point, don't worry too much about the size of the pile; we will come back around to it in a bit. For now keep anything that you use every day, that brings enjoyment to your life, or that makes living easier. For example, this pile might include clothing you wear (and that fits) for work or pleasure; artwork that makes you happy; dishes that are not chipped or cracked on which you enjoy serving food; furniture that's in good condition; family photos and other important documents that hold important memories; financial records; and so on. Tip: If you have even an ounce of doubt about something, put it in the Donate pile and move on to the next item.

SELL

In the Sell pile, put all of the items that you could sell at a garage or tag sale, take to a consignment shop, or list in a local classified ad or online. That would include everything that's in good, usable condition that you no longer use or enjoy—from gloves, belts, and shoes to dishes, appliances, furniture, and even toys your kids have outgrown. Use the money you earn from selling these items to finance your new space-making projects.

DONATE

The Donate pile should consist of everything that you haven't used in the last year, including duplicates (how many blenders do you really need?), as well as building materials, old tools, and anything else that you come across in your purge. Donating to certain organizations can give you some tax relief. At the back of the book, you'll find a list of resources (see page 249) for donating specific and commonly discarded items.

RECYCLE

The Recycle pile should contain items that can no longer be used as-is but may either need to be recycled into something else, repaired, or used as "parts." Even old wall-to-wall carpeting and left-over construction materials (play sand, 2x4s, wire mesh) can be recycled. See the resources chapter for information on where to recycle these kinds of items (see page 250).

TRASH

As you go through rooms, you will inevitably collect the detritus of everyday life—bits of paper with mysterious numbers written on them, dust bunnies, broken items that are beyond recycling, and, yes, you may even discover peach pits, plastic drinking cups, and stale pretzels. And that's just the short list of somewhat embarrassing items we've found behind homeowners' sofas and between the cushions (and it includes items I cannot mention). Put that trash in a bag!

REASSESS

Now it's time to look at your Keep pile again. Was I right? Is the Keep pile the biggest? Okay, let's deal with making it smaller. Separate the Keep pile items into these subcategories:

Daily Use

Weekly Use

Monthly Use

Occasional Use

Never Use

On the Fence

Ease of access and organized storage is key for a functional home.

Once you've sorted the Keep pile, place the Daily, Weekly, and Monthly items (promise me you'll be honest about this stuff) in another room or area. You can put them away later, when you're done with the rest of your so-called Keep items. Focus on the Occasional, Never, and On the Fence items. One by one, go through these items, asking yourself which ones you can get rid of in one of the aforementioned ways. Don't let guilt ("It was Grandma's" or "My best friend gave it to me") sway you, especially if you have no use or real love for the object.

Remember, too, that most of Aunt Rachel's antiques are not all that valuable. So unless you sincerely love that 1920 oak sideboard with the nasty gargoyle carvings, rest assured it will not end up making someone else rich on *Antiques Roadshow*. Besides, relatives and friends would rather see you living well than being weighed down by their castoffs and gifts. One way to test items: Pack them away in a storage system like 1-800-Pack-Rat and store them for six months to a year. Living nicely without them means you really don't need them. If you didn't notice they were gone, it is safe to get rid of them. Remember: our material possessions can tend to own us instead of us owning them, so my golden rule is "lose it if you haven't used it in a year." As for the On the Fence pile, you know deep down inside that you should pass these things along. So why don't you sleep on it? Tomorrow, after you've had your coffee or tea, place those odds and ends in the Sell, Donate, or Recycle piles. Go on; do it!

DEVELOP A CLEAN SCHEME

After a major declutter, an overall dust, sweep, vacuum, and wash is in order. Such a cleaning renews your commitment to keeping your space clutter free. And it's really quite simple. Again, a simple weekly chore chart makes ongoing washing, straightening, picking up, and putting away doable without being daunting, whether you're going it solo or enlisting the help of family or roommates. It's a bit old-fashioned, but what's wrong with using the wisdom of our grandparents?

TIP: The best way to maintain your decluttered lifestyle is to balance everything new you bring into the house by eliminating a similar item. For example, if you buy a new sweater, donate one from your existing wardrobe to charity. Likewise, if you purchase a new piece of furniture, donate one you no longer need to a charity. That way, you will keep your belongings in check and keep your clutter under control.

Living with my family (including a very active little boy) in less than 500 square feet for nearly three years showed me that keeping our possessions organized and put away when not in use and keeping all areas of the house clean and tidy made life easier. We knew where things were when we needed them, meals were easily prepared and happier, and everyday living was predictable in a good way; everyone could get ready for a busy day quickly and efficiently because of our daily maintenance routines.

BREATHE DEEPLY

If you start to feel very emotional or stressed out while sorting through your belongings, take a breather. Go outside, take a walk, or meet a friend for coffee and conversation. Are you afraid someone, such as a relative or friend, will feel hurt? Do you believe that you will lose a memory? If you are fortunate to still have your relatives, discuss this with them up front. This conversation can take a load off your shoulders.

Remember that you will never forget that special person or moment; if you are concerned that a memory will be lost when you let go of the object, take a photo of it and place it in a journal. A journal is much more personal than an item, can be passed on to future generations (who may not want that old silver-plate mirror or whatever), and takes up far less physical room in your life. Finally, know that passing along objects you don't really need or use is a beautiful deed. Remember that you are truly on a path to improving your life.

02
DREAMS VS. REALITY

Every DIY mission starts with a dream. What's yours? Formulate a wish list of space and storage needs and goals. But be realistic. Look at the way you really live, rather than the way you wished you lived. A walk-in closet, for example, may not be feasible right now, but you can do things to double the space you've got (see Chapter 6 for ideas). We can create a lot of space in our homes, but we can't turn a double-wide trailer into a mansion! Once you have your list in hand, you can identify how you can make those dreams come true in your particular space.

NEEDS AND REALITY COLLIDE

Now that your house is cleaned out and all extraneous items have left the premises, you're ready to assess the kind of extra space you really need. The first step is to place in the center of a room everything that you have decided to keep but that does not fit into existing storage.

Into what categories do these items mainly fall? For example, in the bedroom, is your excess mainly shoes, or is it T-shirts? In the kitchen, are your plates and glasses overflowing, or is the pantry unable to accommodate cans of tomatoes or sacks of rice? You see where I'm going here; it's going to be very clear to you what you need more room for. Most of these obvious storage issues will remain consistent, while temporary problems (such as where to put holiday gifts, rented ski equipment, or seasonal items) are just that. We can make a revolving space solution for that stuff, too, but let's focus on everyday life for now.

Next, make a list of every room or area in your home using the Master Space List worksheet (page 17). Underneath each heading, list all of the things you want to store in those spaces. Take a photocopy of this page and keep it because you will use it in the next chapter and throughout the book.

THE 360

Once you have a fairly accurate idea of what you need to store (or to get rid of in another round of clearing out), take a look around each room where those items will be placed. I call this "doing a 360," because I want you to examine the layout of the room, the existing storage, and the areas where you can carve out more storage. Your observations will tell you which projects in this book will fit your needs.

For example, if ten sweaters, fifteen pairs of shoes, and a few laptop bags and briefcases are sitting in the middle of your bedroom, you'll need to find space for them in your room—even if yours is a 10-by-12-foot bedroom with a small closet that you can't expand. While you may not be able to build a deeper closet, you can expand usable space above the high shelf in the closet by building one above it for out-of-season clothing and shoes, those laptop bags, and even important papers that you do not need on a regular basis.

You can also use space under floorboards, as well as space between closet wall studs to create shoe nooks, safe and hidden jewelry cubbies, and additional out-of-season clothing storage. If your bedroom shares a wall with a hall closet or a larger living space within your own walls, you may be able to go deeper in your closet by taking a foot (or more) of space from the room or closet on the other side of that wall. Part 2 has projects to help you do all of these things.

If your kitchen table is stacked with large cans of tomatoes, excess drinking glasses, and large serving trays and baking sheets, I'll help you scout out spaces in your kitchen, not visible right now, that can accommodate these items. My Toe Kick Drawers project (page 54) will give you ample room for all your large baking sheets and trays, while enclosing the space above your cupboards will give you loads of extra square footage when pantry items go on sale at the supermarket.

MAKE AN ACCURATE FLOOR PLAN

You may need to look at the way your rooms are laid out—sometimes moving things around can open up hidden space. I have seen so many bedrooms that actually had ample storage, which was only revealed by rearranging and purging furniture. Do you need every stick of furniture in the room? What clothes must be stored in the bedroom closet, and what items can be put away somewhere else? Seasonal sporting clothes, for example, or formal wear may be better placed in a hall closet or underneath the bed. Is the bed in the right area and placed at the correct angle for optimal floor space, natural light, and views?

On the next page, a before-and-after drawing shows just what I mean.

Defining your space is crucial. The foundation of every Same Place, More Space project requires accurate measurements, and that includes the dimensions of your rooms. A floor plan drawn to scale (¼ inch = 1 foot; see the Metric Conversion Chart, page 28, for metric equivalents) gives you a clear bird's-eye view of your room. While you can buy fancy software to create floor plans, I don't think it's necessary for our purposes. You can do just as well on your own. Most arts-and-crafts stores, and even home stores, carry furniture silhouettes that match the "¼ inch = 1 foot" scale, which will save you time when rearranging your room.

Two room arrangements. Room #2 makes better use of the space.

1

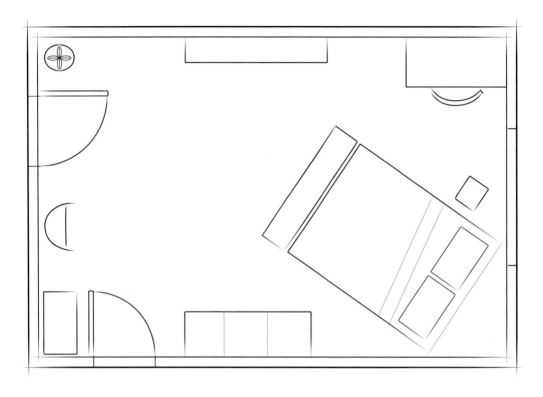

2

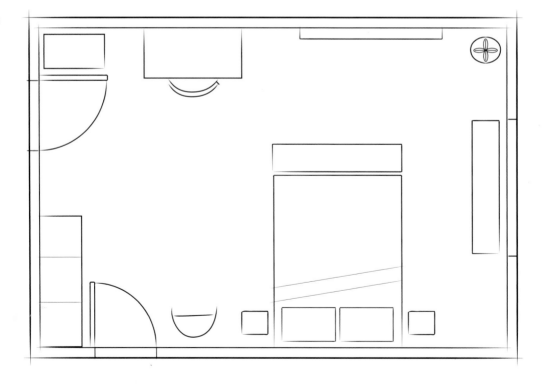

MASTER SPACE LIST

Foyer/Entryway	Hallway/Closet	Mudroom
Kitchen	Living Room	Family Room
Bathroom 1	Bathroom 2	Bathroom 3
Bedroom 1	Bedroom 2	Bedroom 3
Basement	Attic	Crawl Space
Garage	Other	Other

Custom-build your own closet to suit your lifestyle.

02: DREAMS VS. REALITY

You will need:

+ 25-foot flat-blade tape measure
+ Paper
+ Dark pencil sharpened to a point
+ ¼-inch graph paper
+ Eraser
+ T-square
+ Architect's ruler, which has six sides with different scale measurements
+ Furniture templates

Now, using the tape measure, measure and note the length and width of each room or space, including windows, doors, and closets. Also note where electrical outlets and cable or other wires enter the room. Measure twice to ensure accuracy. Jot down each measurement on a piece of paper. Transfer these measurements to your graph paper and include everything—from outlets to windows. When you feel you have created a clear and exact plan, make a few copies to work with. Keep the "master," or original, blank, in case you need more.

TIP: With accurate measurements, it's easy to calculate the area of any floor or wall, as follows:

Floor area = length of room × width of room

Wall area = height of wall × length of wall

Play with your furniture templates on paper until you get a plan that optimizes the floor and wall space. Doing your planning this way is much easier and less exhausting than moving real furniture around and about! Consider not only your space needs (you may have to eliminate one or more furniture pieces from the room) but also views, natural light, and navigation. While the bed may look good underneath a window, does this mean you have no outside view when lying in it—or does this positioning block off one half of the room from the other, making it hard to move around?

Likewise, in the kitchen, would a smaller table be a better idea, or would a round or square table versus a rectangular or oval shape be best? Perhaps a breakfast bar along an empty wall would give you the area you need to eat, especially if you have another dining area in the house. Would short-backed chairs provide more "visual" space than your current high-backed ones? Visual space is important, too—the less cluttered you feel in a space, the more likely you are to feel comfortable in it and use it to full advantage.

All of these are questions that a floor plan can help you answer. Once you have the furniture appropriately placed in the room, or items removed and/or replaced with more appropriate versions, you can move on to assessing the kind of spaces you need to create. Don't forget to take along your Master Space List!

03

THE PROJECT GAME PLAN

You can't wander into the redo and re-org wilderness without a map and a compass. Since you're already armed with floor plans and a Master Space List, the only thing left before you get started on projects is a Game Plan. A Game Plan helps pinpoint the projects in this book that suit your requirements. I never start a project without one, even if it's a basic list or rough sketch (thumbnail dipped in tar will work), because it enables me to create a budget, a timeline, and a breakdown of all the tools and materials necessary for the job.

A Game Plan will also minimize trips to the hardware store. You'll be able to prep in advance and have everything you need at hand. The other benefit of a Game Plan is knowing whether an individual project will take an afternoon, a day, a weekend, or longer. That means better time management—and chances are that you'll finish the project if you are able to estimate and schedule the needed time before you begin.

CALCULATE A REALISTIC BUDGET

Before you do anything else, determine how much you can spend right now on storage and space projects. No matter what your budget, you'll find projects you can achieve in this book. Some projects cost mostly time and effort (under-the-floorboard cubbies), while others require larger outlays of time, talent, skill, and cash (a mezzanine office or under-the-staircase storage). It's better to know what you can afford before you begin, so you won't get stuck with empty pockets or big budget overruns. Naturally, allow for price differences across regions and sources. (Some stores are less expensive than others!)

PRIORITIZE SPACE AND LIFESTYLE NEEDS

Okay, it's time for more lists (but, believe me, lists help). Think about what space you need to create Right Now and what space can wait for The Future. Do you need more storage in the kitchen now and, perhaps, another bedroom later? Or do you need more family or public space now? Are you starting a business? Then a home office is priority number one. Everything else can wait. Some of you might need to carve out a mudroom and storage area for your kids and their stuff, followed by a laundry area and more convenient food prep and storage area. Others may want to tackle a garage workshop and craft area first, followed by a guest room/home office. Some DIYers might need extra bedrooms followed by a hobby area, such as a wine cellar or a photo studio.

Once you have determined your budget and immediate storage needs, browse through the projects in Parts 2 and 3. Note the name and page numbers of each next to the storage issue on your Right Now list. Most of the projects for individual rooms (kitchen, bathroom, bedroom) will be found in the chapters focused on those rooms. However, many projects can be used in a variety of rooms, so I recommend you look through all the chapters before you decide on specific projects. You may find something in the bedroom chapter (such as the floating nightstands) that would be perfect in your bathroom, kitchen, or living room. Each

project has a list of alternative uses to make it easy to select the best place for it in your home.

CREATE A PROJECT TIMELINE

Once you've selected projects, check my estimated completion times at the start of each project. Remember: the timeline is only for the construction period. It does not include the time to purchase materials and to gather the tools. For example, while a floating shelf project can be completed in less than two hours, including drying time, you may need to spread that time over a busy weekend.

You'll want to make a habit of gathering all of your materials and tools before beginning your project. That way, you'll be aware of anything you need to purchase (or locate) and can make just one trip to the store for everything. Certain items, such as a sturdy tape measure, a pencil, and a pad of paper, should be considered a given on the tool list of any project. You don't want to start any project without those tools in hand.

TOOLS

Few projects can be completed without at least a hammer and nails or a staple gun and some glue.

The DIYers toolbox needn't be big, but it should be of good quality to last a lifetime. And it's a great investment! If your budget is tight or you feel you may use certain tools only once or twice, consider renting them. Renting tools is inexpensive, and most large home improvement stores or rental facilities generally have a wide selection of specialized tools. You can also borrow tools from a friend, neighbor, or relative.

Here's a list of my recommended tools (and some finishing supplies), which will allow you to complete the majority of the projects in the book:

Caulking gun: An inexpensive hand tool that holds a cartridge of silicone or caulk and dispenses the silicon or caulk through the tube's nozzle, making for easy application. Caulking guns normally come in two styles: a smooth rod drive and a more old-fashioned ratchet drive. A smooth rod drive is more common, easier to use, and helps prevents drips and oozes. Choose an all-purpose caulk to go with your gun—white caulk is paintable and good for sealing around trim work, while clear silicone is useful when sealing around windows or other clear items.

Chisels: Most household chiseling jobs can be accomplished with a basic set of four wood chisels in ¼-, ½-, ¾-, and 1-inch sizes (from 3 mm to 25 mm). The better the quality of the chisel set, the sharper and more precise the edges are. Cold chisels aren't as sharp and are used on masonry, so they are less useful in terms of the projects here. Pick up a sharpening stone as well. *Always wear safety glasses when working with a chisel.*

Circular saw: A power saw that spins a metal disc or blade with saw teeth on the edge. A 7¼-inch saw with 15 amps provides plenty of power to cut the 2x4 lumber and plywood called for in this book. A good-quality carbide blade is your best bet— thin-kerf blades are cheap and fast when they're sharp. But hit a nail, and you've shortened the life of the blade. Thick-kerf blades have bigger teeth; they're more than twice as expensive as the thinner versions, but you can sharpen them, and they hold up to nails and staples better. Circular saws are also useful for all types of wood, medium-density fiberboard (MDF), and other sheet materials. Hand-held and table-mounted versions are available.

Clamps: I always have two Quick-Grip clamps on hand; they are my second set of hands when I am working on my own. These clamps open up to 24 inches and can steady things that you are working on or help hold glued items together while they dry.

Combination square: Popular, reasonably priced, small, and useful, the combination square does the job of an ordinary T-square but also comes with an adjustable steel-rule-type blade and a 45-degree shoulder for miters. It also contains a scriber and a level vial for checking level and plumb.

Extension cords or leads: A good-quality grounded cord that has a built-in light on the female end is invaluable when using power tools. A cord with three outlets is also very handy.

Extension ladder: Get a step up—an aluminum or fiberglass extension ladder is the way to go. Fiber-glass is the right choice if you are conducting any electrical work. It is also lighter than aluminium, but is more expensive.

Framing square: Also called a carpenter's square, this flat L-shaped measuring tool allows you to set out angles for rafters, stair treads, etc. The legs of the L, which come together at a 90-degree right angle, have measuring tables and marks. It's also a great tool to ensure you're keeping square.

Glues: An assortment of adhesives comes in handy in construction and repair and when reinforcing wood projects that are nailed and screwed together. Keep a few kinds on hand: wood or carpenter's glue and wood putty; white or schoolhouse glue; "super" glue; ceramic adhesive; and a construction adhesive such as liquid nails.

Hammers: The classic 16- to 20-ounce claw hammer is heavy enough for most basic home-repair needs but light enough to carry around without it being a nuisance. Don't be tempted by cheap hammers with wooden handles. Ham-mers with steel, synthetic, or fiberglass handles last longer and won't split or break the way a cheap wooden-handled hammer can. Rubber mal-lets are another form of hammer; they are useful when you are fitting two pieces of wood together and you want to minimize damage to the surface. The wider, softer surface of a rubber mallet is less prone to dent and ding wood than a conventional hammer.

Handsaws: When tool lists mention a "handsaw," what I usually mean is a crosscut saw. Crosscut saws cut against the grain of wood (which, by the way, is exactly what you are doing when you trim a tree or shorten a 2x4). However, when drywall is used, you really need a drywall saw, which is narrower and made specifically for chalky drywall. Meanwhile, when projects require cutting pipes or metal, I list a hacksaw, which typically comes already fitted with metal blades.

Jawhorse by Rockwell: This heavy-duty hands-free clamp not only secures work pieces while you do your thing, but the wide, stable frame instantly provides a go-anywhere workstation to make cuts, drill holes, and more. It can hold doors, 2x4s, 2x12s, and odd-shaped objects. You can even mount miter saws, tile saws, grinders, and other tools to wood panels and use the Jawhorse as a stand. Even better? The horse folds up for simple storage and transportation. It has only three legs because a three-legged stool will never rock!

Jigsaw: This handheld or table-mounted saw is used for cutting free-form curves, stenciled designs, and other custom shapes into a piece of wood, metal, laminate, MDF, or other material.

Laser levels: For precision, laser levels are hard to beat; they range from relatively simple and inexpensive to quite complex and costly. I recommend a 90-degree horizontal and vertical laser level, which usually features dual laser beams and often a magnetic base that can be attached to the metal corner beads on drywall, to help you work hands free. Most levels can be adjusted for flat, angled, or horizontal surfaces. Never look directly at a laser!

Levels: Levels come in all sizes, but a 4-foot level is best. Invest in a good-quality one! Whether you're hanging pictures or installing shelves, a straight line is crucial. Note that when measuring, a horizontal line is called "level," and a vertical line is called "plumb." A 4-foot level is also handy for screeding concrete.

Miter saw: When cutting any wood at an angle, but particularly when cutting trim and molding, a miter saw (also called a chop saw) is the tool of choice. With a miter saw, the blade angle can be adjusted by single degrees and locked to make exact angled cuts. This saw comes in both hand (miter box) and power versions.

Nail guns: Pneumatic nail guns come in two basic types: framing and finishing. A framing nail gun takes nails up to 3¼ inches long and makes framing easy. Finishing nail guns take smaller nails for fit-out work such as trim, baseboards, cabinets, and so on. Choose a good-quality brand nail gun that feels right in your hand and always wear safety glasses when using one! An air compressor and hose are also required equipment when running a nail gun.

Nail set: A spring-loaded nail set lets you drive the head of a nail into a piece of wood without using a hammer (which can dimple or mar the wood). This tool is good for punching the head of the nail below the surface so it can be filled and sanded.

Nails and screws: Keep on hand an assortment of finishing and flat-head nails, from 1 to 3½ inches long, referred to as 2 penny to 16 penny in the United States (which are commonly abbreviated as 2d, 16d, and so on). Also stock a range of wood screws and drywall screws, from 1 to 3 inches long. Pick up a variety of wall anchors and invest in a good storage box with a clear acrylic lid for easy use.

Paintbrushes: Purchase the best-quality paintbrushes that you can afford and clean them well after each use. A good-quality brush is more efficient and will always give you a much smoother quality finish—and years of service—if properly cared for.

Pencils: Keep a bunch of classic number 2 pencils sharpened and with you at all times. A few carpenters' pencils, which have a thick wide lead, are also good to have on hand for framing projects.

Pliers: This gripping hand tool is handy for holding an object still, and for bending an object or turning it (as in a stubborn bolt).

Plumb bob: A plumb line establishes what is "true" or exactly vertical, or plumb. At the most basic, it's a string suspended with a weight at the bottom, and it will be both vertical and perpendicular to any level plane through which it passes.

Power drill: For the jobs in this book, I recommend having an 18-volt cordless hammer drill/driver. Lower-voltage models won't have the power or battery stamina you'll want. In addition, make sure you have a set of wood drill bits that go from ⅟₁₆ inch to 1 inch as well as flat and Phillips head screw bits, preferably with magnetized tips. Also have a set of masonry drill bits. While wood and steel bits are generally the same, masonry drill bits have a special carbide-tipped head that is suitable for drilling into masonry, such as concrete, stone, brick, terra-cotta, tiles, and even glass.

Pry bar: Also called a crowbar, this useful piece of metal has a single curved end and flattened point, often with a small V opening on one end for removing nails. Pry bars come in various lengths; look for a 12-inch bar. A great tool for demolition!

Reciprocating saw: This portable handheld power saw fits blades in a variety of sizes to achieve cuts in a variety of materials by operating in a reciprocating push-and-pull movement. Great for demolition, the saw is a quick-cutting tool, able to cut studs, joists, and drywall in hard-to-get areas where a circular saw cannot reach.

Router: This woodworker's tool is used to rout, or hollow out, an area in the face or surface of a piece of wood for decorative purposes. Also, when fitted with an appropriate jig, a router can recess door hinges and lock faceplates.

Safety gear: I am firm believer in safety gear. Any injury can ruin a fun project. Here's a list of what you should keep on hand:

+ Safety glasses that fit and have good coverage for your eyes
+ Ear protection, such as plugs or noise-blocking earmuffs
+ An assortment of proper-fitting work gloves
+ A good-quality face mask for the type of dust you will be exposed to
+ First-aid kit
+ First-aid chart: It's a good idea to have one on display for larger projects
+ Fire extinguisher: Always good to have a multipurpose ABC fire extinguisher centrally located on any job site!
+ Covered rubber band: Long hair? Tie it back! Loose clothing? Roll it up!
+ Rings and other jewelry? Remove all jewelry while using all tools.

Sawhorses or saw stools: Look for sturdy collapsible stools or sawhorses, so you can store them easily. Remember: you always need a pair. These make working on large projects easier because they can hold up a few wooden planks to form a temporary work surface.

Screwdrivers: No kitchen drawer should be without at least two screwdrivers. A flathead screwdriver has a single flat blade, and a Phillips screwdriver has a cross-shaped or four-star point. Flathead screws are not used as often as they once were, but you'll come across lots of them if you are refurbishing old furniture or repairing a vintage item or removing hinges. More often today, sturdy flathead screwdrivers are used for small pry jobs, like opening paint cans. On the other hand, Phillips screwdrivers are a true must-have. The reason Phillips-head screws are so common, by the way, is that the cross-shape design allows you to apply more torque than you can with a flathead screwdriver, reducing the risk that you'll damage the slots and make them unusable. Have handy a set of three of each type—small, medium, and large, with medium to long handles.

Staple gun: Manual staple guns are easy to use and don't depend on electricity or batteries to run. They are great for quick upholstery projects and a hundred other uses.

Stepladder: A stepladder about 5 or 6 feet tall is useful for many projects, from changing a lightbulb in a ceiling fixture to reaching a high shelf in the linen closet. Make sure the ladder you have or buy is rated for your weight. Test your ladder to make sure it is steady when placed on a level surface and that it has slip-resistant treads, as well as a mechanism for locking it in place when in use. Never use a ladder by yourself, always wear slip-resistant flat shoes on a ladder, and make sure the ladder is placed on a level surface. Never step on the top surface of a ladder.

Adjustable ladders are convenient as they can transform into many levels and make a very handy light scaffold.

Stud finder: Many of the projects in this book require finding wall studs, so always have one of these guys on hand. Stud finders locate the hidden wall studs (the standing 2x4 studs beneath the wall's drywall face). Make your life easy and get a battery-operated one: they are quite accurate and find studs faster. However, my favorite stud finder is simply a strong magnet that picks up the nails and screws that are fastened into a stud. It always works. Called a stud magnet. No joke.

Tape measures: With stiff yet flexible, wide blade, a 25-foot (8-m) retractable metal measuring tape is a must. Look for one with a clip, so you can attach it to your belt or waistband. Those with a magnet on the back are also useful—you can stick it on the fridge, so it's never far away for quick measuring jobs. Other lengths and sizes are useful, too: take a small 12-foot (3-m) measuring tape with you whenever you're buying lumber or rummaging for vintage furniture, and you'll always know if something is the right size or will fit where you need it.

Tool belt or bag: Having a wearable tool belt means never wandering your house looking for a screwdriver, tape measure, or pencil again. Best way to choose one—try on a few at the hardware store to see which one is most comfortable and offers ample storage.

Reclaim valuable real estate.

Making the most of unused space is now a reality.

Utility knife: Every project requires some cutting and scraping, and, in this regard, a utility knife will be one of your best friends. Buy either a straight or an angled version, and for safety, make sure the blade is retractable.

Wet/dry vacuum: A drum-style dual-use vacuum designed to suck up water as well as debris. Wet-dry vacuums are a must for any workshop. You can suck up spilled water, scoop up wood chips and bent or broken nails, and eliminate sawdust in a snap. A wet-dry vacuum is also known as a shop vac, which comes from the brand name "Shop-Vac" that has become synonymous with this type of vaccum.

Whiteboard: I always have a whiteboard mounted on a centrally located wall or door at each of my jobsites. Put one up in your garage or workspace, and it's easy to keep track of even small jobs. Mark it with your project materials list and timeline for a right-in-front-of-you visual reminder of what you need to do and what you've already completed. Jot down materials or tools you need as you think of them, tick off tasks as you finish them, and say good-bye to those scrap-paper lists.

Wrench: A tool specifically designed to fit nuts, bolts, and other standard fasteners, for either securing or removing them. You may wonder if there is a difference between pliers and a wrench. There is: wrenches are made to fit specific-size fasteners, whereas pliers are not sized specifically. If you have a job that could be completed with either a wrench or pliers, use the appropriately sized wrench for best results. The tight fit means the tool won't slip and hurt your fingers or damage the fasteners you're working on. Save the pliers for when wrenches won't work. I recommend buying a socket wrench set because of its versatility—each set includes a handle with an extension, and an assortment of detachable sockets that fit different sizes of nuts and bolts.

WOOD AND OTHER TYPES OF BUILDING STOCK

There are many different types of lumber and wood-based man-made or composite materials on the market that can be used for the projects in this book. Most of the time, I call for lumber or plywood, as they are inexpensive, easy to find, and easy to work with. Of course, every product has its character flaws and its own purpose, drawbacks, and benefits. Here's the lowdown on what to look for:

LUMBER

Western lumber: Western lumber includes more than fifteen Western softwood species, most commonly Douglas fir. It's easy to cut and nail, and it is strong and stable.

Southern pine: This wood has high strength, is resistant to wear and tear, and holds fasteners well. It is often used in homes and is good for framing. It has a clear appearance with a minimum of knots and holes, making it appropriate for furniture and shelving.

Treated lumber: This is lumber that has been pressure treated—the process is not as important to know as the result: pressure-treated lumber resists harsh, wet weather conditions, termites, and fungus. That's why it is often used for decking and other outdoor structures. Wood species typically used in pressure treating include Ponderosa pine, Douglas fir, and Southern yellow pine. When working with this product, wear a mask or respirator, since the treatment process does involve chemicals, which can be released into the air during cutting.

Pine shelving: Wooden boards that are 1 inch thick (lumber that is nominally 1 inch is actually only ¾ inch thick) and of varying widths and lengths. Most of the boards you find at home centers or lumber-yards range from 1x1s to 1x12s, in lengths up to 12 feet long. Most consumer sales will be in 4-foot and 6-foot lengths. No. 4 grade pine is commonly called "garage shelving," and it's cheap and useful for basement and garage and attic shelving, where good looks may not be your number-one priority.

Fine hardwoods: Hardwoods do not grow as fast as softwoods such as pine, therefore they are not as readily available and they are often costly, so should be reserved for special woodworking projects where the material will take center stage.

Common hardwoods include ash, birch, cedar, cherry, mahogany, maple, oak, poplar, redwood, teak, and walnut. Cedar, mahogany, redwood, and teak are good for outdoor projects, as they stand up well to the elements. Cedar and redwood are relatively "soft" for hardwoods, while mahogany is denser, and teak is extremely hard, making it "hard" to work with.

Birch, cherry, and maple work well for furniture projects such as tabletops, floating shelves, and fine cabinetry. Mahogany and oak are also good choices for cabinetry. All of these hardwoods are good choices for flooring as well.

MAN-MADE MATERIAL

Medium-density fiberboard (MDF): MDF is made from fine wood dust mixed with a binder and heat-pressed into panels. The sheets are sold as is, or with a wood veneer such as oak, maple, or birch. Veneered sheets can be stained or painted, but if you plan on painting MDF, go with "blank" sheets, which are called paint grade. They take paint beautifully. MDF is very stable to work with and is consistent from batch to batch (for instance, a ¾-inch sheet purchased today will be exactly the same as one purchased a year from now). In my experience, MDF is easy to saw, but it's darn heavy. That could be a drawback if you're working alone. A ¾-inch-thick, 4x8-foot sheet can weigh as much as 70 to 90 pounds.

Particleboard core plywood (PBC): PBC uses a coarser wood dust than MDF, so it's lighter than MDF. Most melamine products (cabinets, table-tops) use PBC as the substrate.

Veneer core hardwood plywood (VC): VC is made from alternating layers of fir slices with a surface veneer of a finished wood grain, such as birch, maple, or oak. It's lighter weight than MDF, making it easier to handle and move around. VC is not always consistent in thickness from sheet to sheet, or even within the same sheet. When cutting plywood, remember that you may be ripping or crosscutting across the layers. This can make cutting more difficult: saw-cut edges may not be as clean and smooth as they are with MDF.

Melamine: Melamine is a thermally fused, resin-saturated paper finish over a particleboard core. This material comes in a variety of colors and is highly stain and mar resistant, which is why it's used in the cabinet industry for carcass construction. You can often find it precut into 1x12 boards of 5- or 6-foot lengths. It's a great material for shelving, especially in bathrooms, mudrooms, laundry areas, kitchens, and kids' rooms because it's so durable and easy to keep clean.

PROJECTS FOR DIY NEWBIES

Here's a list of projects (and their page numbers) that are perfect for learning basic building skills and easy enough to make a brave new DIYer proud of the results. Once you've mastered what I think are the simplest projects, be bold—and try one that's a bit more challenging.

METRIC CONVERSION CHART

The imperial measurement originally is from England. The foot measurement was taken from the length of the king's foot. An inch was the length of the king's toe. True!

1 centimeter is 10 millimeters.
1 meter is 100 centimeters or 1,000 millimeters.
1 inch is 25 millimeters or 2.5 centimeters.
An example: A 2-by-4-inch stud is 5 by 10 centimeters or 50 by 100 millimeters.
A 2-by-6-inch stud is 5 by 15 centimeters, and so on.
A 4-by-8-foot sheet of plywood is 1.2 by 2.4 meters.

Approximate Conversions from Standard/U.S. Customary Units to SI/Metric Units

SYMBOL	WHEN YOU KNOW	MULTIPLY BY	TO FIND	SYMBOL
LENGTH				
in	inches	25.4	millimeters	mm
ft	feet	0.305	meters	m
yd	yards	0.914	meters	m
mi	miles	1.61	kilometers	km
AREA				
in²	square inches	645.2	square millimeters	mm²
ft²	square feet	0.093	square meters	m²
yd²	square yard	0.836	square meters	m²
ac	acres	0.405	hectares	ha
mi²	square miles	2.59	square kilometers	km²
VOLUME				
fl oz	fluid ounces	29.57	milliliters	ml
gal	gallons	3.785	liters	L
ft³	cubic feet	0.028	cubic meters	m³
yd³	cubic yards	0.765	cubic meters	m³
MASS				
oz	ounces	28.35	grams	g
lb	pounds	0.45	kilograms	kg
	US ton	0.91	metric ton	t

PART

USE-WHAT-YOU-HAVE SPACE SOLUTIONS

Once you've accomplished the cleanout in Part 1, you're more than halfway to having a livable, functional, efficient space to work, rest, and play. With your Master Space List in hand, check out the many ways you can make the most compact kitchen, bite-size bathroom, and cramped sleeping quarters—as well as many other spaces in your home—more expansive.

To prove it, this section bursts with projects and ideas for the individual rooms in your house. Every space in your place should be working for you, not against you. Along with specific space-making projects, I provide plenty of organizational tips and quick fixes that will have your home humming in no time.

04

KITCHENS

The kitchen is the number one room that homeowners would like to remodel. And why not? It's the heart of the home, the command center, and a gathering place for family and friends. Trouble is, a complete overhaul can burn through a budget in no time: with appliances, cabinets, flooring, and countertops, plus labor, the average kitchen renovation costs about $40,000. Even if you don't plan on an intricate mosaic backsplash, imported sandstone flooring, and black granite counters, costs can add up quickly.

If your cabinet boxes are structurally sound and the layout of your kitchen is functional, there is a lot you can do to increase space without major construction or disruption—without sacrificing quality. There are three basic kitchen functions to consider when creating the "ideal" kitchen: storage, preparation, and cleanup. These are the areas our projects focus on.

CUPBOARD AND PANTRY REORGANIZATION

CUPBOARD AND PANTRY REORGANIZATION

Taking inspiration from closet organization systems, we apply the same techniques here to organize drawers and cabinets for optimum functionality and at least 30 percent more storage. In fact, once you go through the process of reorganizing your kitchen, you may find you've got space left over. Then, once your kitchen is organized, the following projects will add even more efficient space, without taking up a lot of (and in many cases no) valuable floor square footage.

TIME:

A few hours to a weekend, depending on the size of your kitchen

DIFFICULTY:

TOOLS:

Purchased organizers may need a screwdriver (or power drill with bits), level, and tape measure

MATERIALS:

Organizing accessories, like drawer organizers, racks, hooks, cupboard "steps," wire baskets, and so on

MAKE THAT SPACE HAPPEN

1..
If you have not already done so, read Part 1 and assess what you have in your kitchen. How many Chinese food containers are you keeping? How about coffee mugs—what's the ratio of cups owned to cups actually used? Are you keeping the can of blueberry pie filling from 1982 for sentimental reasons?

2..
Categorize and purge. Put all like items into groups on the kitchen table: storage bowls with storage bowls, cups with cups, cans of beans with cans of beans, and so on. Any container that does not have a top—or any top that has no bottom—can go in the recycling bin. Cracked and chipped mugs, plates, bowls, and other china, ceramic, or

stoneware items can likewise be recycled. Dented pots and pans, bakeware, and pie plates should be donated or recycled. Extras and duplicates (how many immersion blenders do you need?) can be donated or sold. Toss out expired food packages.

3..
Think about what you use both most frequently and least frequently. Separate the nonfood items into "most used," "moderately used," "least used," and "potentially dangerous and toxic" (such as knives and cleaning products). Separate food items into everyday staples (perhaps dried beans and rice, chicken stock, and cans of tomatoes) and less frequently used items (perhaps baking ingredients or specialty food items like jarred olives and artichokes).

4 ....

Store hazardous items such as knives on a magnetic knife block installed out of the reach of children or in a drawer out of their reach. Store toxic cleaners in a cabinet with a child safety lock installed. These latches are available at department and hardware stores and install easily.

5 ....

Place your most frequently used nonfood items in accessible cabinets, and place rarely used items on high shelves, in the backs of cupboards, or in another area of the house entirely. For example, Granny's Limoges serving platters, which you use only once or twice a year, might be more safely stored in a box under your bed or in a hall closet. Place frequently used food items at eye level in the pantry and keep lesser-used items above and below that shelf. Heavy items should be stored on the bottom shelves, and lighter ones belong on the top shelves. Place short items in front of tall ones, or buy cabinet "steps" that increase the storage space in your cabinet by allowing you to line up cans and jars on three different levels.

6 ....

Store items based on where you use them. This may not create more space per se, but it does create more efficient use of the space you have.

For example, plates, cups, and glasses should be stored in a cabinet with the closest proximity to the dishwasher or drying rack. I have a friend who kept her dishes in cabinets on the wall opposite her dishwasher, which meant she had to walk across the room each time she took items from the dishwasher to put them away. Simply by switching her food cabinets with her china cupboards, she cut in half the amount of time she spent putting things away. Cutting boards should be stored near the sink. Mixers, prep bowls, and knives should be stored near the most expansive work surface. Appliances and tools likewise should be kept near the surface where they are used—the coffeemaker near the sink, the mixer near the oven, pots and pans near the stove top, salad tongs and dressing whisk in the salad bowl, and so on.

7 ....

Expand cabinet space with smart accessories. A lazy Susan can hold cans and jars for easy access; plastic-covered wire plate racks create an extra shelf for dinner or lunch plates; drawer organizers (small boxes that can be mixed and matched to fit your drawers) can hold cutlery, utensils, and small items; wire baskets can be screwed onto the inside of lower cabinet doors to hold old pot lids, paper products, and cleaning items.

KITCHEN STORAGE: RACK, STACK, HANG, RELOCATE

Here are some more ideas to improve your kitchen storage:

Hang: Cup hooks can be screwed under a cabinet or shelf to hold teacups; a pot rack (installed with proper hardware) can hold cookware; a plant hook (installed with anchors in the ceiling or fastened into ceiling joists for safety) can hold hanging fruit and egg baskets.

Nest: Bowls and pots fitted into each other make a neat pile—be sure to place a pad or paper towel between each to prevent chips and scratches.

Rack: Spice racks, sheet racks, plate racks, and over-the-door racks are handy ways to store everything from herbs to extra bottles of ketchup.

Relocate: Consider relocating lesser-used items to a dry cabinet or perishables to a fridge/freezer positioned in a garage (or basement) to help free up extra space.

Slide: Get the trash barrel off the floor of your kitchen and under your sink with a simple trash can glider—easy to install! Place sliding cabinet inserts (available at home centers and organization stores) in deep cabinets or pantry closets to access items placed in the farthest reaches of your kitchen.

Stack: Like nesting, stacking is a simple way to make the most of your space. Stack cans, canisters, plates, saucers, cups, storage containers, and platters.

PROJECT:

BEHIND-THE-DOOR HANGING PANTRY

BEHIND-THE-DOOR HANGING PANTRY

Does your kitchen have a broom closet or a closet holding mechanicals like the hot water tank or an electrical box? Many kitchens do—and people sometimes forget that there is valuable storage space behind, or actually on, these (and all) doors. This simple-to-build behind-the-door 60-inch-high and 21½-inch-wide pantry with five shelves lets you take advantage of that space. Adjust these dimensions to fit a wide or narrow, tall or short door, and adjust the number of shelves to suit your storage needs. Just remember to keep the outside width of the overall unit at least 7 inches narrower (3½ inches on either side of the door) than the door itself to allow for the doorknob and clearance when the door is opened and closed.

TIME:

6 hours

DIFFICULTY:

⚒⚒

TOOLS:

Pencil

Tape measure

Framing (or carpenter's) square

Handsaw or circular saw

Drill/driver with countersink bit and ⅛-inch drill bit

Screwdrivers

Hammer

Nail set

Sanding block

Paintbrushes, roller, and tray

Safety glasses

Ear protection

Level

Combination square

Clamps (optional)

MATERIALS:

WOOD:

1x4 smooth pine stock (6- and 8-foot lengths are standard; quantity determined by size of pantry)

1x2 smooth pine stock (6- and 8-foot lengths are standard; quantity determined by size of pantry)

HARDWARE:

Eight 1½-inch wood screws

Twenty-four 1-inch wood screws

1 box finishing nails

Six 2-inch steel or stainless angle brackets

FINISHING SUPPLIES:

Wood glue

Sandpaper, medium- and fine-grit

1 quart each primer and paint

Construction adhesive (optional)

MAKE THAT SPACE HAPPEN

1..

When measuring and marking, be sure to use a framing square to keep the ends straight and square. With a handsaw or circular saw, cut two 60-inch-long pieces from the 1x4s. These will be the sidepieces. Then cut six 20-inch-long pieces from the remainders. These will be the crosspieces.

2 ....

Put together a rectangular box using both of the 60-inch sidepieces and two of the 20-inch crosspieces, butting the sidepieces over the ends of the crosspieces at the corners. At each corner, drill two holes for 1½-inch wood screws through the face of the long sidepieces and into the crosspieces. Countersink the screw holes so that the screw heads will lie flush with the surface of the sidepieces.

3 ....

Apply a bead of wood glue along both ends of the two crosspieces and to the edges of the sidepieces where the corners of the rectangular box will meet. Screw the box together using the 1½-inch wood screws.

4 ....

With a handsaw or circular saw, cut six 21½-inch-long pieces from the 1x2s. These will be the retaining strips, to hold jars and cans on the shelves. Then cut eight 3½-inch-long pieces from the 1x2s. These will act as shelf supports.

5 ....

Plan how you want to space the shelves. It's best to place the tall items on the bottom shelves and the shortest containers, like spice jars, on the top shelves. Measure your tallest and shortest items, and, with a pencil, mark the shelf positions along each sidepiece. Next, ¾ inch below each mark for a shelf, place a second mark for the shelf support. (The ¾-inch space is to allow for the thickness of the shelf itself.)

6 ....

Using wood glue and finishing nails, attach a shelf support piece at each marked shelf point on each sidepiece. Apply a bead of glue to the support piece and set it flat against the frame, with its top edge flush with the marked line, and nail through the support piece into the frame. Drive two finishing nails into each shelf support.

7...

The remaining four 20-inch-long pieces of 1x4s become the four internal shelves. For each shelf, apply a bead of wood glue to the bottom edges of the board's cut ends, and to the top edge of the two shelf brackets that will support it. Set the shelf into place across the two brackets and secure them at each end by nailing two finishing nails through the sidepieces into the shelves.

TIP: When nailing shelves in place, stagger the nails so they don't hit against each other.

8 ....

To complete the pantry unit, use finishing nails to nail the retaining strips across the front of the unit, 2 inches above each shelf. For tall items, use two retaining strips.

9 ....

Sand all rough spots and edges with medium- and then fine-grit sandpaper.

10 ....

Prime and paint the unit and allow it to dry.

11..

When the pantry unit is dry, hang it on the door, using the 2-inch angle brackets: three across the top of the unit and three across the bottom. First attach the brackets to the unit: mark the screw holes with a pencil, predrill the holes, and then fasten with 1-inch wood screws. Then center the unit on the door and mark the screw holes in the six brackets with a pencil. However, if you have hollow-core doors, locate the solid blocking inside the door by tapping on it. (Most hollow-core doors have solid wood blocking around the sides.) Be sure to attach the brackets to the solid blocking; this may mean extending the unit closer to the edges. If so, just make sure the door can close. Once the position is set and the holes marked, predrill the holes and secure the brackets to the door with 1-inch flathead wood screws.

Here's another option: if it's not possible to attach the unit to solid blocking within the door, add a ½-inch plywood backing piece to the shelf unit. Glue and screw the backing into the frame and then apply construction adhesive to the rear of the unit and screw it onto the hollow-core door.

Exploded view of pantry unit construction.

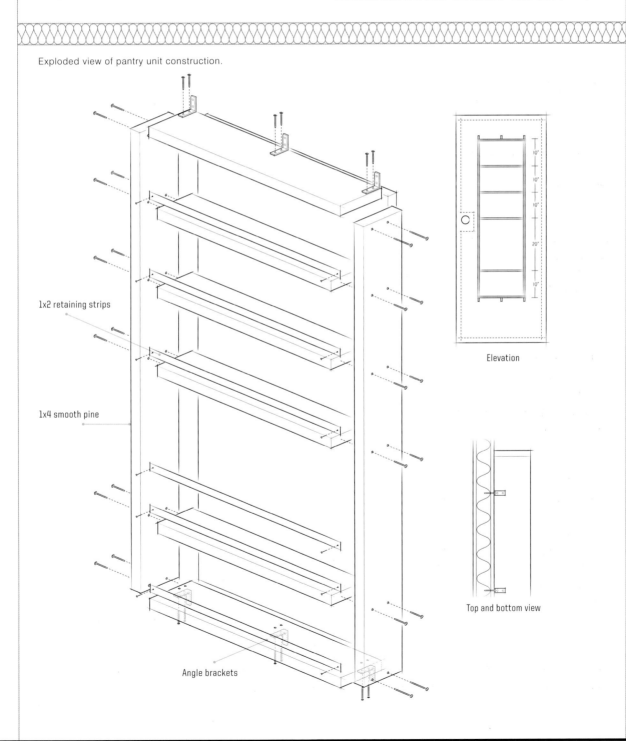

1x2 retaining strips

1x4 smooth pine

Angle brackets

Elevation

Top and bottom view

IN-KITCHEN
LAUNDRY CENTER

IN-KITCHEN LAUNDRY CENTER

Many homeowners have their washer and dryer set behind bifold doors in the kitchen or stacked in a nearby closet. Taking a cue from vintage kitchens, I can show you how to neatly hide the laundry center in or on your kitchen walls without taking up floor space. The projects here include a recessed ironing board cabinet, a fold-down sorting table, and recessed storage shelves to store a clothes steamer, detergent,

and other cleaners—giving you everything you need to wash, sort, fold, and iron your clothes and linens.

TIP: Normally, in modern homes, wall studs will be spaced 16 inches apart "on center," or measuring from the center of each 2x4. This typically leaves a space 14½ inches wide between the studs. However, older buildings may have odd spacing, so always confirm stud locations with a stud finder.

Recessed Ironing Board

Home centers sell ironing board cabinet kits that can be wall mounted or recessed into the wall between studs. Recessing it takes a bit more work, but it is much more unobtrusive than simply hanging the box on the wall so that it protrudes into the room; also, the instructions for wall mounting are generally included with the kits. Recessing is a huge space saver. An unfinished wood ironing board cabinet (also available in kit form) can be painted or stained to match your existing kitchen cabinets.

TIME:
4 hours (plus paint or stain drying time)

DIFFICULTY:
↑↑↑

TOOLS:
Paintbrush (optional), roller, and tray
Tape measure
Stud finder
Hammer and nail set
Pencil
4-foot level
Drywall saw
Drill/driver with bits
Miter saw (optional)
Safety glasses

MATERIALS:
1 recessed ironing board kit

WOOD:
Two 14½-inch pieces 2x4 pine
1x2-inch pieces trim stock slightly longer than the total dimensions of your ironing board kit
Shims

HARDWARE:
Four 2½-inch wood screws
1 box finishing nails

FINISHING SUPPLIES:
1 gallon each primer and paint or 1 quart stain (optional)

MAKE THAT SPACE HAPPEN

1 ....

If you bought an unfinished cabinet kit, prime and paint or stain the box and its door—as well as the boards you'll be using for trim—to match your existing cabinetry (see "Stain Matching 101," page 53, for help doing this).

2 ....

Choose and measure a location as close to an electrical outlet as possible so you don't need to plug your iron into an extension cord to use it. (That's dangerous!) Keep in mind that the board will extend outward 42 inches when it's pulled down, so make sure that you have enough space in the room for the board. Also take into consideration your favorite side of the ironing board. Mine is neither!

3 ....

Use the stud finder to locate the two adjacent wall studs closest to your chosen location. With a pencil, mark the wall between the studs at the height at which the cabinet bottom will be. Use a level to draw a level line along the mark.

4 ....

Using the tape measure and the level, measure the cabinet and mark its outline on the wall. Before cutting this large hole, knock out a small inspection hole between the studs to ensure your space is free. See Step 2 of Project: Carved-Out Wall Niche (page 122) for details.

5 ....

Use a drywall saw to begin cutting open the wall along the cabinet template you marked. As you cut, keep checking the space to avoid any wires and pipes that you may have missed before! Hold the saw at an angle with the blade along the inside of the line for the best control. The cut does not have to be precise but try to stay on the line.

6 ....

Attach the two 14½-inch pieces of 2x4 flush with the top and bottom of the cutout with 2½-inch wood screws by screwing them in at an angle from the end of the boards directly into the studs on either side. (This is called toe nailing.) These pieces will help support the weight of the cabinet and give the trim something to nail into. For easier placement, drill pilot holes diagonally into the 2x4s before placing them in the opening. Toe nail or screw them into position.

7 ....

Place the cabinet in the cutout. Use shims to adjust the cabinet so that it's level and plumb (use your level to check). Then secure it with the screws that came with the ironing board kit.

8 ....

Assemble the ironing board according to the manufacturer's instructions and attach it to the cabinet.

9 ....

Cut and fasten the trim with finishing nails to surround the cabinet. For a more professional look, miter the corners where the trim pieces meet.

10 ....

Attach the door to the cabinet according to the manufacturer's instructions.

Fold-Down Laundry Table

This ingenious table works wonders in a space-strapped house that has no room for a dedicated laundry area. In a kitchen, it can double as a dining table or a place to do work or craft projects.

TIME:
6 hours

DIFFICULTY:
⌁⌁⌁

TOOLS:
Miter saw or circular saw

Pencil

Drill/driver with bits

Stud finder

Hammer

Screwdriver

4-foot level

Tape measure

Paintbrushes, roller, and tray

Safety glasses

Ear protection

MATERIALS:

WOOD:
1 standard sheet ¾-inch birch plywood, cut to the size of your table

1x4 wood trim to fit the dimensions of 4 sides of your table size

One 1x6 cut to the length of the table

2 premade table legs, 1x1 lumber, or 2 balusters that can be cut ¾-inch less than the desired height of your table

HARDWARE:
8 to 10 screws and anchors (optional)

1 box finishing nails

1 piano hinge the length of your table

Two 2-inch folding butt hinges

Two 12-inch folding metal support brackets

1 box 3-inch wood screws (optional)

FINISHING SUPPLIES:
Wood glue

Wood putty

Sandpaper, 220-grit

1 quart each primer and paint or 1 quart stain

MAKE THAT SPACE HAPPEN

1 ....
Measure the wall area in your kitchen or adjacent hallway to calculate how long and wide a fold-down table you can build—and to know how much lumber to buy. When determining the height of the table, take into account the fact that you'll be standing in front of the table (or maybe even sitting at it) to sort and fold laundry.

2 ....
Cut the plywood to the desired size of your table or ask the home center to do it for you. (They typically do two cuts for free and will do more for a small fee.)

3 ....
With a miter saw or a circular saw, cut three pieces of the 1x4 for the front and sides of the tabletop. This trim will cover the raw edge of the plywood. If you are using a miter saw, cut mitered joints to frame the front and sides of the tabletop; otherwise butt joints are okay. The trim will hide the legs when the table is folded against the wall. Attach the trim to the front and sides of the plywood surface (the back side will sit against the wall) with wood glue and a couple of finishing nails per side.

4 ....
With a circular or miter saw cut one piece of 1x6 to the exact length of the tabletop.

5 ....
Screw one side of the piano hinge to the bottom of the 1x6 board; screw the other side of the hinge to the back of the tabletop. This is the hinge that allows the table to flip up and down. The 1x6 board also serves as a cleat to secure the table to the wall.

6 ....
With a circular saw, cut the two premade legs, 1x1s, or balusters ¾ of an inch shorter than the desired table height. Dry fit the legs before installing them on opposite sides of the tabletop to ensure that they are level and that both fit within the trim when the desk is folded down. Screw the folding hinges into the tops of the legs and then screw the other half of each hinge to the underside of the table.

7 ....
Add a folding metal support bracket to each leg, which will enable you to fold the leg up so the table hangs flat against the wall when not in use. This will also lock the leg into position when folded down. When this table is not in use, the legs fold up underneath and the tabletop collapses down against the wall.

8 ....
Now that construction is finished, sand the tabletop, legs, cleat, and trim pieces.

9 ....
Stain or paint the laundry table to match your décor and allow it to dry overnight.

10 ....
Attach the cleat to the wall at the desired table height using four screws and anchors if you are going into drywall. If you can, attach the board into the wall studs with 3-inch wood screws. Make sure that the legs sit flush and the table is level before securely fastening the cleat. Touch up upon completion.

Top: Piano hinges are long and require many screws—so grab your power drill/driver.

Bottom: Note how the legs tuck neatly behind the desk surface when the table is not in use.

Piano hinge

1x4 wood trim

Butt hinges

Mitered corners

Recessed Laundry Storage Niche with Shelves

This niche project is similar to other recessed cubby projects in this book. However this one is designed with tall shelves for holding detergent, an iron and a steamer, and other laundry products and accoutrements. If possible, position the niche in a wall alongside your laundry closet.

TIME:
6 hours

DIFFICULTY:
↑↑↑

TOOLS:
Tape measure

Stud finder

Pencil

Framing square

Utility knife

Hammer

Drywall saw

Circular saw

Nail gun

Nail set

Miter saw or miter box

Paint brushes or stain applicators, roller, and tray

Level

Drill/driver with bits

Scoring knife

Safety glasses

Ear protection

MATERIALS:

WOOD AND SHELVING:

1 sheet ¾-inch plywood precut with grooves for adjustable shelves (readily available at home improvement centers)

1 sheet ¾-inch birch plywood

1 sheet ½-inch white acrylic

Decorative wood trim (if making the fold-down laundry table, get the same trim to coordinate)

HARDWARE:

Twelve to fifteen 1½-inch brad nails

Six to eight 1½-inch wood screws and drywall screws

1 box finishing nails

FINISHING SUPPLIES:

Wood glue

Sandpaper, fine-grit

Tack cloth

1 quart stain, or primer and paint

Wood putty

MAKE THAT SPACE HAPPEN

TIP: Cut the two pieces of grooved plywood so the grooves line up with each other when the piece is assembled. If they don't match up, the shelves will be askew.

1 ....
Make sure that you have all of your supplies before beginning the project and then decide on the wall location and height of the storage unit. Take into consideration the size of the items you will be storing: measure the detergent bottles and other items and then add at least 2 inches to the height of your items to accommodate the ¾-inch shelving material and clearance. You may be able to tuck this unit into a wall next to the closet housing your laundry machines. Avoid placing the unit directly above or below wall switches, outlets, or lighting fixtures, as there will likely be wiring behind the wall; this would be challenging (and potentially dangerous) to deal with. It's also a smart idea to check the other side of the wall in which you intend to place the niche.

2 ....
Once you've decided on the location, use a stud finder to locate the nearest wall studs. As with the ironing board cabinet, this shelving unit will be recessed between the studs.

3 ....
Using the tape measure and pencil, mark the wall to show the dimensions of the shelving unit and the location of individual shelves. Then use the framing square and utility knife to score the drywall. If you are still unsure whether there is any wiring behind the wall, use a hammer to carefully knock out a section of the inside corner and look behind the drywall to check.

4 ....
If no obstacles are in the way, use a drywall saw to cut along the lines that you just scored into the wall. Continue checking for any electrical wiring while cutting the drywall.

5 ....
Measure and mark the plywood for the shelving unit. For the sides, use the precut plywood with grooves for adjustable shelves. Use the plain plywood to create the top, bottom, and back of the unit. Using a circular saw, cut out the pieces.

6 ....
Use wood glue and a nail gun to assemble the box using butt joints.

7 ....
Use a miter saw or miter box to cut the decorative wood trim to fit around the face of the box; this will cover the raw plywood edges and help hide any gaps between the box and the drywall. Attach the trim with wood glue and finishing nails.

8 ....
Sand the unit and wipe the dust away with a tack cloth.

9 ....
Now either prime and paint or stain as desired. I recommend using a white semi-gloss latex paint if your laundry area is white. It's easy to see dirt and clean it off, and it will coordinate with the easy-to-clean white acrylic shelves (detergent drips and circles being an inevitable part of any laundry room).

10 ....
Anywhere the drywall opening is not flush to a wall stud, slip 3-inch strips of plywood behind the drywall so they run the length and width of the opening, lining them up with the edges of the hole. Secure these to the drywall with drywall screws to provide support for the recessed shelves.

11 ....
Slip the box into the hole in the drywall. Use a level to check the box for plumb and secure it by nailing through the front trim and into the wall studs (or screw into plywood strips) behind the drywall.

12 ....
Install the shelves. One sheet of acrylic from the home improvement store will yield about six shelves. It's best to have the store precut the acrylic to the correct size. If not, cut the acrylic with a scoring knife. (With ½-inch acrylic, this will take some work.) Remove the protective plastic and slip the shelves into the grooves.

PROJECT:

TAKE-IT-TO-THE-TOP
CABINET MAKEOVER

TAKE-IT-TO-THE-TOP CABINET MAKEOVER

Many kitchens have standard 30-inch upper cabinets that leave empty space between the top of the cabinets and the ceiling. Why aren't taller cabinets put in to begin with? Often kitchens are built with a full soffit above the cabinets that contains mechanicals or wiring. Yet even when no soffit exists, many builders use the same 30-inch upper cabinets because they are the least expensive options available. At first many homeowners think that the top of the cabinets is a good place to store large bowls, decorative items, and even plants. Soon enough they realize that this is one of the dustiest, grimiest parts of the kitchen—largely because it is unprotected from the airborne grease and other particles that the kitchen kicks up. Still others simply leave the space empty.

If you have such a situation, you have wasted space! You can enclose that space and convert your cabinets to 42 inches high by building simple cabinet boxes to fill the space overhead. Then add ready-made 12-inch wood or glass doors to the top (you can order doors in any size you need from several online manufacturers, such as rawdoors.net or nakedkitchencabinetdoors.com) or replace the old lower doors with longer 42-inch stock doors, matching or coordinating them to your existing lower cabinets. If time and budget allow, you can reface the lower cabinet doors to match the upper. The good news is that some cabinets built even twenty years ago are more solidly constructed than many modular laminate or chipboard cabinets of today—so those carcasses are worth keeping.

By doing this relatively straightforward job, you'll gain one-third extra space in the kitchen. Stock doors, both 12-inch and 42-inch, are available online and from large home centers. You can find unfinished oak doors that can be painted or stained to match the rest of your existing cabinets (see "Stain Matching 101," page 53). Or, you can choose a door (and a color) that coordinates with the lower cabinets, so you can leave them as is, especially if they are in good condition. Remember to always take note of your existing light fixtures as they can sometimes cause a problem with your new upper cabinet doors. If this is the case, it may be worthwhile having them changed so they are a closer fit to your ceilings, as space is key!

TIME:

A weekend to a week, depending on the size of your kitchen

DIFFICULTY:

⇡⇡⇡

BUILD AND INSTALL THE CABINET BOXES

TOOLS:

Tape measure

Table saw (optional)

Nail set

Framing square

Handsaw or circular saw

Hammer or nail gun

4-foot level

Pair of Quick-Grip Clamps

8-foot sturdy ladder

Stud finder

Screwdriver or drill/driver with bits,
plus countersinking bit

Combination square

Pry bar (optional)

Safety glasses

Ear protection

MATERIALS:

WOOD:

1 sheet ¾-inch melamine or birch plywood
(depending on quantity of cabinets)

HARDWARE:

Four 3-inch wood screws per unit

1¼-inch wood screws

1 box nails

Shelf pins for adjustable shelving (optional)

FINISHING SUPPLIES

Wood glue

Screw caps

Wood filler

MAKE THAT SPACE HAPPEN

1 . . . .

Plan to build as many five-sided cabinet boxes as necessary to match the existing cabinets underneath. Use plywood or a material similar to the existing cabinetry so all cabinets look like one unit. Melamine shelving is always a good option as it is easy to keep clean because of its vinyl coating. Plan for the new cabinets to be the same width as the underneath cabinets, but approximately 1 inch shorter in height than the available open space, so installation is not a headache. If you order 12-inch or 42-inch cabinet doors from a supplier, then the box height will be 1 inch less in height. The 1-inch gap can be filled in with a wooden strip or left for the new doors to cover. For step-by-step instructions on building the boxes, see Project: Modular Storage and Floating Cube Nightstands, page 116.

2 . . . .

Add additional shelves to the new cabinets if you wish. Consider carefully what you want to store in each cabinet to help you decide. For step-by-step instructions on building and installing fixed shelves, see Build Side Shelves, page 105.

3 . . . .

Prior to installation, finish the new cabinet boxes with stain or paint; see the next section for step-by-step instructions on finishing. Make sure to match the finish of the boxes to the finish on the new doors (and/or on the existing cabinets).

4 . . . .

Install the cabinet boxes before attaching the doors. If any light fixtures or fans might get in the way of cabinet installation, temporarily remove them. Position each new cabinet so it lines up perfectly with the one below. Ensure it is flush at the front and then clamp it to the cabinet below. Use four 3-inch wood screws to attach it directly to the cabinet below, evenly spaced at each corner and screwing through the bottom of the new cabinet into the top of the existing cabinet. Ensure the screws are slightly shorter than the two thicknesses. This method will anchor the unit nicely. When anchoring the cabinet boxes, it is always a good idea to fasten the rear of the cabinets to the rear wall directly into the studs. However, this is easier said than done, as it is a tight space, and you are working on a ladder at this point! See the next section for instructions on attaching the new doors.

FINISH THE WOOD AND ATTACH THE NEW DOORS

TOOLS:

Paintbrushes or stain applicators, roller, and tray

Muffin tin, teaspoon, and artist's brushes (if mixing stain)

Sander

Pry bar (optional)

Screwdriver or drill/driver with bits

Pencil

Safety glasses

Ear protection (if using sander)

Face mask

Disposable gloves

MATERIALS:

WOOD:

42-inch or 12-inch replacement doors

HARDWARE:

Hinges (3 per door for 42-inch; 2 per door for 12-inch)

Pulls or knobs, 1 per door

1 box finishing nails

FINISHING SUPPLIES:

Sandpaper, 120-, 150-, and 220-grit

1 gallon each primer and paint, or 1 quart stain (that closely matches existing cabinetry)

Polyurethane (optional if painting or staining)

Masking tape

MAKE THAT SPACE HAPPEN

1 . . . .

Before painting or staining, thoroughly clean the new doors and the existing cabinets. If either new or old cabinets are made of particleboard or medium-density fiberboard (MDF), do not wash them with water, as the wood will swell. Instead use a general all-purpose spray cleaner.

2 . . . .

Sand the unfinished wood doors and the faces of the new cabinet boxes with a sander, one pass with 120-grit sandpaper and then another pass with 150-grit sandpaper. If you will be refinishing the existing cabinets, sand those as well. If the new cabinet doors are laminated or prefinished, don't sand or refinish them; instead, skip the finishing steps.

3 . . . .

Once that's dry, paint the wood, sanding between coats with 220-grit paper for a smooth, brush-stroke-free finish. Two coats should be adequate. Try to use a good-quality zero-VOC (volatile organic compounds) semi-gloss paint for easy maintenance. Or apply two clear coats of a water-based polyurethane.

TIP: If you are painting, prime the wood with a tinted primer that matches the color you have chosen. This will save you time and money.

4 . . . .

If you are staining, confirm the stain color first by testing it on a hidden area, such as the back of the new cabinet boxes or the back of the wood door. Sand the area, wipe clean, and then follow the manufacturer's directions to prepare the stain. Apply the stain and allow it to dry fully before deciding if it's a good match. If it seems acceptable, I recommend applying one clear coat of polyurethane as a final test, as this can darken the overall result. If the color isn't right or doesn't match the existing cabinets, then you need to stain match. See the instructions in the sidebar "Stain Matching 101" for help.

5 . . . .

Before installing the new doors, use a pry bar to remove any crown molding from around the top of your existing cabinets. Save it, as you may need it later to trim the top of your new cabinet configuration.

continued

STAIN MATCHING 101

Stain matching is all about testing, trial, and error—and, eventually, success. Be sure to keep notes so you can re-create your exact finish recipe in the future.

Mix the stain with paint thinner in separate cups of a muffin tin (which, thereafter, can't be reused for food!). Use these four ratios: stain straight from container; 4 parts stain to 1 part thinner; 2 parts stain to 1 part thinner; and 1 part stain to 1 part thinner. (One teaspoon equals one part.) Stir each combo to mix completely.

Apply a small amount of each solution to the cabinet according to the stain manufacturer's instructions (with an artist's brush, paper towel, or clean rag). When each stain area is dry, apply one coat of polyurethane, which will darken each stain sample.

When the polyurethane is completely dry, one sample will match (or nearly match) your existing cabinetry. Use that recipe to stain your doors. If none of these shades matches, try mixing different stain colors together, along with thinner, always keeping track of your ratios, until you hit the right combination. However, today stain manufacturers offer a variety of shades that mimic many wood species so you will likely not have to do a lot of mixing to find the right color.

Safety First: If stain is not water-based, dispose of rags in a bucket of water as they may self-combust.

6 ....

Attach hinges to the back of each new door:
If you have 12-inch doors, attach two hinges,
placing them 2 inches from the top and bottom.
If you have 42-inch doors, attach three hinges,
placing the third at the midpoint between the top
and bottom hinges. Use masking tape to mark
a reference line on the top face frame rail of the
cabinet you built. This will help you keep the tops
of the doors in line and level. The door should be
centered horizontally over the door opening.

7 ....

Position the door over the opening, aligning the
top edge with the tape reference line. With masking tape or a pencil, mark hinge locations on the
face frame.

8 ....

Open the hinges and position the door against the
edge of the face frame so the hinges are aligned
with the markings and the hinge locations. Drill
pilot holes in the face frame and anchor the hinges
to the face frame with the mounting screws. Then
remove the masking tape.

9 ....

Attach door hardware, such as knobs or pulls,
following the manufacturer's instructions. But
always drill from the face side of the door as some
materials can chip or blister. I often use tape here
as it is easier to mark and prevents the drill bit
from dancing across the face of the door.

10 ....

Finally, if you desire, reattach the crown molding
to nicely finish off your reclaimed space.

CHOOSING HINGES AND PULLS

You can find many types of hinges and pulls (or handles) on the market. Indeed, new hardware
can dramatically change the appearance of any kitchen—even if it's the only change you make. For
visual harmony throughout the room, be sure to choose fittings, handles, and knobs that comple-
ment each other and have a finish that matches your existing hardware. When it comes to kitchen
and cabinet hardware, two of my favorite companies on the planet are Blum (www.blum.com) and
Häfele (www.hafele.com). They have tons of great gadgets and mechanics for hard-to-access areas,
and their products are affordable, durable, and innovative.

Try to choose hinges that match your existing cabinets. You will be surprised to find that the right
hardware is still available 95 percent of the time. Your existing hardware will be your guide to
installing them. Hinges that are fully adjustable can make the installation process much easier
and also can give a better result. Self-closing hinges are also the way to go.

PROJECT:

TOE KICK DRAWERS

TOE KICK DRAWERS

This is one of my favorite projects. Behind the toe kick under the cabinets lie all sorts of space—very valuable real estate in the kitchen. This space is perfect for storing trays, cooling racks, platters and oversize baking trays, linens and towels, and even a small folding step stool. Toe kicks vary in type and size. Some are simply clipped onto the legs of the cabinet, while others are built in. First determine what type of kick board you have: get down on the floor and see if you can pry one off. If you can, you are golden. You can build a toe kick drawer just as you would any standard drawer. If the toe kick is built in, you can still build a drawer, but it's trickier, and it turns this 3-hammer job into a 4-hammer one. Another option is to add four casters to the bottom of the drawer. But you will make this decision when you discover what's down under! I outline the second option separately after describing the easier project.

TIME:

7 hours

DIFFICULTY:

⌃⌃⌃

TOOLS:

Hammer

Measuring tape

Pencil

Jigsaw (with fine wood blades)

Screwdrivers or drill/driver with bits

Framing square

Paintbrushes, roller, and tray

Pry bar

Combination square

Wood chisels

Safety glasses

MATERIALS:

WOOD:

1 sheet ¾-inch birch plywood per unit

HARDWARE:

1 pair fully extendable drawer slides, runners, or casters

1 drawer pull or push catch latch per unit

1 box 1½-inch finishing nails

Three 2-inch wood screws per unit (optional)

2x2-inch brackets (optional)

Eight 1½-inch screws per unit

FINISHING SUPPLIES:

Rubber stopper

Wood glue

1 quart each primer and paint, or stain

Sandpaper, 120-grit

MAKE THAT SPACE HAPPEN

1 ....
With a hammer, pry off the toe kick where you want a drawer. Examine the space: Is it free and clear of wires and obstacles? If so, have it say hello to a vacuum cleaner.

2 ....
Measure the space's width and depth and the height of the toe kick and then sketch a drawer on paper. This will include a tray (or frame) in which the drawer itself will fit. A cutout portion of the toe kick will become the drawer face. Make sure the drawer is large enough for whatever you want to store in it.

3 ....
Using a jigsaw, cut an opening in the toe kick that is the same height and width as the planned drawer. This should be a U-shaped rectangular opening that leaves a strip of wood along the bottom of the toe kick.

NOTE: Go slow with the jigsaw and try to keep the blade straight to the line. Ideally, the piece you cut out will become the drawer face.

4 ....
Using the ¾-inch plywood, build the tray that will hold the drawer. The tray should be the same width and height as the cutout opening on the toe kick; the depth extends as far as possible or desired. The tray must have a bottom, two sides, and a backing piece. Attach all sides using wood glue and nails. Glue is essential here. You can also add a few 2-inch screws for additional support. You can use butt joints for this project, since it's located where you can't see it.

5 ....
Attach the wooden tray to the toe kick by using screws and wood glue or using small 2x2-inch brackets and 1½-inch screws* fastened to both the tray and the rear of the toe kick to conceal the fixings. If using brackets, use two for each side to give adequate support.

*NOTE: Make sure your screws are short enough so as not to protrude through the face of the toe kick. When attaching the tray, you will be matching the toe kick's cutout to the tray's open side.

6 ....
Next, using more ¾-inch plywood, build the drawer the same way as you built the tray, adding a front side to make a five-sided box. Measure the inside of the tray to get the necessary outer drawer dimensions, which should be slightly smaller than the opening, as it must fit inside the tray. Be sure to leave enough room in your measurements to accommodate the drawer slides in the tray also.

TIP: Drawer slides can be mounted on the sides and some are available that can be mounted on the bottom.

7 ....
Attach the drawer slides to the drawer and the tray, using the screws included with the slides.

8 ....
Attach the cutout of the toe kick to the front of the drawer by attaching screws from the drawer side into the rear of the drawer face. This keeps the fasteners secret. Be sure to align it so there is an even gap all around.

continued

9 ....

Sand and prep the edges of the drawer face and cutout. Slide the drawer in and out, making any necessary adjustments.

10 ....

Paint, stain, or seal the drawer to match the face of the toe kick.

11 ....

Install a drawer pull to match existing hardware, or a push catch latch that requires no surface handle, or just a simple notch.

12 ....

Attach a small block of wood under the wooden tray, so it stays level and secure. Also attach a small rubber stopper to the back of the drawer to prevent it from pushing in. When closed, the drawer face needs to be flush with the toe kick.

13 ....

Slide the entire unit into its original position. Screw or nail the toe kick back into place on the cabinet legs.

TIP: Is your cutout of the toe kick a little rough? No worries. Using the same material as the toe kick, cut out another drawer front that's slightly larger and fasten it to your drawer front to cover up your practice cut.

Toe kick drawers are incognito when closed, but offer a wealth of storage space for cutting boards and trays.

A simple center notch makes the drawer easy to open and close.

Existing toe kick board is reused as the drawer face.

Drawer hardware is easy to install and gives the drawers a professional look and enables smooth operation.

The bottom piece slides into grooves on each side of the drawer. (See "Get in the Groove," page 172.)

TOE KICK DRAWER VARIATION

This variation is a little trickier than the first! If you were unable to pry off the toe kick, you will have to cut the drawer opening from the toe kick where it is—under the cabinet. Since you can't see what's behind the toe kick before cutting, keep away from cabinets between your dishwasher and sink as well as your oven and gas outlet, as the open space may contain mechanicals or wiring. What's there depends on how the previous tradesperson placed these lines on the floor. You do not want to cut them, however they can be rerouted or pushed back further to enable the toe kick drawer to function. Note: Use the appropriate tradesperson for this if you are not confident doing this yourself.

TIME:

10 hours

DIFFICULTY:

↑ ↑ ↑ ↑

TOOLS:

Same as those listed above, plus:

Oscillating tool or reciprocating saw

¾-inch spade drill bit

MATERIALS:

Same as main project

Packing block

Material to match cabinets (oak or maple veneer ¾-inch plywood that can be stained to match existing cabinets [see Stain Matching 101, page 53] or matching laminate material), or if existing toe kick is painted, simply prime and paint to match. If you plan to use plywood for the toe kick face, you may wish to edge band it. If so, the veneer edge banding is generally available and can be ironed on or adhered using a contact adhesive.

MAKE THAT SPACE HAPPEN

1...

Choose your position within the width of the cabinet above and mark out your level rectangular area to be cut. Ensure the top of the cutout is lower than the opening door above.

2...

Use a drill and a ¾-inch spade bit to drill a hole in each corner of the rectangular area, making sure your bit stays within the lines.

NOTE: Try to prevent the drill bit and saw blade from cutting in too deep in case there are services beyond.

3...

Using an oscillating tool or a reciprocating saw, cut out the drawer opening; place the saw blade within the drilled holes and cut straight lines from hole to hole. If you don't have a reciprocating saw, a jigsaw may be used to make the cuts, but often the space is too tight. If you use a SoniCrafter oscillating type saw, you won't need to drill pilot holes.

4...

Following the instructions on page 57, measure and build a wooden tray to the desired or allowable depth, and whose width and height match the internal size of the cutout, so the tray can slide into the cutout.

Drawers on wheels offer flexible function as these boxes can be used in other areas of the house.

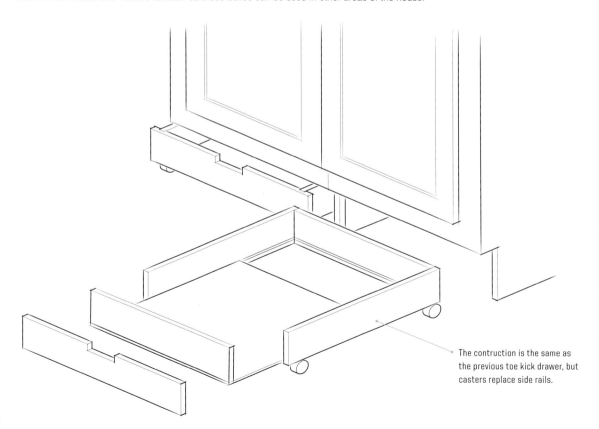

The contruction is the same as the previous toe kick drawer, but casters replace side rails.

5 ....
Fasten two fully extendable drawer runners to the tray (unless you're using casters; see Step 7).

6 ....
Before attaching the tray, place a packing block inside the opening to ensure the tray is level. Now attach the tray to the toe kick; fasten with screws from the inside front ends of the tray into the edges of the toe kick cutout, taking care not to drive the screws through the face of the toe kick.

7 ....
Build the drawer, per the instructions on pages 57 and 58, and attach the drawer runners to it. However, I have often used small wheels/casters for this more difficult project, as attaching the runners can be challenging. This makes it a simpler project, as the drawer face is the toe kick, which is cut from top to bottom.

8 ....
Cut, attach, and finish a front to the drawer, using oak or maple veneer ¾-inch plywood or matching laminate material. Cut the plywood or laminate material with a jigsaw, making the drawer face slightly larger than the opening, so that the drawer face will act as the drawer stop. Stain the drawer face to match existing cabinets (see "Stain Matching 101," page 53), or, if the existing toe kick is painted, simply prime and paint to match.

9 ....
Finish the edges. Attach the drawer face in the same way as in step 8 on page 57.

10 ....
Insert the drawer into the tray along the runners, then stand up, straighten your back, and admire your work!

PROJECT:

STORAGE ISLAND

STORAGE ISLAND

Whether they were built midcentury or yesterday, many tract and planned development homes often have a common feature: a knee wall that separates the family room or dining room from the kitchen. This slim divider marks one area from another and can be useful in some applications (in a large bedroom or family area, for example). But in a kitchen, I think knee walls represent a lost opportunity. Since these partial walls are not structural or load bearing, they can be removed fairly easily and replaced with counter and storage space that has much more function and aesthetic appeal. Stock cabinetry topped with laminate, stone, or tile adds prep space, a buffet for serving meals, and even a place to eat, do homework, or pay bills. For the most attractive look, consider putting in your own tile or stone countertop, which I've described under Optional Finish: Tile the Countertop (page 67). You need a buddy to help with this project because some lifting, setting in place, and holding are required. Remember to be organized up front by ordering all the necessary materials before you start.

TIME:

3 days

DIFFICULTY:

ΛΛΛΛ

TOOLS:

Pry bar

Sledgehammer (if knee wall is brick)

Hammer

Protective painter's sheets or drop cloths

Screwdrivers

Pencil

Measuring tape

Miter saw

Handsaw

Circular saw

4-foot level

Drill/driver with bits, plus masonry carbide bit (if necessary)

Paintbrushes, roller, and tray for painting or staining

Safety glasses

Ear protection

Face mask

Work gloves

MATERIALS:

Two 30-inch base cabinets that match or coordinate with existing rooms

One precut 39-x-73-inch or 25-x-64-inch piece laminate or solid surface countertop (if tiling countertop, see page 67)

WOOD:

One 1x30-inch piece wooden corner trim (to cover seam at back and side of island)

Four 1x4 pieces paint-grade wood (optional)

1 sheet ½-inch medium-density fiberboard (MDF) or bead board paneling (to fit the back of the island)

Shims

HARDWARE:

Six 1½-inch wide 2x2½ metal L-brackets

1 box finishing nails

1 box 1¼-inch screws

1 box 1⅝-inch screws

1 box 1-inch nails

Knobs or pulls to match existing cabinetry hardware.

FINISHING SUPPLIES:

Construction adhesive

1 gallon each primer and semi-gloss paint, or 1 quart stain (for bead board only, to match wall or kitchen décor)

MAKE THAT SPACE HAPPEN

1......................................
Demolish the knee wall. Wear safety glasses at all times during demolition as pieces of dust, drywall, wood, nails, and screws can go flying no matter how careful you are. If there is a wooden or laminate top on the wall, remove it with the pry bar. Save it if you think it is salvageable for another project, such as a shelf. Knock out the drywall with your sledge hammer, pry up any nails from the floor with a hammer, and unscrew any screws. Sweep the area clean and, ideally, use a shop vac (see page 27) to scoop up all the debris.

2......................................
Make a sketch of your island and measure the space. Typically, I use two 30-inch flat-packed stock cabinets from a home center as the base of the island; this results in a 24-by-60-inch island topped by an oversize 39-by-73-inch countertop. The large top provides room on one side for bar stools. If you do not have enough room for a counter this large, reduce the size to a 25-by-64-inch countertop, which will make a good prep and serving surface. It's your design, so the size is up to you.

3......................................
Assemble the cabinets according to the manufacturer's instructions, except for the doors. You will attach these at the end of the project.

continued

A countertop with storage beneath doubles the amount of usable space in small kitchens, providing a great space to dine or chat.

The drawer and cabinet finish, countertop material, and hardware should all match the existing finishes and features.

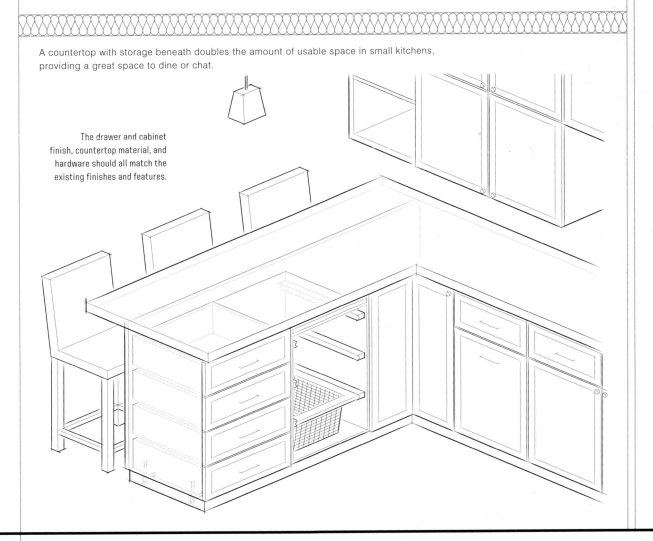

4 ....

Build the toe kick (if the cabinets did not come with their own). Use the 1x4 pieces (height to suit) to build a separate box measuring 21 by 54 inches. Put the box together with simple butt joints and screws; for instructions on constructing a butt joint, see Tip, below.

TIP: A butt joint is the easiest of all joints to make, but it is also the least strong. For this joint, two pieces of wood are butted together at a 90-degree angle. Cut the ends to be joined as straight as possible (a miter saw is helpful for this). Glue one end of one piece to one side end of the other to form a corner. Tack finishing nails along the side for added strength or support.

Remember to utilize this space by also including a toe kick drawer (see page 55).

5 ....

Using your 4-foot level, set the toe kick box into place on the kitchen floor and attach it to the floor using the L-brackets (place two on the long sides and one on each of the narrower sides). This stabilizes the box so it will not tip over. If you have a ceramic or stone tile floor, drill holes using a masonry carbide bit and insert the anchors and screws into the grout lines to avoid damaging the tiles. If you decide to remove the island later, you can fill in the holes with grout. If you have a wood or vinyl floor, mark and drill pilot holes first. Wood floors can be repaired if the cabinets must be removed, using wood putty and matching stain.

6 ....

Ask for help setting the cabinets on the toe kick box. Then, secure the cabinets to one another using 1¼-inch screws (or shorter depending on the thickness of the two sides). Secure them to the toe kick box with screws.

7 ....

Set the counter on the cabinets. If you are using the oversize counter, make sure there is a 1½-inch overhang on the kitchen or front side of the cabinet island and a 15-inch overhang on the back side of the cabinet (where the stools will be). If you are using the smaller countertop, set it with an even ½-inch or so overhang on both sides.

8 ....

Attach the countertop. For a laminate counter, screw up through the underside of the cabinet using 1⅝-inch screws.

If you are using a stone or solid surface countertop, check with your supplier to make sure your solid surface can safely span the distance without any additional support. A granite or marble top, for instance, may be heavy enough to hold itself in place, but it may need an additional sheet of ¾-inch plywood underneath. For extra strength, run a bead of construction adhesive that can be used on stone or solid surface around the top edge of the cabinet. Set the counter in place.

If tiling the countertop, screw the plywood onto the top of the cabinets. See Optional Finish: Tile the Countertop, facing page, for tiling instructions.

9 ....

Attach the MDF or bead board paneling to the back side of the island cabinets. Apply construction adhesive to the back of the paneling according to manufacturer's instructions. Then place the paneling and attach it with a hammer and a few finishing nails. You can also attach with some short screws driven from inside the cabinet.

TIP: Rub the head of your hammer with sandpaper to give it some "grip." This should prevent the head of the hammer from slipping off the nails . . . and hitting your thumb. Ya gotta love that!

10 ....

Place the corner trim along the side of the island where the back panel meets the side to cover the unfinished seam. Attach with 1-inch nails.

11 ....

Stain or prime and paint the surface of the island cabinetry to match your existing cabinetry or décor.

12 ....

Attach the doors using the manufacturer's included hardware; add knobs or pulls. Put your stuff away and enjoy your new island peninsula!

OPTIONAL FINISH: TILE THE COUNTERTOP

TOOLS:

Tape measure

Pencil

Manual tile cutter or 4-inch grinder or circular saw with tile-cutting blade (see Tip, page 69)

Bucket (for mixing thinset)

Notched trowel

4-foot level

Large sponges

Grout float

Miter saw (optional)

Hammer or nail gun

Nail set

Safety glasses

Ear protection

MATERIALS:

Tiles, enough to cover the surface evenly (Always grab a few extra for a future repair job or just in case your tile-cutting skills need a little honing.)

WOOD:

One ¾-inch plywood sheet cut to countertop size

1-inch flat wood trim to fit dimensions of countertop

HARDWARE:

1 box finishing nails

FINISHING SUPPLIES:

Sandpaper, 120- and 220-grit

Wood glue

Wood putty

Tile spacers (⅛ inch) or tile wedges appropriate for tile size (Your supplier can assist you but the general rule of thumb is the smaller the tile, the smaller the spacer.)

Thinset mortar suitable for a plywood application (Your supplier can assist you.)

Grout

Grout sealer

Rubber gloves

Construction adhesive

MAKE THAT SPACE HAPPEN

1 . . . .

Using a tape measure and a pencil, find and mark the middle of the counter area. Measure from the middle of each side and draw a line; the point where the lines cross is the middle of the tiling area.

2 . . . .

Lay your tiles out in a "dry run," using spacers to make sure they fit. Start with a tile in the center and then add tiles on the sides, working your way out to the edges. Mark any cuts you may have to make—but don't make them until you actually lay the tiles, as they may change slightly in the actual installation. Take your time and try to arrange the tiles so you end up with full tiles covering the entire surface, or so that any tiles that need to be cut are placed at the edges of the counter and not in the center.

3 . . . .

Once you have settled on an arrangement, take up the tiles and place them on a surface nearby in the pattern you've just set so you can easily replicate it during installation.

4 . . . .

Prepare the thinset in a bucket according to the manufacturer's instructions; it should be the con-sistency of frosting. Trowel the thinset directly onto the middle of the plywood surface using a notched trowel, pulling it toward you in an arc at a 45-degree angle away from your lines. Cover an area large enough for only the first stage of tiling you are comfortable with; thinset starts to set quickly. Take note of your set-out lines and always try to work cleanly. Put any excess thinset back in the bucket.

5 . . . .

Carefully place the first tile in the center as you did in the dry run. Twist the tile just slightly to set it in place and proceed with the rest of the tiles, applying thinset as you go. Occasionally place your 4-foot level on top of the tiles to ensure that the surface is flat. Set spacers between tiles as you work to make sure the grout lines will be

evenly spaced. Remove the spacers once the tile adhesive is set or push them down so the grout will cover them.

6 . . . .

Once you've finished laying all the tiles, carefully wipe away any excess thinset with a just-damp sponge, moving on the diagonal and keeping the joints clean and open.

7 . . . .

Let the thinset set overnight. Wash out the bucket and clean all your tools.

8 . . . .

Mix the grout to the consistency of cake mix—somewhat looser than the thinset. Apply it to the tiles with the grout float, moving across the surface on a diagonal to the tiles. The edge of the float should remove most of the grout from the face of the tile but leave it in the joints.

9 . . . .

Wait about 20 minutes and then wipe away as much grout as you can with a slightly damp sponge, also moving on a diagonal so as not to pull the grout back out of the joints. This is an important step, as grout is next to impossible to wipe away once it's dried—at least without using a caustic chemical.

10 . . . .

Allow the grout to dry and then wipe away any "haze" with a slightly damp sponge. Polish with a soft, dry clean rag or paper towel. Consider seal-ing the grout a couple of days after installation using a penetrating clear sealer. Believe me; it's worth doing. Aqua Mix is a good product.

11 . . . .

Cut the 1-inch trim to finish the countertop, hiding the edge of the tile and the thinset. Attach the trim using construction adhesive and finishing nails. (This step can also be done prior to installing tiles to avoid any gaps between the trim and tiles.) A butt joint will look fine, but a 45-degree angle cut, made with a miter saw and box will look even more finished and professional. It's worth the time and energy to do. Two 45-degree angled cuts make a 90-degree corner like a typical picture frame. Slightly sand the sharp corners with 120-grit sandpaper followed up with 220-grit sandpaper.

TIP: You needn't use an expensive wet saw to cut tiles. A far-less-expensive and versatile circular saw and a good-quality tile-cutting blade can make any necessary cuts. My favorite tool for this job is a 4-inch grinder with a good-quality industrial diamond tile-cutting blade; it's great for intricate curves. Make sure you purchase a blade that has a continuous, unbroken diamond surface all around the blade. This surface is for finer-detailed cuts. This is an outdoor project. Always wear your mask, safety glasses, and ear protection when cutting tile. It is similar to working with glass! You will look ridiculous, but at least you won't end up blind. You want to see your finished project when it's complete.

Tiling a countertop: Set the tiles in place before adhering them to the surface to make sure your design fits.

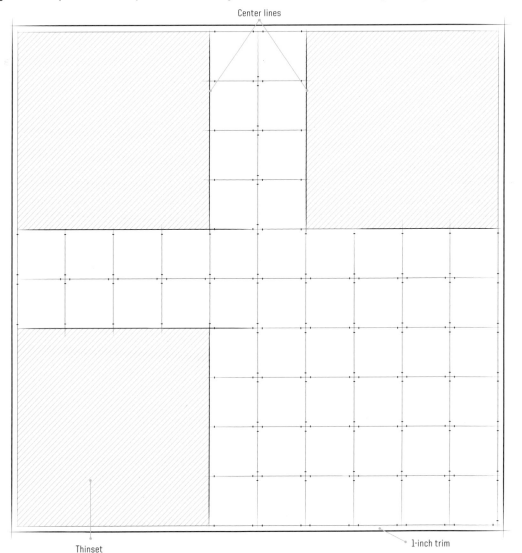

Center lines

Thinset

1-inch trim

05
BATHROOMS

After kitchens, bathrooms top the wish lists of home-bodies who want a serene spa space to retreat to after a hard day. Unfortunately, like kitchen redos, bathroom redos can cost plenty—expensive and sometimes complex plumbing fixtures, labor, and special material costs can send budgets into five figures very quickly. Add to that the fact that many bathrooms in a typical home or apartment may be no bigger than a 5-by-6-foot area—maybe less if you have a place in the city—and that's not a lot of room to work with, so every inch, literally, counts. Here, we tackle the top trouble spots and space takers of every bathroom, to make yours work better and even more luxuriously, for you, your mate, your kids—and even the family dog.

ADJUSTABLE SHELVING
LINEN CLOSET

ADJUSTABLE SHELVING LINEN CLOSET

Linen closets often become dumping grounds for unused pillows and blankets; extra paper products; candles and serving platters—even shoes. This project creates an orderly linen closet and increases accessibility to toiletries and linens; plus, adjustable shelves are, by definition, adjustable, so they are easy to rearrange and add to as your storage needs change. Adjustable shelves are a boon for almost any closet, but they are especially helpful for bath and bedroom items.

And just as important a consideration, linens need to be stored in a way so that they can "breathe," and using wire shelves allows for better airflow. If you have existing stationary wood shelves, I suggest removing and replacing them with adjustable tracks and wire shelves. Of course, despite being tidy, adjustable shelf tracking systems are not terribly gorgeous, so I do avoid using them in areas where they will be seen or on display. But in a linen closet, they are perfect—easy to install, affordable, and flexible.

TIME:

2 hours (depending on closet size)

DIFFICULTY:

TOOLS:

Nail set

Screwdriver or drill/driver with bits

Hammer or pry bar (optional)

Putty knife (optional)

Painting supplies (optional)

Stud finder

Tape measure

Level

Pencil

Safety glasses

MATERIALS:

SHELVING:

Adjustable wire shelving

Adjustable shelf tracking

Wicker or wire baskets, sized to fit the width, depth, and height of your shelves (optional)

HARDWARE:

4 to 6 screws and wall anchors per unit depending on length (if not supplied with shelving units). Ensure that they are 2½ inches long or long enough to bite into the studs.

FINISHING SUPPLIES:

Acid-free tissue paper (enough to cover your shelves and wrap any antique linens; available at art supply stores)

120-grit sandpaper or sanding block

Spackle (optional)

1 gallon each primer and paint (optional)

Wood putty

MAKE THAT SPACE HAPPEN

1 ....

Purge! Similar to Project: Cupboard and Pantry Reorganization (page 33), first take everything out of your linen closet and make some hard decisions about what you really need to store there. Then get rid of or move what you don't. See that project, or Chapter 1, for my systematic approach to clutter reduction.

2 ....

Clean. Wipe down the interior of the closet with a damp cloth and dry thoroughly; vacuum the floor of the closet and remove any dust and cobwebs that might be in the top and bottom corners of the closet. You'll be amazed at how much dust collects in this (or any) closet.

3 ....

Plan and buy adjustable shelves.

4 ....

Remove any stationary shelving from the closet. Inspect to see how it was attached and use the necessary tools to detach it. Generally, a screw-driver and pry bar is enough to work with. However, a persuader (hammer) is also a convenience. If any damage occurs to the wall during this process, no worries; take the time to fill any holes with spackle and give the closet a new prime and paint job.

5 ....

Once the spackle and paint have dried completely, use the stud finder to mark the location of the studs on the back wall of the closet. Ideally, the studs will be spaced appropriately for installing the shelf tracks into them using screws. It's not a tragedy if the studs are not well placed; simply use wall anchors with

the screws to install the tracks in the drywall (the shelving units may include all the necessary screws and anchors). With a pencil, mark the placement of the tracks so they are about 2 inches in from either side of the closet walls, and with a dot, mark the placement of each screw hole.

NOTE: When screwing through drywall directly into a stud behind it, use a cordless drill/driver to drive the screws into the wood. No studs? With the drill, drill pilot holes slightly smaller than your plugs or anchors. Tap them in with your hammer and then screw into place where you marked.

6 ....

Using the screws and wall anchors (if needed), hang the first shelf standard track. Place a level against it to ensure it's straight (or plumb). Then hang the second track and check to see that it's straight and aligned (level) with the first track.

7 ....

Install the brackets, which will snap easily into place, and set the shelves on the brackets, according to the manufacturer's instructions. (Most shelves just sit on the brackets, but some snap into the brackets.) Check the shelves for level.

8 ....

Depending on your storage needs, consider investing in a few add-ons, like snap-on undermount wire baskets or shelf dividers. Baskets are excellent for keeping toiletries and paper products corralled and for keeping sheets and blankets neat. Also, lay the shelves (and wrap antique linens) with unbuffered acid-free tissue paper; this prevents yellowing and won't discolor fabrics over time. You can find this paper at art supply stores or ArchivalUSA.com.

FOLD-AWAY DRYING RACK

FOLD-AWAY DRYING RACK

This nifty wall-mounted drying rack could work just as easily in a laundry room (for drying delicates) or a kitchen (to dry dish towels or even herbs)— and probably in a lot of other places (craft room, garage, potting shed). It's especially useful in the bathroom, as a handy place to dry hand washables (most often cleaned in the sink) and washcloths, and as a place to hang shirts, pants, and dresses to de-wrinkle while you shower. When not in use, the rack lays almost flush with the wall, taking up very little space. If you install the D-ring hangers into wall studs, you can use the hooks on the bottom of the rack for bath towels and robes— making it even more functional.

TIME:
3 hours

DIFFICULTY:
⚒⚒

TOOLS:
Drill/driver with ⅜-inch drill bit

Handsaw

Screwdrivers

Hammer

Mallet

Nail set

Stud finder

Tape measure

Pencil

Safety glasses

Combination square

MATERIALS:

WOOD:
One 2x2 piece ½-inch birch plywood

One 1x2 poplar board, cut to 8-foot length

Two ⅜-inch dowel rods, 48 inches long

HARDWARE:
1 sash lock

Two 1½-inch narrow loose pin hinges

2 D-ring hangers

1 lid stay or chain with small screw eyes

1 box framing nails

Four 2-inch hooks or knobs to match your bathroom décor (glass or porcelain work well)

FINISHING SUPPLIES:
Wood glue

Wood putty or wood filler

Sandpaper, 120- and 220-grit

Tack cloth

1 can each semi-gloss spray primer and spray paint

MAKE THAT SPACE HAPPEN

1..

Measure and mark the 1x2 poplar board to create frame pieces. With a handsaw, cut two 2-foot-long pieces (for the top and bottom of the rack frame), and two 20-inch-long pieces (for the sidepieces of the frame).

TIP: Before you cut your boards to size, use a square to make a 90-degree line to ensure your cuts are always square.

2..

Measure the internal width between the two side-pieces of the frame. Cut the dowel rods into four pieces that are 1 inch longer than that measurement.

3..

Fit the drill with the ⅜-inch drill bit and make ½-inch-deep holes on the inside of the sidepieces to accommodate the dowel rods. To make sure that the holes on one side line up exactly with the other side, measure 3 inches down from the top, and 3 inches between each hole.

4..

Apply wood glue to each drill hole and use a mallet to secure the dowel rods in the holes.

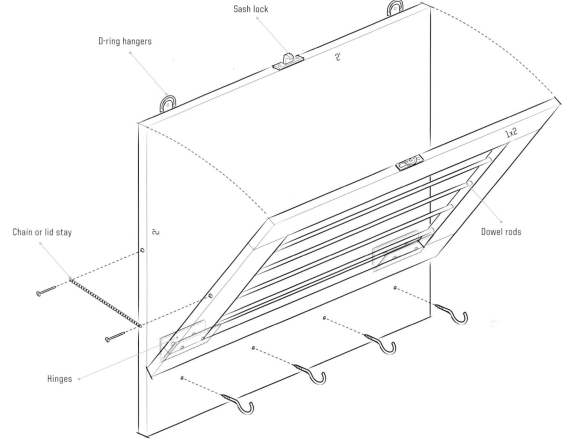

Exploded view of a simple drying rack assembly.

Sash lock

D-ring hangers

2'

1x2

Chain or lid stay

Dowel rods

Hinges

5 ....
Assemble the frame by gluing and nailing the pieces together using butt joints. Drill pilot holes first when nailing.

6 ....
Attach the pin hinges to the bottom of the rack; place them 1½ inches in from either side with a screwdriver. Next, attach the other side of the hinge to the 2x2 piece of poplar: line up the top of the frame with the top of the board and screw the hinge plate to the bottom part of the board. (The frame should reach to about 3 inches above the bottom of the board.)

7...
Fill nail holes with paintable wood filler or wood putty. Once it's dry, lightly sand the entire frame and board. Wipe with a damp paper towel or tack cloth.

8 ....
Prime the drying rack and then paint it with your color of choice. For easy application, especially on dowels, use a can of semi-gloss spray primer and paint for a smooth finish.

9 ....
Once the paint is dry, attach the sash lock to the top of the drying rack. Drill pilot holes first, so you don't split the wood when you drive in the screws.

10 ....
Drill holes to attach four hooks across the bottom of the plywood, below the folded down rack.

11 ....
Next, attach a lid stay, or a chain with screw eyes, to keep your drying rack at your desired angle when open. Attach a minimum of two D-ring hangers to the back of the 2x2 plywood and hang on your bathroom wall. If your bathroom is drywalled, fasten your screw into studs. If it's tiled, use wall anchors and be careful of plumbing pipes!

DESIGN TRICKS FOR CREATING A SENSE OF SPACE AND SERENITY

+ Replace a minuscule mirror with a larger one—for more depth and light. Caution: Never hang one mirror facing another (unless you want a Las Vegas vibe).

+ Replace dark-colored bathroom tiles with lighter-colored tiles. If that's not possible, tone down darker tiles by painting walls with a lighter version of the tile color. Monochromatic schemes seem larger.

+ Keep decoration to a minimum: instead of bold colors and big, bright patterns, add interest through texture such as wicker, waffle-weave towels, and fluffy cotton bath mats.

+ Allow as much natural light into the room as possible. Install blinds that can be opened when the bathroom is not in use. Spray-on window frosting lets light in while maintaining privacy. A sun tube installed in the ceiling is less expensive and easier to install than a skylight.

+ Replace a swinging door with a pocket door (see Project: Install a Pocket Door, page 96).

+ Replace a vanity with a floating, wall-mounted unit to create more visual space.

+ If replacing a shower, think about installing a corner shower unit with a curved front. They take up much less floor space while still providing plenty of room.

+ Tile the floor and wall with the same product to stretch its boundaries.

PROJECT:

FLOATING SHELVES

FLOATING SHELVES

Floating shelves can be used in any room of the house: they make great side tables in tiny bedrooms, for example, or ledges for books and art work in family rooms. But in the bathroom, they are a wonderfully sleek and visually subtle storage solution for some of the most attractive accoutrements of the bath: fluffy towels and washcloths, soaps, lotions, and sleek cups that hold cotton balls, makeup, toothbrushes, and razors—and whatever else you regularly use.

Simple, strong, and attractive, floating shelves are also easy to make—even for the DIY novice. The shelves get their name because they appear to "float" on the wall without any visual support: the cleat (or batten) that mounts each shelf to the wall is hidden within the shelf's hollow interior. The shelves are similar to hollow-core doors that have a lightweight interior framework and a "skin" on the top and the bottom of the frame. In fact, it is possible to use hollow-core doors to make floating shelves. In terms of construction, a table saw is preferred

for cutting the plywood, but a circular saw can be used. If you have none of these, use a handsaw or ask the lumberyard to cut the plywood to your dimensions for you. I recommend using birch plywood, as it has a smooth surface that's excellent for painting or staining.

When measuring your lumber, keep in mind the following: each hollow shelf has a top and bottom, so double each shelf's area to come up with the amount of plywood you need. Each shelf needs an internal three-sided frame of 1x2s equal to the shelf's perimeter; the 2x2 wall batten will make the unseen fourth side of the frame. The ¼-inch trim is used to cover the three sides of the shelf that will be showing. The depth of your trim needs to be the same thickness. If not, make it flush at the top and let it extend lower at the bottom. If you're in doubt about your measurements, take your drawings with you to the lumber store, and the salesperson can help you get the right amount of wood.

TIME:
2 hours per shelf

DIFFICULTY:
⌁⌁⌁

TOOLS:
Stud finder

Level

Measuring tape

Handsaw

Table saw or circular saw

Miter saw or miter box

Hammer

Staple gun (optional)

Nail set

Drill/driver with bits

Paintbrushes, roller, and tray

Framing square

Carpenter's pencil

Safety glasses

Ear protection

SAME PLACE, MORE SPACE

MATERIALS:

WOOD:

1x2 lumber, for framing (quantity determined by your needs and measurements)

2x2 lumber, for the batten (quantity determined by your needs and measurements)

¼-inch sheets birch plywood (quantity determined by your needs and measurements)

¼-inch flat trim

HARDWARE:

1 box brad nails

1 box each 1- and 3-inch screws

FINISHING SUPPLIES:

Sandpaper, 120- and 220-grit

Wood glue

Spackle

Wood putty

1 quart each primer and paint, or 1 quart stain

MAKE THAT SPACE HAPPEN

1..
Based on your space and needs, design one or more floating shelves: where will they go on the wall and how wide and deep will they be? Using a stud finder, locate the wall studs, mark them with a pencil, and then adjust the design or placement of each shelf so that it spans two studs.

2..
Cut all the wood to size, based on your measurements. A handsaw can be used for the lumber and the plywood, or use a circular saw. For the plywood, the straightest cuts will be made on a table saw; if you want, have the lumberyard cut the plywood for you. (You may be charged a small fee.) For the ¼-inch trim, use a miter saw to cut three pieces per shelf: where the pieces meet at

the front corner of each shelf, cut a 45-degree angle, in which the interior point of the angle is the exact length of that side of the shelf.

3..
Arrange all the cut pieces in front of you on a sturdy worktable and assemble the three-sided frame. Glue and nail the two sidepieces of 1x2 to the one long piece of 1x2.

4..
Apply glue around the top of the frame and set one piece of plywood in place. Using a hammer or staple gun, nail or staple the plywood to the frame all the way around. If the nails or staples are protruding, use a nail set to set them. Complete one side, then flip the shelf over and repeat the process.

5

Next, attach the mitered trim to the three exposed, outside edges of the shelf (to hide the edge of the plywood and the seam where it meets the frame). Do the front piece of trim first and make sure that the inside of the mitered angle is directly aligned with the shelf's front corners. Apply a thin, even bead of glue to the trim and attach with brad nails (if you have one, a pneumatic pin nailer is ideal for this). Once the front trim is attached, glue and nail the sidepieces.

6

Fill any nail or staple holes with spackle and sand the shelves smooth to the touch. Wipe off dust with a damp paper towel (or a tack cloth).

7

Prime and paint or stain the shelves. Allow them to dry completely before installing.

8

Finally, install the shelves. Using your original wall markings (from Step 1) as a reference, drill a pilot hole into each wall stud where you will attach a 2x2 batten (which is also the missing fourth side of your shelf frame). Using 3-inch screws, securely attach each 2x2 batten, or mounting strip, to the wall studs, along the marked level lines. The hollow opening in the back of the shelf fits over the batten and is secured with 1-inch screws, from the underside and topside.

9

Fill, sand, and apply one final coat of paint.

Exploded view of simple floating shelf construction.

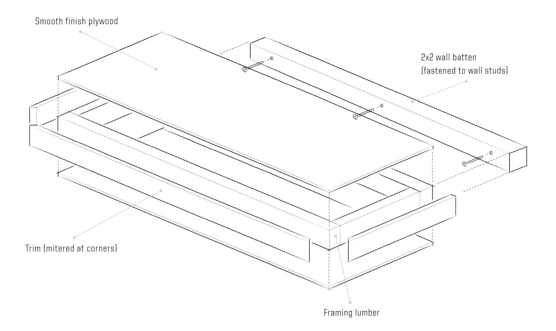

Smooth finish plywood

2x2 wall batten
(fastened to wall studs)

Trim (mitered at corners)

Framing lumber

MAXIMIZE THE MEDICINE CABINET

MAXIMIZE THE MEDICINE CABINET

This project takes advantage of an ample 7-inch-deep medicine cabinet—which can be slipped into a wall with typical 2x4 studs with only minimal intrusion into the space over the sink (if your walls have 2x6 studs, even better!). Only 1 inch protrudes from the wall—sleek, simple, and understated. Everyone is surprised when opening a recessed cabinet to see its practical storage depth. Even more surprising? It's a relatively quick and easy project, as most medicine cabinets are built to fit between your existing studs (or 14½ inches wide). However, if you need your cabinet to line up exactly to a lavatory or faucet, you will have to cut a stud and provide some additional blocking. Internal walls are best, but external walls are also usable. If you place the medicine cabinet within an external wall, you will have to reduce the depth slightly to accommodate some insulation. The toughest part will be choosing a cabinet, since there are so many styles available from home centers and online sources. When selecting your cabinet, make sure it is a recessed style. You can also find hinged-door and sliding-door models, with one, two, or three doors. I suggest a one-door hinged style, which I think looks very clean and modern.

When shopping, buy the best quality you can afford. It's one area where you may not want to cut corners, since a cabinet receives a lot of use, especially if it is located in a family bathroom. Cabinet boxes made from wood and/or aluminum are good choices since they hold up to humidity well. Plastic does, too, but it may not be as sturdy as you like. Steel cabinets with baked-on enamel finish resist rust a bit better than cheaper models with a sprayed-on finish. I personally love the Kohler cabinets, as they have three mirrors: one each on the front and rear of the door and one behind the tempered glass shelves. They also contain a ground fault circuit interrupter (GFCI) receptacle.

The variations in hinge quality can be huge; in a way, a cabinet is really only as good at its hinge. A high-quality hinge will provide good support for the heavy mirror on the front. Hinged-door cabinets and spring-loaded, self-closing hinges hold doors closed more firmly than do magnetic catches. European hinges often include this extra feature, while piano hinge cabinets do not. Other features you may want to look for include: adjustable shelves so you can customize your storage space; distortion-free mirrors; fog-proof mirrors; and door-activated interior light cabinets (which need to be wired).

TIME:

4 hours

DIFFICULTY:

↑↑↑

TOOLS:

Tape measure

4-foot level

Stud finder

Utility knife

Wire coat hanger

Flashlight

Drywall saw

Short-bladed handsaw, reciprocating saw, or oscillating tool

Drill/driver with bits

Hammer

Caulking gun (optional)

Carpenter's pencil

Paintbrushes, roller, and tray

Safety glasses

Ear protection

MATERIALS:

Medicine cabinet, 7 inches deep

WOOD:

2x4 or 2x6 lumber (quantity determined by your wall's framing)

Shims

HARDWARE:

1 box 3-inch drywall screws

1 box 6d drywall nails

FINISHING SUPPLIES:

Sandpaper, 120 grit

Small pieces of drywall or scraps

Drywall compound

Drywall tape

Acrylic caulk (optional)

½ gallon each primer and paint

MAKE THAT SPACE HAPPEN

1 . . . .
Potential cabinet placements are typically limited to above or next to the sink, so choose your spot first, and then see what's behind the wall. However, any wall position that tickles your fancy works. I have three in my master bath. If you are replacing a small cabinet with a larger one, remove the old cabinet from the wall—it's generally affixed with screws through the sides. If you are installing a cabinet where none exists, mark the wall with the cabinet placement. A good height is for the bottom edge of the mirror to be about 40 inches off the floor; however, adjust cabinet placement and height from the floor to suit the needs (and sizes) of the people who will be using it.

Use a tape measure to mark off the height and then draw a horizontal reference line at that point with a carpenter's pencil and level. If the cabinet will be above the vanity or pedestal sink, measure the width of the sink and divide by two—that's the centerline. Transfer the measurement to the wall. If the medicine cabinet has a template, tape it to the wall, aligning it with your two reference lines. If you don't have a template, measure the width and height of the back of the cabinet and add ½ inch to each measurement to give you some wiggle room when you place the cabinet. Mark these dimensions on the wall.

2 . . . .
Next, before you saw the cabinet opening, check the wall for studs, water lines, and wiring. Use a stud finder to check for studs within your layout lines. If you find one, use a utility knife to cut an 8-inch-square access hole in the wall that spans across the stud. If you don't find a stud, use the knife to cut the access hole at the center of your layout. Look inside the wall for obstructions; also feel behind the wall with your hand and/or with a bent wire coat hanger and a flashlight. If you find wiring and/or pipes, you may have to surface-mount the cabinet or recess it only partially. But since you are likely to find a stud or two, I will guide you next in cutting them and building in blocking to support both the wall and the cabinet.

NOTE: It is good practice to add a blocking piece at the top; this is a horizontal piece cut out of a removed stud. This enables the general weight of the wall to be evenly distributed to the other two studs. Never cut a double stud or any stud that is 3 inches or greater, as these may be carrying load.

3 . . . .
If you do find wires or pipes, you will need to reroute them, which may require a plumber or an electrician. But if the space behind the wall is completely clear, cut the opening with a drywall saw (or a reciprocating saw), but use the utility knife to cut away the drywall where it overlaps the studs. In this case, measure and cut the drywall and the obstructing studs themselves, 1½ inches above and below the cabinet opening to provide clearance for the blocking. Once the drywall is cut to this measure, use a short-bladed handsaw, an oscillating tool, or a reciprocating saw to cut through the studs. An oscillating cutting tool is perfect for cutting nails that have been used to support the drywall to the adjoining room. If you do not have access to this tool, try to tap the stud at an angle toward you so you can pull the nails or screws through the back of the adjoining drywall.

4 . . . .
Frame the opening. Cut the 2x4s or 2x6s (whatever matches the existing wall studs); you need at least two and possibly four pieces. Two pieces are horizontal blocking to fit between the studs. At the top and bottom of the opening, screw that blocking into place, using 3-inch drywall screws driven at an angle. If you cut the blocking to the exact size, it should stay in place while you drive in the screws.

With the horizontal blocking in place, install two vertical pieces of 2x4 (or 2x6) with 3-inch drywall screws to match the opening exactly, placing them behind or inside the drywall. If your opening is already flush with existing studs, you don't need these vertical pieces. If you had to cut studs for the opening, take the stud pieces you removed, recut them to the correct length and use these for the vertical sides.

continued

5

If you cut studs and, therefore, had to cut extra drywall at the top and bottom of the cabinet opening, you will need to patch the cutout areas. Cut sections of new drywall to match the cutout areas and cover the blocking. Nail the patch pieces in place with 6d drywall nails. Cover the joints with drywall tape and drywall compound. Allow the compound to dry completely, lightly sand, and then prime and paint the surface. Allow the primer to dry completely before proceeding.

6

Install the cabinet. Remove the door(s) and place the cabinet box in the opening. Check that the box is level and plumb in the opening. Shim it if necessary. Screw the cabinet to the side studs on each side of the opening. Don't overtighten the screws, because you can distort or even damage the cabinet. Attach the door(s) and check and adjust for level and alignment.

7

Many recessed cabinets have a lip that projects over the drywall opening to trim and cover the wall opening. If the wall surface is uneven, there may be gaps between the edge of the lip and the wall. If that's the case, use a caulking gun and acrylic caulk to fill and seal the sides of the cabinet. Smooth the bead with your wet finger and wipe away any excess. Paint it with your wall color, and it will disappear.

Another option is to cut and nail a small wood strip around the cabinet. You can then paint or stain it to match the finish of the cabinet or wall.

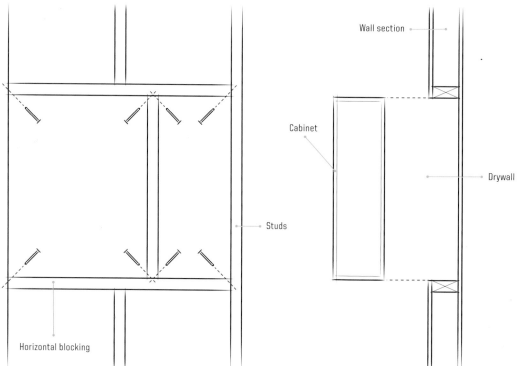

Wall framing elevation.

Wall section

Cabinet

Drywall

Studs

Horizontal blocking

PROJECT:

RECESSED SHOWER SHELF

RECESSED SHOWER SHELF

Recessed shelving in a shower stall gives you a place to stow shampoo, soap, sponges, bubble bath, rubber duckies, and other items that may otherwise clutter up a ledge. A niche does not need to be small—I have built some floor to ceiling in size—but I can tell you that a niche makes an enormous amount of difference in terms of storage and clutter control.

Construction is similar to that for Project: Carved-Out Wall Niche (page 120)—with some important caveats. If you are retrofitting the niche in an already-tiled shower wall, the job becomes more time-consuming and complex; you have to take extra care when doing the partial demo on the old wall, the rebuild requires the use of waterproof drywall (or cement board) and a waterproof membrane, and then you have to re-tile the new space properly. This is a much easier project if you are in the planning stages for, or in the construction phase of, a new shower—and thus have exposed studs and open access. Also, in some cases, your shower may have only a partially tiled wall or walls, and the recessed shelf can be situated in a nontiled section of wall, making it almost exactly the same job as the Carved-Out Wall Niche.

Here I provide two options: either installing a niche in a new build, or installing one in an existing shower.

RECESSED SHELF IN A NEW SHOWER

This project assumes that the shower wall is exposed. If you are making this niche on a finished, non-tiled portion of the wall, see Project: Carved-Out Wall Niche (page 120) for instructions on making a hole in the drywall.

TIME:

2 hours

DIFFICULTY:

↑↑

TOOLS:

Circular saw

Drill/driver with bits

Tape measure

4-foot level

Framing and combination squares

Hammer

Tiling and grout equipment

Pencil

Safety glasses

Ear protection

MATERIALS:

WOOD:

2x4 or 2x6 lumber (quantity to match existing wall studs)

HARDWARE:

1 box each 2-and 3-inch drywall screws

90-degree metal drywall setting angle, long enough to cover external edges of niche (sold in 8- to 10-foot lengths)

FINISHING SUPPLIES:

Marine or bathroom-grade waterproof Sheetrock or cement board

Drywall compound

Drywall tape

Waterproof membrane

MAKE THAT SPACE HAPPEN

1 ....

Take note of where your shower valves and shower-head will be located, and then choose your desired location. Ideally, use an edge of an existing stud for your niche or use the entire width (usually 14½ inches). However, it is always a wise idea to plan in advance in terms of your tile size, so you can cleverly position your niche to fit in with a full tile—eliminating the need for cutting. While this is not a necessity, it does make for a more stream-lined result.

2 ....

For constructing the recessed niche, consult the instructions for Project: Carved-Out Wall Niche (page 120). Cut the appropriate size lumber and screw the pieces into place ensuring they are plumb, level, and square.

3 ....

Sheet the walls and the niche using marine- or bathroom-grade waterproof drywall or cement board. Set the metal angles and use drywall com-pound to fill in all joints.

4 ....

When the compound is dry, apply your choice of waterproof membrane. You'll find many varieties available on the market. I like to use the approved paintable membranes. The walls and shower floor are done at the same time. There is often a primer, with reinforced mesh for the corners, followed by two to three coats of membrane applied by roller and brush. This is truly a DIY project!

5 ....

Begin tiling when the entire shower membrane is completely dry, as per the manufacturer's recom-mendations. For tips on basic tiling, see Project: Storage Island, "Optional Finish: Tile the Counter-top" (page 67).

RECESSED SHELF IN A TILED SHOWER WALL

Before starting this project, decide on what tiles you wish to use. If you are trying to match the existing tiles, note that you may need to order them, and this can take up to a month (or more!). So wait for the tiles to arrive before starting your project! However, if you can't match your tiles, you can use contrasting tiles instead: they will really make your niche stand out.

TIME:

3 days (due to membrane drying time; time varies by product)

DIFFICULTY:

⚒⚒⚒⚒

TOOLS:

Drywall saw

Tape measure

4-inch angle grinder with diamond blade

Cold chisel

Circular saw

4-foot level

Drill/driver with bit

Hammer

2-inch paintbrush for membrane

Tiling and grout equipment

Combination square

Pencil

Safety glasses

Ear protection

Face mask

Work gloves

MATERIALS:

WOOD:

2x4 lumber (quantity determined by niche dimensions)

Cement board

TILE:

Tile, enough for niche, plus 10 percent

HARDWARE:

1 box 3-inch drywall screws

FINISHING SUPPLIES:

Construction adhesive

Waterproof (paintable) membrane

Insulation, small piece

Thinset mortar

Grout

Shelving and silicone (optional)

Sponges

Lint-free cloths

MAKE THAT SPACE HAPPEN

1 ....

Choose your desired location. On the other side of the wall, cut out a small inspection hole in the drywall (see Project: Maximize the Medicine Cabinet, page 82, for instructions). Making an inspection hole in drywall is easy, and it's imperative to determine that no plumbing pipes are in the wall before you cut through the existing shower tile. If you see plumbing lines, move the location of your niche, or call in a pro. Plumbing pipes are not necessarily hard to relocate—if you have the know-how. If you don't, get a plumber to help you out.

2 ....

Measure and transfer the dimensions of your niche onto the tiled wall using a common wall for reference. It is a good idea to cross check your dimensions, as a wall thickness can vary. Do this by running your tape measure across the room to another adjacent wall. Triple check this as your location needs to be exact.

3 ....

On the tiled wall, use a small 4-inch angle grinder with a diamond blade to cut out the opening and chip out the corners and any chipped tiles. Be sure to place some old towels on the floor to protect the tub or floor tile from falling tile pieces. Also, ensure that a window is open; or if there is no external window, have a mate use a shop vac to suck the dust directly as you cut. Tape the door around all the gaps to eliminate the flow of dust.

4 ....

Construct the niche frame following the instructions in Project: Carved-Out Wall Niche (page 120). Cut framing pieces from the 2x4s and screw them into place using 3-inch screws, making sure that the framework is level, plumb, and square. Provide some insulation at the rear of the niche, especially if it backs onto a bedroom!

5 ....

Line the niche with cement board, plasterset all edges, and allow everything to dry.

6 ....

Apply a minimum of two coats of paintable waterproof membrane to the niche. Allow to fully dry and then begin tiling.

7 ....

Finish the niche with the tile. For the basics in how to apply thinset and to lay and cut tiles, see Project: Storage Island (page 62). When tiling the base of the niche, remember to slope the tiles slightly from back to front so water will fall into the shower and not pool in the niche. To do this, just apply a little more thinset to the rear of the base prior to placing your tile. Then use a small level to ensure it is out of level; you can use your square placed against the rear wall to check as well.

TIP: A great way to finish the tiled edges is to use a chrome-plated brass strip surround. It is widely available. This gives you the opportunity to change the tile direction or color in an aesthetically pleasing way.

8 ....

Mix grout to match the existing material and apply it to the tiled area. You may have to mix a few colors to get it right. Or, if you are using different tiles altogether, find a grout that matches the tile. Lucky you if your tile is standard white—it's the easiest to match.

9 ....

If you have built a tall niche, you will want to install some shelves to take advantage of your new space. You'll have many to choose from. Tempered glass, acrylic, stone, or tile will fit into the niche, depending on your décor and tile choices. Tiles can be built in and glass can be installed afterward using a neat silicone seal all round.

DOUBLE VANITY

DOUBLE VANITY

I've seen a lot of 40- and 46-inch bathroom vanities that have one lonely sink plopped in the middle of their countertops. This does not make a lot of sense to me, especially for people who have a partner or kids who need to get ready at the same time for work or school. Replacing that single fixture with two sinks is a simple plumbing job that can be accomplished by a confident DIYer (though you may need another pair of hands to lift and remove the old countertop). In fact, this is an excellent project not only for doubling the function of your bathroom, but for building basic plumbing skills as well. A word about plumbing materials before we begin: everything you need for this project can be found at the hardware store. I recommend using a PVC P-trap kit with compression fittings, which are easy to align and less likely to leak than metal fittings because the joints or connection points can be made very secure and tight very easily.

A PVC T-connector with compression fittings is also a must for the same reason. Plumber's putty is a gooey paste that is most often used when installing sink drains to compress to seal between the flange and the sink. Plumber's (or Teflon tape) is used to create a seal on any threaded fittings that do not have a rubber washer fitting.

TIME:

8 hours

DIFFICULTY:

↑↑↑↑

TOOLS:

Jigsaw

Hacksaw

Utility knife

Hammer

Electrical pliers

Grooved pliers

Pipe wrench

Crescent wrench

Level

Drill/driver with bits

Caulking gun

Pencil

Safety glasses

Ear protection

MATERIALS:

A snazzy new countertop to your liking

2 new sinks or 1 to match your existing (measure to ensure it will fit into your vanity)

PLUMBING SUPPLIES:

1 PVC P-trap kit with compression fittings per each sink

1 PVC T-connector with compression fittings per each sink

2 shutoff valves with dual outlets

Small length of drain pipe (usually 2 inches in diameter) for wider runs

FINISHING SUPPLIES:

Silicone caulk

Plumber's putty

Plumber's tape (Teflon tape)

Acrylic sealant (optional)

Shims

MAKE THAT SPACE HAPPEN

1 . . . .

Turn off the water at the shutoff valves located under the sink. Turn on the faucet to remove any standing water and drain the sink. Remove the supply lines going from the faucet to the shutoff valve and loosen the drain line.

2 . . . .

Loosen the caulk between the vanity top and the wall with a utility knife. Gradually lift and remove the top, moving carefully so as not to damage the wall. You will likely need an extra set of hands for this.

3 . . . .

Make sure you have shut off your main water supply. Then, remove the old shutoff valves from under the sink and recycle them. Be careful not to damage the existing supply pipes.

4 . . . .

Attach the faucets to the new vanity top, according to the manufacturer's instructions, before installing the vanity top. Most of the time, faucet instructions recommend attaching the flexible supply lines to the faucet by tightening the compression nuts to the threaded posts on the faucet. Then insert the faucet through the predrilled holes in the vanity top and tighten the nut that comes with the faucet kit to hold it in place.

5 . . . .

Next, install the drain assembly included with each faucet by putting a bead of plumber's putty under the rim of the drain trim and pushing it down through the top of the drain hole in the sink. From underneath, tighten the nut until the excess putty oozes out on all sides to seal the drain from leaks. Use a rag and your finger to remove the excess putty. Screw the tailpiece from the drain assembly to the drain trim and tighten. Install the lift lever and stopper by aligning the lift lever through the hole in the back of the tailpiece and inserting it into the hole in the stopper.

Plumbing pipes are put together quite logically, as you can see—nothing to be afraid of, folks!

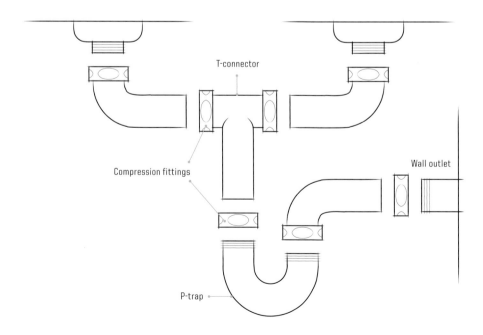

T-connector

Compression fittings

Wall outlet

P-trap

6 ....
If you chose a laminate top or tile on a plywood surface, fasten with screws from the underside. If stone, simply run a bead of acrylic sealant around the perimeter and around each cutout, then lay it onto the vanity. Secure the new vanity top to the cabinet. Make sure the top is level in both directions. If it's not, bring out the shims.

7 ....
Install the new dual-outlet shutoff valves by inserting the valves onto the supply pipes (usually ½-inch copper pipes). Slide the compression nut from the shutoff valve onto the pipe with the threads facing the open end. Then slide on the compression ring. Attach the shutoff valve. Slide the compression nut and ring up to the shutoff valve and hand-tighten the nut.

8 ....
Hook the flexible supply lines from the faucet or handle fittings to the hot and cold shutoff valves. Once all your compression fittings are attached, use an adjustable wrench to tighten them. Be careful not to over-tighten, as this can bend the soft copper pipe.

9 ....
Hook up the new drainpipes and fittings to the old drainpipe using a T-connector and the new P-trap. Tighten all connections.

10 ....
Turn on the new shutoff valves slowly. Check for leaks in the supply lines. Turn on the faucets (slowly) and check for drain line leaks. You will find that the faucet makes all sorts of scary sounds, right out of the soundtrack for a horror movie! Don't worry—this is just the air escaping out of the lines. Fill the sink with water and let drain all at once to check for leaks under pressure.

11 ....
If you are drip-free up to your sink, run a bead of silicone caulk around the sink cutouts and set the new sinks into the top of the cabinet.

TIP: To catch small drips you might miss otherwise, lay a piece of newspaper or paper towel on the floor of the cabinet under the pipe you installed. Any size drip will leave an obvious spot on the paper; if you find one, tighten the fittings without overdoing it.

12 ....
Caulk the back and sides of the vanity top where it meets the wall. Allow to dry for twenty-four hours before using.

NOTE: If you have an electrical outlet close to the sinks, it will need to be a GFCI (ground fault circuit interrupter) outlet to prevent anyone from being electrocuted (such as if a plugged-in hair dryer were to accidentally drop into a water-filled sink). This is important. If you are not confident installing and testing this yourself, hire a licensed electrician.

The second sink can be hooked up to the existing sink's water supply.

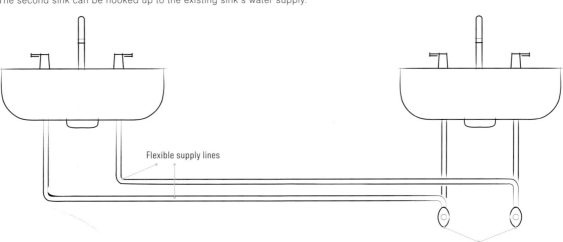

Flexible supply lines

Dual shutoff valves

INSTALL A POCKET DOOR

INSTALL A POCKET DOOR

A slim, discreet pocket door is a great way to add usable floor and wall space to a tiny powder room. Pocket-door kits are reasonably priced and available at many home centers. However, installation is not without its challenges. A portion of the wall must be removed to make room for the split studs that replace the wooden ones and for the track on which the new door hangs. Demolition is always rather messy, and this project does require some knowledge of framing carpentry. If you're concerned about your skill level, I recommend working with an experienced friend.

Before you start, check to see if the wall into which the door will slide (when open) contains wiring or plumbing. A wall with pipes is not a good candidate for a pocket door, but you can work around wires. If you have attic and basement access, electrical cables can be rerouted. Concealed wiring can be detected by using a stud finder that has a built-in voltage detector. In addition, wire splices need to be made in a permanently accessible electrical box. This is a job you may want to hire a licensed electrician to take care of—then you can tackle the pocket-door installation yourself.

You also want to make sure you have enough room in your wall to fit a sliding door. A rough opening that's a bit more than twice the width of the door is necessary; if that works in the wall you have chosen, the next step is to determine if the wall is a load-bearing or a nonstructural partition. Load-bearing walls are usually near the center of the house and run perpendicular to the floor joists (check joist direction in the basement). Doors placed in load-bearing walls have headers over their openings. Installing a pocket door in a load-bearing wall requires replacing the old header with a longer one and creating a temporary ceiling support while the header goes in. If this is the case, you may want to consult or hire a pro to install the door.

Because this is a 5-hammer job, the instructions assume a higher level of experience and familiarity with both the tools and the techniques required.

TIME:

2 days

DIFFICULTY:

⋀⋀⋀⋀⋀

TOOLS:

Screwdriver or drill/driver with bits

Utility knife

Reciprocating saw with wood- and metal-cutting blades

Drywall saw

Hammer

Nail set

Pry bar

Circular saw

4-foot level

Handsaw

Hacksaw

Tape measure

Drywall knife

Sanding block

Wood chisel

Paintbrush, roller, and tray

Safety glasses

Ear protection

MATERIALS:

1 pocket door kit

1 door jamb kit

WOOD:

2x4 lumber (quantity determined
by width of header)

HARDWARE:

1 box 1-inch drywall screws

1 box 2-inch nails

1 box finishing nails

FINISHING SUPPLIES:

1 sheet of ½-inch drywall (or thickness
to match existing)

Construction adhesive

Drywall tape

Drywall compound

Molding (quantity determined by door
surround dimensions)

Wood putty

Topping compound

120-grit sandpaper

1 gallon plus 1 quart primer and paint

Panel adhesive

MAKE THAT SPACE HAPPEN

1 ....

Using a drywall saw, remove a section of drywall above the door to allow you to inspect prior to removal of the drywall. If you see wires or other services, consider consulting a professional.

2 ....

Remove the existing door by unscrewing the hinges. First, put on your safety glasses (no exceptions). Pry off the trim on both sides. It is good practice to use your utility knife to cut the corner where the drywall meets the trim to avoid tearing the drywall paper when removing the trim pieces. Then remove the doorjamb. Use a reciprocating saw fitted with a wood-cutting blade to cut across the side of the jamb horizontally a couple of inches from the top jamb to break the side jamb away from the top jamb.

3 ....

Remove drywall and the existing header by slicing through the nails that fasten it to the studs with the reciprocating saw fitted with a metal-cutting blade. Remove the drywall above the header but stay a few inches below the ceiling to avoid extra finish work later. The use of a utility knife will make this easy. Use a reciprocating saw to remove the existing header and cut away the studs to make room for the pocket door's new framing.

NOTE: If your wall turns out to be a load-bearing wall, a temporary ceiling support wil be required before removal. Placement should be directly under the load. I suggest consulting a structural engineer if this is the case—better safe than sorry.

4 ....
Remove the door frame's bottom plate by prying it
off with the claw end of a hammer. If the threshold
is made of stone or marble, pry it off or, if absolutely necessary, break it into pieces and remove
it. (Don the safety glasses.)

5 ....
Using a circular saw or handsaw, cut a length of
straight 2x4 to form the new header. Some 2x4s
are shaped like bananas, which would make the
project difficult.

continued

Note how the pocket door fits neatly inside the wall when open, saving valuable floor space.

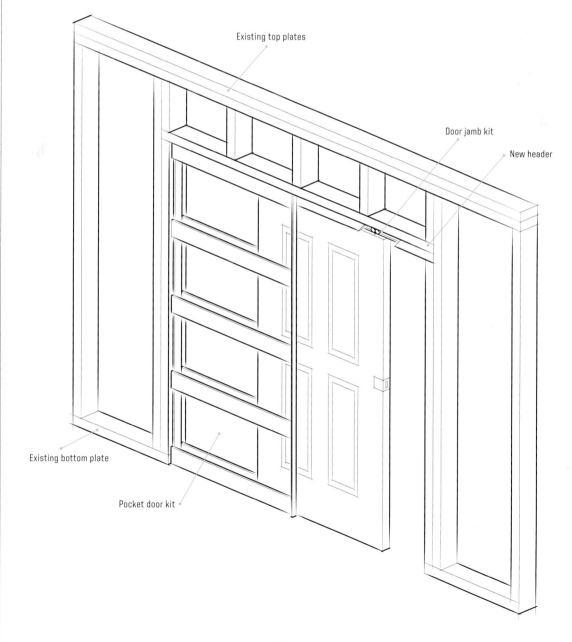

Existing top plates

Door jamb kit

New header

Existing bottom plate

Pocket door kit

6

Cut the studs to the length needed to support the new header at the correct height. To determine the new header height for your door kit, figure the height of the new door, plus 3¼ inches, plus the height of the new threshold, if any. However, always check the kit manufacturer's instructions.

7

Determine the rough opening width and install a new stud this distance from the existing stud on the opposite side. Nail or screw the new header in place and then cut the pocket door header-and-track-assembly to length with a hacksaw. Install it at the specified height using the fasteners and brackets supplied with the door. The assembly must be level.

8

Attach the jamb stiffeners (thin, metal-reinforced supports for the wall material) to the floor brackets. Attach them to the header, as directed by the manufacturer. Then plumb them with your 4-foot level and nail or screw the brackets to the floor. Once complete, install the door bumper in the face of the stud at the back of the pocket using a 2-inch screw. (Jamb stiffeners, floor brackets, and door bumper should all be included in your door jamb kit.)

9

Secure the door plates to the top of the door with the long screws supplied in the door jamb kit; put the two wheel hangers in the track. Then hang the door on the two hangers and use the adjusting nuts to adjust the door for height and plumb. Try out the door. When it glides perfectly, install the door handle and latch.

TIP: Paint or finish the door before you install it. Be sure to paint all edges including the top and bottom to prevent excessive moisture vapor from damaging the door and causing it to warp.

10

Install drywall over the door pocket using construction adhesive and 1-inch drywall screws.

11

Tape all joints and then apply drywall compound with a drywall knife. Allow to dry. Use your drywall knife to take off any high spots, then apply the topping compound. Allow to dry completely and then sand using a 120-grit sanding block.

12

Using the screws supplied in the kit, install the door guides on the jamb on the inside and outside of the door at the entrance of the pocket. Adjust the guides to center the door in the opening and allow just enough clearance for the door to slide smoothly.

13

Nail the two-piece strike and head jambs on either side of the door so they are flush to the finished wall surface. Use wood screws (supplied) to install one side of the head jamb so you can remove the door in the event of a problem. Install a full-width jamb on the opposite side jamb (called the strike jamb). Drill a hole and, using a wood chisel, carve out a shallow mortise in that jamb for the strike plate to line up with your handle and lock.

NOTE: The size of the door hardware will determine the size of the drill bit and chisel width.

14

Install door trim/molding, nailing it to the jamb and to the pocket door stud with finishing nails no longer than the thickness of the trim, plus the drywall, plus the ¾-inch stud thickness. Otherwise you will nail the door shut! Also nail the existing baseboard you had removed or matching profile in place to make it look like it was always there.

15

Prime and paint the door wall and trim.

06
BEDROOMS

Bedrooms are a place to get away from the hustle and bustle of household activities, relax and unwind, read a book, snuggle and cuddle, and, of course, sleep. Even children need an "isolation chamber" where they can decompress, study, draw, read, play, dream, and fantasize. Unfortunately, too much stuff bulging from closets, overstuffed dressers, and limited floor space doesn't make for sweet dreams.

For more than three years, my wife and I lived in a 7-by-7-foot bedroom area in the tiny cottage we called home while I built our house. A standard 10-by-12-foot tract house bedroom would have seemed quite princely to us! I used every inch of space to build shelving, platforms, nooks, and hooks so we had room to put away our clothes, stack books, and set a glass of water and an alarm clock on the surface next to our bed. So I know it is possible to create a functional, restful, and beautiful space in any size room.

PROJECT:

CLOSET MAKEOVER

CLOSET MAKEOVER

You don't need to hire an expensive closet system firm to remake your closet. There is so much you can do to maximize your existing closet space at a fraction of the cost of what a pro would charge you. This closet makeover consists of five easy, individual projects; do them all or do only one or two, depending on your needs. A good cleaning and evaluation gets you started. Then turn the sides you never see into convenient sweater shelving. Add double rods to double your hanging space. Make a simple shelf 6 inches from the closet floor to create a convenient extra rack for shoes. And add high shelves to take advantage of the air space close to the ceiling. In fact, these strategies can be applied to every closet in your house—to enlarge a linen closet, punch up a pantry, or increase a coat closet or china cabinet.

Clean, Plan, and Paint Your Closet

TIME:
1 to 2 hours per project

DIFFICULTY:

TOOLS:
Tape measure
Putty knife
Paintbrushes, roller, and tray
Painter's drop cloths
Pencil
Safety glasses

MATERIALS:

FINISHING SUPPLIES:
Joint compound or spackle
Sandpaper, 120- and 200-grit
1 gallon each primer and paint

MAKE THAT SPACE HAPPEN

1...

You know the routine: clear everything out of the closet and discard or relocate everything that isn't in use or doesn't need to be there. See Chapter 1 for a refresher. Then, clean the closet, top to bottom.

2...

Measure the dimensions of the closet height, width, and depth. Measure the depth and height of the sides from the back to the door opening, and from the bottom of the top shelf to the floor. Using the measurements, create a diagram of the closet before you begin. This will prevent you from having to adjust anything after you begin construction.

3...

Is your lighting suitable? Consider this prior to your closet build. Inexpensive battery-operated touch lights are easy to install and operate. This can save you from doing another DIY project or hiring an electrician.

4...

Patch any dents or holes with spackle, sand them smooth, and then prime and paint the ceiling and interior. A good washable semi-gloss paint is recommended to ensure ease of cleaning. Or you might consider using a metallic or pearlescent glaze to add a bit of glamour to your closet.

Build Side Shelves

Side shelves expand your closet storage options by giving you a place to stow shoes, clothing, towels, or anything that you do not want on the floor or a hard-to-reach upper shelf. These are the most basic types of shelves and an easy project for the novice builder.

TIME:
3 hours

DIFFICULTY:

TOOLS:
4-foot level

Tape measure

Drill/driver with bits

Stud finder

Handsaw or circular saw

Table saw (optional)

Iron, for melamine edging (optional)

Paintbrush, roller, and tray (optional)

Framing Square

Pencil

Safety glasses

MATERIALS:

WOOD:
1 sheet ⅝-inch paint-grade birch plywood or white melamine

Edging for plywood or melamine

HARDWARE:
4 shelf brackets or one 1x2 wood strip (ledger board) per shelf

1 box each 2½-inch and ¾-inch screws

1 box 1-inch nails

FINISHING SUPPLIES:
Construction adhesive

Screw caps (optional)

Sandpaper, 220-grit (optional)

½ gallon each primer and paint (optional)

MAKE THAT SPACE HAPPEN

1 . . . .

Using a level and a pencil, mark lines for shelf placement on the wall prior to attaching the shelf supports. Remember to account for the thickness of the shelf itself when calculating the distance between shelves.

2 . . . .

Using a stud finder, locate and mark wall studs. Then attach shelf supports to the wall studs following your level lines, using either brackets or a 1x2 wood strip. If you use brackets, drill pilot holes through the drywall and into the studs before screwing them in. (Drilling pilot holes will prevent you from struggling with issues such as wood grain and drifting screws.) If you use wood strips, use a handsaw to cut the 1x2 into two equal lengths that are at least 2 inches shorter than the dimensions of the shelf itself. Center these pieces on the wall marks where the shelf will be; drill pilot holes before screwing to avoid splitting the wood. Set screw heads flush with brackets or wood strips. Make sure screws are long enough to fasten into the studs, taking into account the thickness of the ledger board and drywall. Generally 2½-inch screws will do the job.

3 . . . .

With a circular or table saw, cut the plywood or melamine to desired width and depth for shelves.

You could also ask the lumberyard to cut the boards to the correct dimensions for you.

NOTE: Since you may need to bring the shelf in at an angle when installing, cut the material ¼ inch shorter than the exact full width to guarantee a hassle-free fit.

4 . . . .

Attach edging to the front edge of each shelf. Cut, glue with construction adhesive, and nail on wooden edge strips or iron on melamine edging.

5 . . . .

If using plywood, this is a good time to paint your shelves! Sand, prime, and paint all exposed surfaces. A smooth foam roller gives you a smooth finish in a jiffy. Make sure you sand between coats using a 220-grit sandpaper. A good quality VOC-free semi-gloss paint is a good choice.

6 . . . .

Place the shelves on the supports and fasten them with screws. If using brackets, fasten from below with short screws (making sure they do not penetrate through the top surface), and begin with the highest shelf. If using 1x2 supports, install 2½-inch screws from the top of the shelf into the 1x2 (ensuring the screwheads are flush or countersunk), and begin with the lowest shelf. There are screw caps available in a variety of colors to cover these screws if visible.

Whether you use metal brackets or wood strips for support, side shelves are easy and provide space for closet overflow.

Front edging   Ledger boards   Angle brackets

Hang Double Rods

Adding a second rod doubles your space for hanging clothes. Most closets are tall enough for double rods; depending on your space, the second rod can be put above or below the current rod. Before installing the second rod, determine how much space each rod needs. Measure your clothes (on hangers), from the top of the hanger to the bottom of the clothing. If placement of the second rod doesn't leave enough hanging room, consider moving and reinstalling the first rod higher or lower and/or dedicating one rod to short-hanging clothes (like pants folded twice). These considerations are why it's best to diagram your entire closet before starting these projects.

TIME:

1 hour

DIFFICULTY:

TOOLS:

Handsaw (if a wood dowel; optional)

Hacksaw (if a pipe; optional)

Tape measure

2 clamps

Level

Screwdriver or drill/driver with bits

Pencil

Safety glasses

MATERIALS:

One 1¼-inch-diameter wooden or chrome metal pipe closet dowel

HARDWARE:

2 dowel brackets

Four 1½-inch screws (with anchors if necessary)

MAKE THAT SPACE HAPPEN

1 ....

To cut the dowel, first measure the exact width of the closet and then deduct ¼ inch (to make installation easy). Then mark and cut the dowel, using a handsaw for a wooden dowel or a hacksaw for a metal pipe. Use two clamps (or preferably a mounted vise) to hold the dowel to a solid surface, or this event can turn into an unattractive dance. However, bracing the dowel with your knee on a saw stool can quite often do the job.

2 ....

Determine the correct height for the rod by hanging the longest clothes on the rod and holding it at your desired height. With a pencil, mark this position on one end. Using a level, draw a line to transfer this point to the other side.

3 ....

Fasten the brackets to the side walls using screws, preferably into a stud. However, that's like winning the lottery in a closet space, so use wall anchors as the alternative. (I prefer using screws as I can easily adjust the rods at a later date). Then place the rod in the brackets.

Install a Shoe Shelf

A shoe shelf is always great to have, and it feels like a luxury item if you've never had one before. If you're hanging double rods, then clothes on the lower rod may be too close to the floor to allow for a shoe shelf, but if you've got a foot or so of clearance on the floor, don't waste it.

TIME:

2 hours

DIFFICULTY:

TOOLS:

Handsaw or power saw

Drill/driver with bits

Level

Combination square

Pencil

Safety glasses

Paintbrushes, roller, and tray

MATERIALS:

WOOD:

1 half sheet ¾-inch birch plywood or melamine

Three 1x2 ledger boards (wooden strip, size equal to three sides of the shelf)

One ½-by-1½-inch trim piece (front edge, equal to width of shelf)

HARDWARE:

Eight to ten 1½- and 3-inch wood screws

Finishing nails

FINISHING SUPPLIES:

Wood glue

Screw caps (optional)

Sandpaper, 220-grit (optional)

½ quart each primer and paint (optional)

MAKE THAT SPACE HAPPEN

1 ....
Cut the board for the shoe shelf to length. The back of your door will determine how far out you can extend your shelf.

2 ....
Glue and nail on the trim piece (with finishing nails) to add a small lip to the top front edge of the shoe shelf.

3 ....
Fasten the ledger boards at your desired height and to the sides of your closet; position them at an angle. If your floor or closet base is level, then, as an example, create your angle by measuring up 8 inches at the back and 6 inches at the front edge. Adjust the angle to best suit you. If the closet base is not level, draw a level line at the base and take your dimensions from there. It is best to use screws, as you can easily change the height or angle. Ensure your screws are long enough to bite into the studs or side panels of your closet. If your shoe shelf is long or sags, add an additional ledger strip on the rear wall.

4 ....
Install shelf. Fasten from the top with a couple of small nails or 1½-inch screws on each side directly into the ledger boards.

5 ....
Touch up nail heads or use screw caps to cover screws. Sand, prime, and paint all exposed surfaces.

The angled shelf conveniently holds shoes.

Shoe stop trim

Ledger boards

Mount a High Shelf

If storage of rarely used items is a main need, consider adding a second high shelf, above the primary one. But remember not to overload this shelf with too much weight, or it will sag, and be sure to build it less deep than the lower shelf to allow easier access to that wasted space.

TIME:

1 hour

DIFFICULTY:

↑

TOOLS:

4-foot level

Tape measure

Drill/driver with countersink bit

Framing square

Stud finder

Circular saw or handsaw

Iron, for melamine edging (optional)

Paintbrush, roller, and tray

Pencil

Safety glasses

Ear protection

MATERIALS:

WOOD:

1 sheet ¾-inch birch plywood or melamine shelving (to span width of area)

One 1x2 ledger board (wooden strip, size determined by width of area) or brackets (1 every 32 inches/every 2 studs; 2 for each end)

Edging for plywood or melamine (to fit width of shelf)

HARDWARE:

Six to eight 1½-inch screws and anchors (if necessary) for ledger board or four 1½-inch screws per bracket

1 box finishing nails

FINISHING SUPPLIES:

Construction adhesive

Screw caps (optional)

1 quart each primer and paint

Sandpaper, 220-grit

MAKE THAT SPACE HAPPEN

1...

To make this shelf, follow the instructions for "Build Side Shelves" (page 105); cut the board material to length and width, and edge as needed. When measuring, remember to make this shelf less deep than the one below. Allow enough clearance so you can access your belongings.

2...

Install shelf supports, using either brackets or 1x2s (ledger boards), as in "Build Side Shelves" (page 105). Be sure to attach supports to wall studs.

3...

Sand, prime, and paint the shelf.

4...

Attach the shelf board to the supports using screws from below. If, after loading the shelf with items, you find it starts to sag, clear the shelf and add more brackets (or lighten the load on the shelf).

UNDER-BED STORAGE

UNDER-BED STORAGE

If you have a traditional bed that sits on a frame, you'll find loads of usable space beneath it. In this project, we take sturdy wooden dresser drawers whose shell (the dresser frame that holds the shelves) is no longer useful and make them into storage units on wheels. Before you start, measure the space under your bed to make sure the drawers will slide easily under it, and factor in the height of the wheels (casters can add up to 2 inches). A coat of paint will make these recycled pieces look less like drawers and more like customized storage boxes. Then, to protect what you're storing and add visual pizzazz, I provide an optional step of creating removable fabric covers for the boxes.

If you can't find a set of drawers that suits your space or décor, you can easily make them—they're just boxes. To make your own boxes, follow the first three steps of Project: Modular Storage and Floating Cube Nightstands (page 116), adjusting the measurements of the box so it fits under your bed.

TIME:

2½ to 3 hours

DIFFICULTY:

⌐

TOOLS:

Drill/driver with bits (optional)

Screwdriver

Paintbrushes or roller and tray

Tape measure

Pencil

Safety glasses

TIP: If the surface of the old drawer has already been painted or sealed, there is no need for a primer. Just clean it, sand it lightly, and paint it.

MATERIALS:

Old drawer(s)

HARDWARE:

4 screw-on casters (per drawer)

Handle(s) (optional)

FINISHING SUPPLIES:

Sandpaper, fine-grit

1 quart each primer and paint

Clear polyurethane (optional)

Wood putty (optional)

TIP: Instead of using a handle on your drawer (particularly if you're making your own box), consider making a cutout for your hand to grab instead. Then nothing will protrude past the face of the drawer, and it will not cost you a cent. A jigsaw is the perfect tool for this job. Use a compass with a pencil to mark your circle or oval. Start by drilling a hole on the inside of your mark with a ½-inch drill bit. Then, insert the jigsaw blade into the hole and slowly and carefully cut along your outline. If you move the jigsaw too fast, the blade could snag and possibly break.

MAKE THAT SPACE HAPPEN

1 . . . .
Remove the drawer handle and any side rails (older drawers usually do not have these, but newer ones may). If you plan to use the existing handle, set it and the screws aside in a safe place. If you have more than one handle, mark each handle so they can be reattached to their original positions, otherwise they may not fit correctly. If you'll be attaching new, different-size handles, fill the old holes with wood putty, let dry, and sand down. Do the same with any holes left by the removal of side rails.

2 . . . .
Sand down any rough spots. Clean up any paint or sawdust with a brush or vacuum, wipe down the drawer inside and out with a damp cloth, and let dry.

3 . . . .
Paint the drawer inside and out—except for the outer bottom—with a stain-killing primer. This will cover up knotholes and the original finish on the drawer front and provide a clean slate. After the primer is dry (in about an hour), paint the drawer with the color of your choice. Let the paint dry completely before proceeding, about two hours.

TIP: Tint the primer to the same color as the final coat. This will allow you to finish the job in two coats, not three. Less money and less time—we all like that!

A clear coat of polyurethane is also a good idea to further protect the painted surfaces in many applications.

4 . . . .
Mark the caster placement; one caster in each corner. The wood on the bottom of your drawer should be soft enough to easily screw into by hand. If not, make pilot holes for the screws, either by making a shallow indentation with a large nail or by drilling a hole slightly smaller in diameter than the screw. Then, attach the four casters to the corners with the screws, using the pilot holes as a guide.

TIP: Lubricate screws with liquid soap or bar soap. You'll be surprised how easily your screws will drive into the wood.

5 . . . .
Reattach the drawer handle(s). If you're using new handles, mark the new screw holes, drill pilot holes, and attach the new handle(s) with a screwdriver.

SEVEN SURPRISING BEDROOM REPURPOSING IDEAS FOR NON-BEDROOM FURNITURE

1. **Kitchen cabinets:** If you're redoing your kitchen or have a spare cabinet from a past remodel, turn it on its back so the door is facing up and use it as a toy box. Install a self-locking hinge to the inside so it's safe for little ones.

2. **Small kitchen island or microwave cart:** These rolling storage centers make great arts-and-crafts centers for kids' bedrooms. The shelves can store flat paper, the dishtowel holder can instead hold a roll of craft paper or a roll of paper towels for clean up.

3. **Small square or rectangular dining tables:** These can hold books and magazines, a clock, and water on top—a basket underneath holds extra blankets or even the family pet.

4. **TV armoires:** Make this into a freestanding closet, storage for toys, and/or a workstation in a child's bedroom.

5. **Dining room sideboard or credenza:** These tables do double duty as changing tables and clothing storage in the nursery.

6. **Planters:** Yes, planters! Large plastic, foam, or fiberglass planters make great stackable stools and storage for kids' toys. Just be sure to clean the planters well, using warm soapy water.

7. **Coffee tables:** These make great drawing tables for kids; if rectangular, they make terrific end-of-the-bed benches for grownups.

Optional Finish: Make a Fabric Cover

A cover made of heavy canvas or denim creates an attractive, removable dust shield.

TIME:
2 to 3 hours

DIFFICULTY:

TOOLS:
Tape measure
Scissors
Sewing machine (optional)

MATERIALS:
Heavyweight canvas or denim

FINISHING SUPPLIES:
Thread (optional)
Fabric glue (optional)
Velcro strips, self-stick

MAKE THAT SPACE HAPPEN

1 ....
Measure the top of the drawer front to back and side to side, using the top of the sides and the back as a starting point. You want the fabric to sit on top of the sides and back and just meet the front of the drawer. The drawer front is usually higher than the sides and back, and since you want the fabric to sit flat, you will only attach the fabric to the sides and back.

2 ....
Cut a piece of the fabric 1 inch larger than the measurement all the way around.

3 ....
Hem the fabric by turning it under ½ inch twice all the way around, so the hemmed fabric sits on top of the sides and back rails of the drawer and just meets the front of the drawer. Sew or tack down the hem with fabric glue.

4 ....
Attach self-stick Velcro strips right on top of the two sides and back edges of the drawer. The width of the Velcro might be slightly wider than the drawer sides. If this is the case, simply press the Velcro so it fits snugly on the sides. Take the Velcro tape off the top piece, lay the fabric on top, and attach it.

PROJECT:

MODULAR STORAGE AND FLOATING CUBE NIGHTSTANDS

MODULAR STORAGE AND FLOATING CUBE NIGHTSTANDS

Not all of us have an expansive master suite complete with a lounging area and a spalike bathroom. I know firsthand what it's like to sleep in a bedroom that barely has room for the bed. This project is perfect for space-conscious settings. These cubes or rectangles—make 'em by the dozen in any size you need—can act as modular storage or as tables that take up no floor space. You can make them with hand tools or power tools (or have the lumberyard cut the plywood for you). This is an ideal project for novice carpenters, as making these simple structures builds your confidence. They look sleek and contemporary and can be painted or stained any color or shade. Make them just the right size for your books and bags, kids' toys and sports gear, or, as "floating" wall-mounted tables for your alarm clock, a water glass, a book, and a box of tissues. What more do you need?

While you can make these boxes with either plywood or MDF, I prefer MDF. The edges of MDF can be sanded smooth, which eliminates the need for edge trim. However, it is always important to wear a mask when cutting or sanding this product!

TIME:

About 1 hour per box, not including paint-drying time

DIFFICULTY:

TOOLS:

Tape measure

Handsaw or circular saw

Screwdriver or drill/driver with bits

Hammer or nail gun

Nail set

Framing square

Level

Stud finder

Countersinking bit (optional)

Pencil

Paintbrushes, roller, and tray

Safety glasses

Ear protection

MATERIALS:

WOOD:

1 sheet ½-inch or ⅝-inch smooth paint-grade plywood or MDF

Edge trim (optional)

HARDWARE:

Brad nails

2 L-brackets per shelf (long enough to extend approximately halfway to the underside of the box)

1 box screws

Wall anchors (if brackets will not be not attached to wall studs; optional)

FINISHING SUPPLIES:

Wood glue

Wood putty

Sandpaper, 220-grit

Felt pads for base (to avoid scratching floor)

1 quart to 1 gallon each primer and paint (depending on size and quantity of cubes)

MAKE THAT SPACE HAPPEN

1..

For modular storage, decide what size you want your boxes to be. For hanging bedside tables, measure each side of your bed (or just one side, if you need only one table) to calculate the width and height of your cube nightstand. Here, I'll guide you through building a small four-sided cube with a 13-inch-square opening on either end. Whatever your cube size or dimensions, remember to factor in the width of the plywood before cutting. (See illustration for how the boxes go together.)

2..

For a 13-inch-square box, cut two 12-by-14-inch pieces and two 12-by-13-inch pieces from the ½-inch plywood or MDF. Line up the pieces to build a square that's 12 inches deep. The 12-by-13-inch pieces will fit inside the 12-by-14-inch pieces.

3..

Attach the pieces using simple butt joints, being sure to keep the edges flush all around. First attach the two narrower pieces to one wider side and then attach the final, fourth side. When joining, apply a strip of wood glue where the pieces meet and then attach with brad nails (or a nail gun). If the measures and cuts are true, the opening should be square.

Box construction is simply a matter of getting the measurements and cuts right, then securing the pieces properly.

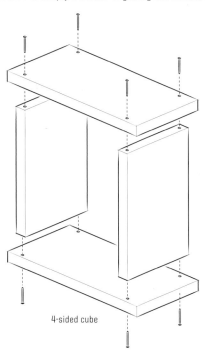

4-sided cube

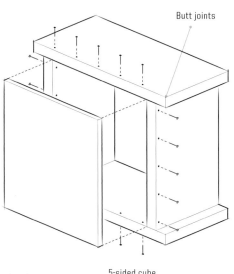

Butt joints

5-sided cube

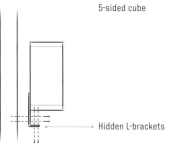

Hidden L-brackets

SAFETY ALERT: If you use a nail gun, be sure to wear eye protection. Be extremely careful when using any compressed-air tools: They are extremely powerful and can be dangerous if used incorrectly. Be careful of your fingers, too, as nails can fire through the sides of your materials if you are not holding the nail gun plumb or 90 degrees to the surface.

4 ....
If using plywood, glue and nail on the edge trim to cover the exposed edges.

5 ....
Prime and paint the box, sanding with 220-grit sandpaper between coats. Allow the paint to dry completely before installing the cube.

6 ....
If you'll be using the top of the box as a tabletop or nightstand, mark the wall where you want the top to sit. Using the level, mark the placement of the L-brackets at the bottom of the box so they are level with each other and about 10 inches apart (as a rule of thumb, make sure the L-brackets are 2 to 3 inches in from either side). Ideally, use a stud finder to locate at least one wall stud and screw one L-bracket into it (drilling a pilot hole first). For L-brackets that are attached only to drywall, use wall anchors with screws. The larger the box, and the more weight it must support, the more important it is to attach it to at least one stud.

7 ....
Put the cube in place on the wall, with the bottom of the cube resting on the L-brackets. Drive screws from below, attaching the L-bracket to the underside of the cube bottom. Make sure the screws are not too long; they should screw in flush to the bracket without penetrating through the face of the cube.

Another great way to hang a cube is to mount the brackets to the wall, flush with the cube sides. Then position the bottom of the cube on top of the bracket legs and screw up to the underside of the cube. This will hide the vertical section of the bracket.

OPTION: The Five-Sided Cube

Another option is to add a back panel to your cube and create a five-sided box. This method ensures the cube is square and eliminates the need for brackets (or hides them entirely).

1 ....
After building a four-sided cube, measure the interior dimensions of the cube's open side and cut a piece of plywood or MDF to fit. Run glue along the edges of the fifth piece, insert it into one end of the cube (keeping it flush with the sides) and, using 1½-inch nails, nail it several times on all sides. Allow the glue to set fully overnight.

2 ....
Locate the wall studs and fasten the cube directly into them. First drill several pilot holes, followed by a countersinking bit through the rear panel into the wall studs, and then drive 2½-inch screws into the studs to secure the cube. Sink the screw heads below the wood surface. Or, if you wish, use brackets to hold the cube from the bottom, similar to Step 6 at left.

3 ....
Apply wood filler over the screws, sand, and then prime and paint or stain the cube. The rear piece can be painted to match the wall color so it looks like an independent cube.

CARVED-OUT WALL NICHE

CARVED-OUT WALL NICHE

There's so much wasted space behind drywall. In the bedroom, you can use this space for book-shelves, display spaces, shoe cubbies, CD holders, and more—without taking up any valuable floor space. This project is similar to Recessed Laundry Storage Niche with Shelves (page 46), and, in fact, wall niches can be useful in just about any room in the house: the bathroom, the family room, hallways, and more.

For this project, I provide two options. The first creates a simple and easy single recessed shelf. The second is only a little more complicated, but it allows for as many internal shelves as you have room and desire for.

Note: It's handy if you have some spare paint that matches your bedroom to finish the niche when it's done; otherwise, you'll need to buy more, or choose a contrasting color.

TIME:

3 to 4 hours per niche

DIFFICULTY:

⚒⚒

TOOLS:

Stud finder

Tape measure

Utility knife

Wire coat hanger

Drywall saw

Circular saw or jigsaw

Hammer or nail gun

Level

Putty/drywall knife

Paintbrushes, roller, and tray

Pencil

Safety glasses

Ear protection

MATERIALS:

WOOD:

2x4 lumber (quantity determined by niche dimensions)

HARDWARE:

1 small box of 3-inch nails

1 small box of drywall screws

1 box drywall nails

90-degree metal drywall setting angle, long enough to cover external edges of niche (sold in 8- to 10-foot lengths)

FINISHING SUPPLIES:

Drywall, small pieces

Construction adhesive

Drywall tape

Drywall compound

Sandpaper, medium- and fine-grit

1 quart to ½ gallon each primer and paint (depending on size and quantity of niches)

MAKE THAT SPACE HAPPEN

1...
Use a stud finder to locate studs. Measure and mark the stud locations. Decide the height you want the niche to be and mark the top and bottom of it.

2...
Use a utility knife to cut a small 6-by-6-inch inspection hole to check for services behind the drywall. In addition to looking, use a bent coat hanger to "feel" for wires and pipes you might not see. Always check the other side of the wall, too, as there may be an outlet positioned there.

3...
Using a drywall saw, follow your lines and cut out your niche.

4...
Measure the width between the studs. Using a circular saw, cut two lengths of 2x4 to that length; these are the framing pieces for the top and bottom of the niche.

5...
Place construction adhesive on the ends of the framing pieces and place them inside the wall (and behind the drywall), so the edges face out. Make sure the ends make good contact with the existing studs and then, using a hammer or nail gun and the 3-inch nails, toe nail the 2x4s into the studs. (These can also be screwed in with a drill.)

TIP: Before nailing, screw a couple of drywall screws through the drywall into the framing pieces to hold them in place and prevent them from slipping.

6...
Using your utility knife, cut four pieces of new drywall to cover the interior sides of the added framing and the exposed wall studs. Drywall varies in thickness from ¼ inch to ⅝ inch. If the area is very small, you can use construction adhesive to hold the drywall in place. If it is large enough to nail in, use drywall nails and hammer them in. The back of the niche should be the back of the drywall from the adjoining room.

7...
Fasten the metal drywall angles around all the external (or front) corners using drywall nails; check that the angles are plumb and level as you go. Tape the internal corners with drywall tape and then apply drywall compound (otherwise known as mud) over the tape and angles using your putty/drywall knife. Allow the areas to dry and then sand them. Repeat the process with drywall compound until the wall is smooth and you can no longer see the joints.

TIP: Fold drywall tape in half, lengthwise, when placing it into internal corners of a niche for a sharp 90-degree corner.

8...
Prime and paint the niche and the wall outside the niche. If it's a small niche, you can install trim around the outside to match the door and window trim in the room—but that's completely optional. Consider painting the niche, or just the back wall of the niche, a different color or darker shade to add contrast and depth.

Or here is another great idea: Have a mirror cut to the internal dimensions. Put a little construction adhesive on the back of the mirror and place it at the rear of the niche for a nice effect.

Wall Niche with a Box and Internal Shelves

For this niche, you'll fabricate an open box unit out of ½-inch paint-grade plywood and recess it between wall studs just as you did for the preceding wall niche.

TIME:

4 to 5 hours per niche

DIFFICULTY:

⚒ ⚒

TOOLS:

Stud finder

Tape measure

Utility knife

Circular saw

Drywall saw

Hammer or nail gun

Nail set

Screwdriver or drill/driver with bits

Miter saw or handsaw and miter box

Table saw (optional)

Level

Putty/drywall knife

Paintbrushes, roller, and tray

Pencil

Safety glasses

Ear protection

MATERIALS:

WOOD:

1 sheet ½-inch paint-grade plywood or lumber

2x4 lumber (quantity determined by niche dimensions)

Trim to match existing room

HARDWARE:

1 box 1-inch nails

1 box 1-inch wood screws

FINISHING SUPPLIES:

Construction adhesive

Wood putty

1 quart to ½ gallon each primer and paint (depending on size and quantity of niche)

MAKE THAT SPACE HAPPEN

1..

Follow Steps 1 through 5 for Project: Carved-out Wall Niche on page 122: Locate studs, measure your space, check for wires and pipes, cut the opening to your dimensions, and then cut and install the two lengths of 2x4 as top and bottom frames.

2..

Measure the dimensions of the recessed space (height, width, and depth) and use these to design a boxed frame with internal shelves (and a backing piece) made of ½-inch paint-grade plywood. With a circular saw, cut the plywood pieces to the dimensions you recorded.

3..

First nail together the outer frame, then the internal shelves, and finally the backing piece, which helps ensure your niche is square. Using a hammer is fine, but a nail gun is the perfect tool for assembling this box.

4..

Place constructor adhesive on the ends of the framing pieces and place them inside the wall so the edges face out. Install the box into the recessed wall by driving screws through the box into the studs. Remember to sink the screw heads and then fill the holes with wood putty.

5..

Cut and affix your trim pieces to match your existing trim. Miter the ends so you have a picture-frame effect. You may need to use a little caulk for your joints. I won't tell.

6..

Prime and paint the niche and trim once installed. Consider painting the niche or just the back wall of the niche a different color or darker shade from your existing paint colors to add contrast and depth.

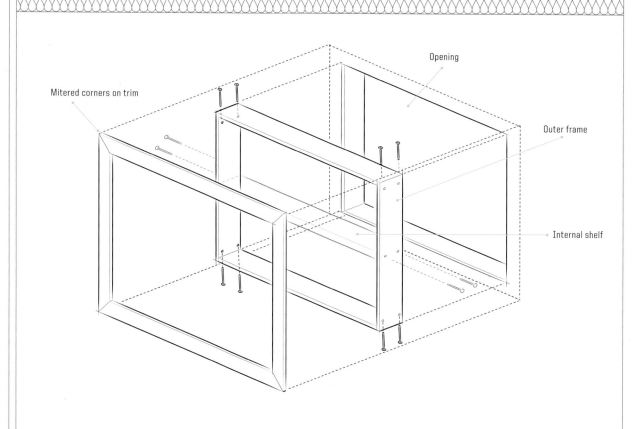

Mitered corners on trim

Opening

Outer frame

Internal shelf

PROJECT:

FLUSH-WITH-THE-FLOOR HIDEY-HOLES

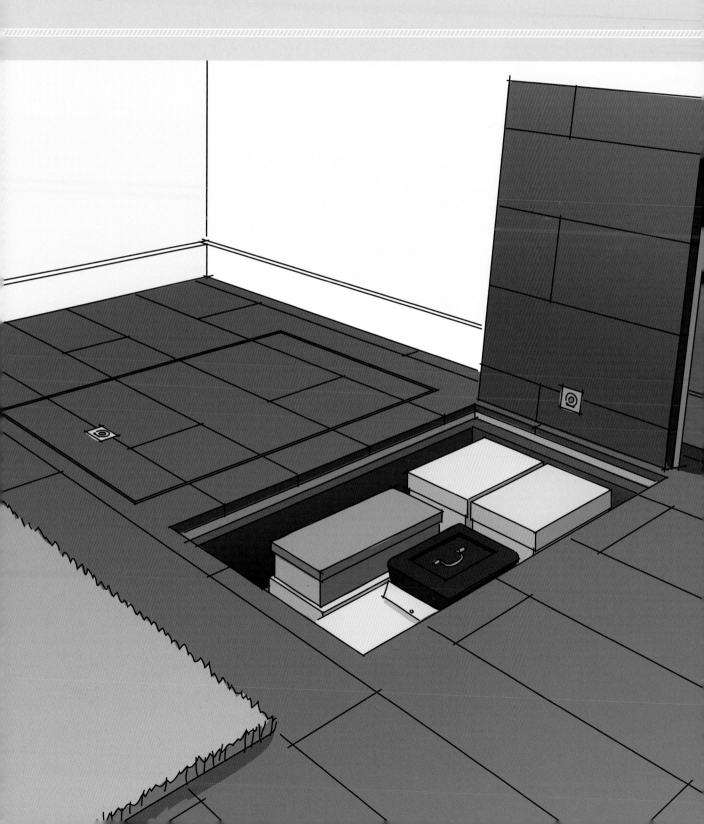

FLUSH-WITH-THE-FLOOR HIDEY-HOLES

There's nothing more fun—and useful—than a secret compartment, whether it holds family valuables (important papers, jewelry) or treasures picked up on a walk (arrowheads, marbles). These hidey-holes are easy to install—you'll cut slots between the floor joists and install a brass flush-mounted ring handle. You can use this trick anywhere, of course, but closets are a good location for storing valuables. Kids' hobby rooms are another good spot, as children love secret hiding places for their special odds and ends.

While this project is not particularly difficult, it has a few tricky aspects. The first is finding a space between floor joists clear of wires or plumbing. To do this, you must make an exploratory hole first, in exactly the same way as you did for Project: Maximize the Medicine Cabinet (page 82), but in this case you'll cut through the drywall ceiling directly beneath the floor. The other is that the hole you cut out in the floor becomes the hidey-hole's lid, so you need to take extra care while cutting and use a plunge cut with a circular saw (see Step 2).

TIME:

About 6 hours

DIFFICULTY:

ʌʌʌ

TOOLS:

Stud finder

Utility knife

Tape measure

Framing square

Circular saw, with a new saw blade for fine cuts

Jigsaw

Drill/driver with bits

Hammer or nail gun

Wood chisel

Paintbrushes, roller, and tray

Pencil

Safety glasses

Ear protection

MATERIALS:

WOOD:

Half of a sheet ¾-inch birch plywood

Quarter of a sheet ½-inch plywood (optional)

HARDWARE:

2 flush-mounted drawer pull per unit

1 box finishing nails

1 box 1½-inch wood screws

1 box 1¼-inch wood screws (optional)

FINISHING SUPPLIES:

Wood glue

Sandpaper, medium- and fine-grit

Painter's tape

Less than 1 quart each primer and paint or stain and polyurethane per unit

Shims (optional)

MAKE THAT SPACE HAPPEN

1 . . . .

Choose an area of flooring for the hidey-holes and check that it is free of any wiring or plumbing. Closet floors are ideal locations. First determine where the floor joists are. If you have wooden floors that are surface nailed, you can determine where the floor joists are by the location of the nails. If your floorboards are secret nailed or glued, you'll have to search for floor joists from below, checking the ceiling with your stud finder; if you're on the ground floor, this requires accessing a basement or crawl space under the house.

NOTE: The reason you can't check for joists from above is that electronic stud finders work by detecting wood and magnetic stud finders work by detecting nails, and both can give a false reading in this situation.

Next, in the same way as in Project: Maximize the Medicine Cabinet (page 82), use a utility knife to cut an exploratory hole in the drywall ceiling: both look and feel for wires and pipes between the joists of the area you intend to use. This hole will require repair, but a hole in drywall is far easier to fix than wooden floorboards, and it is essential that you confirm no services exist before cutting the floor with a saw.

From below, mark out the clear section between the joists. Measure this space, mark its distance from walls that are shared with the room above, and use these to transfer the hole dimensions to the correct spot on the floor surface above, using wide painter's tape.

TIP: Painter's tape is your best friend on this project. First, place painter's tape on the area to be cut, then make marks on the tape, not the floor. Then, to further protect the wood floor from scratches, before you start cutting, cover the shoe plate of your circular saw with painter's tape.

2 . . . .

Using a circular saw along the taped markings, carefully cut out the section of flooring between the joists for the storage compartment. First adjust the depth of the blade so it is no deeper than the floor thickness, usually ¾ inch; if you are unsure about the depth, start with as shallow a cut as you can. Then start the cut in the middle of each side, using a plunge cut, and continue cutting on a straight line almost but not quite to the corner. Take your time here and play it safe with the circular saw. Do not twist the blade as it may catch and kick back. It is also important to have the saw fully running before you make the plunge and let the saw stop running completely before pulling it out! Practice these cuts on some scrap wood before you attempt to cut into your floor. Use a jigsaw to finish the cut all the way into the corner, making square or rectangular openings. Go slow and steady to make as clean and straight a line as possible and to ensure you do not overcut or damage the finished wood flooring. Set the cutout sections aside; these will become the lids for the storage compartments.

continued

Painter's tape helps guide your cutting while protecting the surface of your floor.

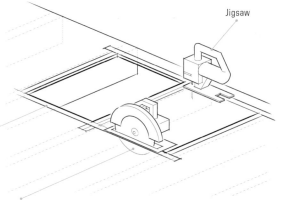

Painter's tape

Jigsaw

Circular saw

Be careful not to overcut!

3 . . . .

If the removed flooring becomes loose and the pieces separate, no worries. Cut a ½-inch sheet of plywood to the same dimensions and attach it underneath the flooring section. Reassemble the loose flooring pieces on top, flip the section upside down, and screw through the plywood to secure the pieces, making sure that the screws do not penetrate the surface.

4 . . . .

To build the boxes to the proper dimensions, measure the openings in the floor and then the depth from the underside of the floor to the bottom of the space between the joists. Don't make a box taller than the underside of the wood floor, since the lid must sit flush with the floor. Assemble the boxes using ¾-inch plywood, wood glue, and finishing nails; join pieces with simple butt joints (see Project: Modular Storage and Floating Cube Nightstands, page 116, for instructions on making a box with butt joints).

5 . . . .

Sand and then prime and paint or stain and poly coat the interior of the boxes; allow them to dry.

6 . . . .

Attach the flush-mounted pull to the cutout sections of floor that will form the lids, following the manufacturer's instructions that come with the hardware.

7 . . . .

Attach the boxes to the floor joists, so that they sit recessed at the proper height. Sink two wood screws into each side of each box, driving them directly into the joists. If you have a gap between your box (and your opening) and the joist, use shims or blocking to make up the difference. Be sure to fasten the shims or blocking first before fastening the box into the joists.

8 . . . .

Carefully drop the lid into place. There is no need for a hinge; leaving it off means that the lid can be lifted out completely if desired. However, if you want, you can secure the lid to the floor with one or two hinges.

TIP: If the floor is insulated, reduce the depth of the box and add a thin layer of insulation to the base. Do not compress the insulation as it will become ineffective. If using fiberglass, tear it in half to reduce the thickness and place it while wearing your mask. The insulation will just go at the bottom.

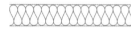

Great extra storage that can be placed anywhere in the home.

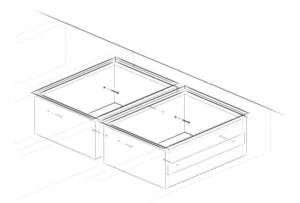

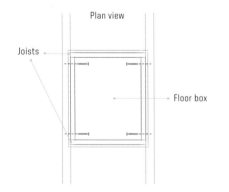

Plan view

Joists

Floor box

FOLD-DOWN CHANGING TABLE

FOLD-DOWN CHANGING TABLE

This changing table is perfect for small-space dwellers who also happen to be new parents. Standard floor model changing tables can take up a lot of extra room, but this version folds right into the wall and takes up zero floor space. Best of all, this project will grow with the child, so that after baby is out of diapers, your child can use it to store all sorts of small items, books, and toys. Or you can cover the fold-down surface with another piece of plywood to make a snappy homework center. The only room requirement is a wall with studs and enough clearance to allow the table to unfold. If the skills required for this project are beyond your capabilities, consider hiring a carpenter to build this for you; the price may be equivalent to buying a freestanding changing table, but this fold-down version has so many more benefits.

TIME:

8 hours

DIFFICULTY:

ʎʎʎʎ

TOOLS:

Tape measure

4-foot level

Stud finder

Utility knife

Drywall saw

Table saw

Circular saw

Hammer or nail gun

Nail set

Putty knife

Paintbrushes, roller, and tray

Tin snips

Router with ¼-inch round-over bit

Framing square

Miter saw

Drill with bits and countersink bit

Small bolt cutters or wire cutters

Pry bar

Pencil

Safety glasses

Ear protection

Work gloves

MATERIALS:

1 changing pad

WOOD:

One 1x6 pine board, cut to 8-foot length

One 1x4 pine board, cut to 8-foot length

One 1x2 pine board, cut to 8-foot length

1 sheet ⅛-inch birch plywood

1 sheet ½-inch birch plywood

Decorative trim

HARDWARE:

1 piece sheet metal, approximately 30 by 14 inches (have a piece cut to suit your dimensions or cut with tin snips)

One 30-inch piano hinge

1 chain or hydraulic support hinges (long enough for both sides)

Two ¼-inch bolts, washers, and nuts

1 hook-and-eye latch, roller catch or cupboard catch

1 box 3-inch drywall screws

1 box finishing nails

Four ½-inch screws

FINISHING SUPPLIES:

1-inch insulation (if installing unit on an exterior wall)

Medium- and fine-grit sandpaper

Wood glue

Spray contact adhesive

Wood putty

½ gallon each primer and paint

TIP: This project can also be installed in the kitchen as a fold-away work and bill-paying area; in an entryway as a family mail, key, and message center; and on the wall of the exterior of your house (use treated wood and exterior-grade paint) as a garden center or outdoor serving area. In the den or living room, it makes a great fold-down bar, and it's a perfect solution for a tight garage as a place to keep tools and car detailing items.

SAFE NURSERIES; HEALTHY BABY

There's a lot of planning that goes into the arrival of a little one. Be sure you paint the room designated as nursery with low- or no-VOC paint; install hardwood floors with a natural fiber room-size rug as opposed to wall-to-wall carpeting, which contains many toxins such as formaldehyde. Or look for carpeting made from organic fibers, which have no off-gassing issues. If you do have wall-to-wall carpeting, keep the room open so it airs—otherwise you may create a gas chamber. I mention this because, with today's energy-efficient windows and doors, our rooms are now sealed tight. So try to create a little natural ventilation so the room can breathe.

MAKE THAT SPACE HAPPEN

Measure the Dimensions and Cut the Opening

1
Measure the changing pad you intend to use and add 2 inches to the length and width to determine the size of the changing table. If you have the space, it is a good idea to make it a little larger to give yourself more table space. I recommend you choose a changing pad that can be fastened to its table with a small strap for the bub.

2
Using a stud finder, locate wall studs, and be sure to center the dimensions on a stud. Transfer the dimensions to the wall with a pencil and a 4-foot level. Also, consider the height of the changing table; the bottom should be a comfortable height for the parents who will be changing diapers, typically above waist height.

3
Cut an exploratory hole in the drywall with a utility knife to check for mechanicals. If you discover nothing inside the wall, then, following the lines, use a drywall saw to cut out the drywall between the studs (see Project: Carved-Out Wall Niche, page 120).

4
Leave the small drywall strip on the center stud. If it breaks off, no worries: just tack on another small strip of drywall. Later this will be used as a spacer.

Build the Wall Insert

1
Measure both the spaces between each stud and the available depth. The maximum depth for in-wall storage in a 2x4 wall is about 3½ inches.

2
Measure and build two boxes with shelves (and a backing piece), to fit on either side of the center wall stud; follow the same techniques as the Wall Niche with a Box and Internal Shelves (page 123). Once you have your dimensions, use a table or circular saw to rip down ½-inch plywood into the necessary pieces: each box has four sides, a back, and internal shelves. Using wood glue and a nail gun, assemble the two boxes.

3
Connect the boxes with a center trim strip of plywood that's as wide as a stud, using glue and nails. This will bridge the stud in between the recessed holes and act as the primary attachment point of the unit.

4
Fill the nail holes with wood putty. Sand and paint the wall insert.

5
Install the insert. If you're working on an exterior wall, provide a thin layer of insulation first and then set the insert in the wall and check for level and plumb. Secure the shelving insert with finishing nails to the studs on the left and right. Fill the nail holes, sand, and touch up paint.

Build Changing Table Box

1
Next build the changing table box; when finished, it will have four sides and a plywood-and-metal bottom. The frame dimensions must match the cutout in the wall. So, if the hole you cut in the wall is 14 inches tall by 30 inches wide, cut the frame to 14 by 30 inches.

2
Cut four lengths of 1x6 pine on a table saw. For finished corners, cut the ends at 45-degree angles with a miter saw. You should have two long and two short pieces.

3
Using a table saw, set the blade height at ¼ inch. Rip a ¼-inch dado (slot) ½ inch from the bottom, along the length of the four pine pieces that make the box sides. (The guard on the table saw must be removed to make the cut. Be sure to replace the guard prior to using the saw again.) This is a dangerous process, so if you are not familiar with

continued

A fold-down changing table frees up floor space.

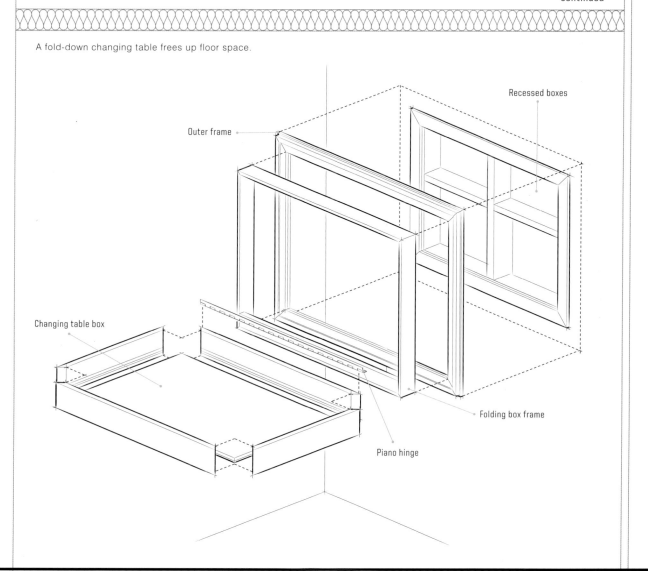

Recessed boxes

Outer frame

Changing table box

Piano hinge

Folding box frame

how to cut a dado, I recommend you enlist the help of a carpenter or friend with experience. This dado is essentially a groove for the base of the box to slide into; for more detail, see the Chapter 8 sidebar "Get in the Groove" (page 172).

4
Assemble three sides of the box—one long piece and two short pieces—gluing them and nailing them with finishing nails. Make sure the dado grooves line up and that the corners join properly.

5
Cut a piece of sheet metal about ¼ inch larger on all sides than the inside dimension of the pine box frame. Cut a piece of ⅛-inch plywood to match. Cut the sheet metal with a good pair of tin snips and make sure you wear gloves; this metal is extremely sharp! The sheet metal is needed only for the message center panel (see page 137), so if you are not comfortable cutting sheet metal and/or don't want the panel, this step can be skipped. But remember: you can always have a piece cut from a local sheet metal shop. Some shops may not even charge you for the cut.

6
Glue the metal and plywood together using contact adhesive and slide the two into the dado with the metal facing out. When using contact adhesive, spray or apply it to both surfaces. Wait until it's tacky to the touch and then press both surfaces together. Be careful here as you have only one shot! Line it up correctly the first time, as you cannot realign it once it makes contact.

7
Place the last side of the box on and nail on with finishing nails.

8
Lay the box flat and use a router with a ¼-inch round-over bit to rout the inside and outside edges of the box. The simple pine frame will be the anchor that holds the folding unit to the wall.

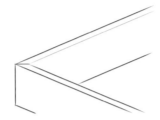

Mitered corners.

SAFETY ALERT: Always wear safety glasses when operating any power tool. Also be super careful if you are pregnant!

Build the Frame

1
Use the assembled changing table box to determine the dimensions for the frame. When calculating the dimensions, allow for a ¼-inch space or gap between the changing table box and the interior dimensions of the frame on all sides so there won't be friction when the table is folded down. The frame consists of two parts: a box of 1x2s set on a frame of flat-sided 1x4s, both of which have this same interior dimension.

2
Cut four lengths of 1x4 (using 45-degree diagonal cuts) and four lengths of 1x2 (using 45-degree angled cuts) to length on the miter saw. The interior points of each diagonal or angle cut should match the dimensions you measured for the frame.

3 ....
Lay the four pieces of 1x4 down on the flat side and assemble them with glue and finishing nails.

4 ....
Set the four pieces of 1x2 on the short edge, so they stand up like the earlier box frame, and assemble them with glue and finishing nails.

5 ....
Attach the two frames by first laying the 1x2 box frame on the table and setting the 1x4 flat-sided frame on top; align the inside edges. Glue and nail the two together, using finishing nails through the 1x4 frame into the 1x2 box frame.

6 ....
Sand, prime, and paint the frame and the box.

Attach the Frame with the Piano Hinge

1 ....
Place the changing table box and the frame on a table and align the edges.

2 ....
Piano hinges, or continuous hinges, are perfect for long surfaces that need to pivot.

Use the screws that came with the piano hinge to secure it to the changing table box and the frame.

SAFETY ALERT: The piano hinge is strong enough to hold a baby, but the changing table will also be outfitted with a sturdy chain for extra support. The chain prevents the changing table from unfolding past perpendicular to the wall. Important note: Make sure the chain at no times is a danger to children—never leave a child unattended on a changing table. Or, alternatively, you can use a hydraulic support hinge; these are available at cabinet hardware supply stores.

3 ....
Fill the nail holes and touch up with no-VOC paint.

4 ....
Set in the changing pad and secure the straps to the base with ½-inch screws or by following the manufacturer's instructions.

Note that the piano hinge is screwed into the table box itself and the frame.

Install the Changing Table on the Wall

1
Set the table on the wall over the wall insert, and have an extra set of hands hold it steady while you work. It should already be level because the wall insert is level.

2
With a countersink drill bit, drill through the outer frame and into the wall studs beneath at the left, right, and center.

TIP: It is best to use a countersink bit to predrill for the screws so they drive flush to the frame.

3
Drive 3-inch drywall screws into the predrilled holes. Cover the screws and outer frame with decorative trim.

Add the Chains and Latch to the Folding Box

1
First, add the chains (or the hydraulic support hinges). Predrill holes for bolts through each side of the fold-down box. Do this approximately 4 inches from the front edge.

2
Hook the chain on one bolt and secure it with a washer and a nut. On the wall, twist an angled hook through the left and right sides of the wall insert and into the stud.

3
With small bolt cutters, cut the chain to the length that will allow the table to rest perpendicular to the wall and place it on the hook. Hook a second piece of chain onto the other bolt and secure it with a washer and nut. Cut the chain to match the first length of chain and place it on the second hook.

4
Next, install the latch by placing the eye on top of the frame and screwing the hook into the edge of the pull-down table, being careful to align them so that the hook fits securely into the eye.

SAFETY ALERT: Before placing a baby on the table, test it first. Fold the table down and place an item on it that is twice as heavy as the baby to be 100 percent sure it is sturdy.

Attaching chains provides extra support and ensures the changing table remains level when in use.

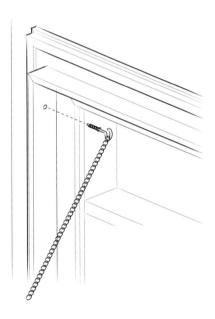

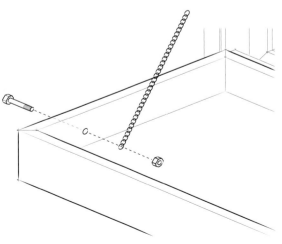

Optional Finish: Exterior Message Center Panel

When folded up, the changing table bottom can double as a message center or a place to display your child's growing artistic talents. All you need to do is glue magnetic strips to the back of a Masonite panel, and it will stick firmly to the sheet metal on the bottom of the fold-down box. Variations are endless, but here are two—one for writing messages and the other for displaying whatever you wish.

TIME:

1 to 2 hours

DIFFICULTY:

↑

TOOLS:

Tape measure

Circular saw

Utility knife (optional)

Straightedge (optional)

Pencil

Safety glasses

Ear protection

MATERIALS:

Trim to fit dimensions of unit

Masonite dry-erase panel to fit dimensions of insert

Cork panels (optional)

FINISHING SUPPLIES:

Flat magnetic strips

Super glue

Spray contact adhesive (optional)

MAKE THAT SPACE HAPPEN

1 ....

Measure the bottom of the folded up box. Cut Masonite dry-erase panel to size using a circular saw.

2 ....

Attach a trim finish around the edges of the Masonite panel with super glue. Choose something that suits the room's theme or décor.

3 ....

On the backside of the panel, use the super glue to adhere magnets to it. Use strong magnets and space them evenly to ensure the panel will stick to the sheet metal. If what you want is a dry-erase

message board to write on, then you're finished. Simply place the magnetized panel onto the bottom of the fold-down table.

4 ....

To turn this into a corkboard display space, use a utility knife and a straightedge to trim a cork panel so that it fits over the Masonite surface inside the trim.

5 ....

Spray contact adhesive on the back of the cork and on the Masonite panel. When the glue is tacky to the touch, press the Masonite and cork panels together. Line it up correctly before pressing as you only get one shot!

07

GATHERING ROOMS

The public spaces in your home—family and living rooms, great rooms, dining rooms, and dens—often lead double or triple lives, serving as home offices, playrooms, hobby and study areas, and workshops. Given their multiple uses, it's not uncommon for these rooms to devolve into a hodgepodge of furniture styles and disparate storage solutions. They can look messy even when they're not, and they certainly don't promote family time or creative pursuits. The good news is you can create a multitasking room that's streamlined and hardworking. Storage solutions, dual-purpose furniture, built-ins, and creative room dividers can all work together to serve a family's specific needs. In this chapter, I'll show you how to transform a little-used dining room into a room that can be both a quiet space for reading, thinking, working, and creating, AND a space that instantly turns into party central when the need to celebrate arises. A dining room can also become a nursery when a little one arrives. Window seats with storage and a platform help family rooms serve a variety of functions.

MULTITASKING CHANGING TABLE

MULTITASKING CHANGING TABLE

A standard chest of drawers or dining room credenza found at a tag or rummage sale can easily be converted to a changing table. While you probably wouldn't want to use a fine antique or new piece of furniture in this way, simply adding a removable lip around the top of the chest creates a spot where a changing pad can sit snugly. The repurposed piece of furniture is perfect in a multiuse dining room. Unused dining rooms make great nurseries, especially if your master bedroom is on the first floor.

Moreover, in a smallish home, converting a dining room into a temporary nursery is smart, since the dining room is often centrally located and offers tired parents easy access to their little one. And true to the nature of the project, the changing table can become a serving area once the nursery has been converted back to a dining room. Of course, you can create this project for a standard nursery room, too. It's an economical solution to what can be an expensive proposition: nursery furniture.

TIME:
4 hours

DIFFICULTY:

TOOLS:
Drill/driver with bits

Paintbrushes, roller, and tray

Tape measure

Handsaw or circular saw

Pencil

Safety glasses

Ear protection

TIP: Whenever you plan on staining a finished project piece, try to use the same wood for your project as you have in your existing furniture—or, at the very least, try to match the color of any new wood (such as trim) with that of the old. Both birch and maple take paint and stain beautifully.

MATERIALS:
1 credenza or dresser, approximately 36 to 38 inches high, 19 to 20 inches deep, and 33 inches wide

1 changing pad

WOOD:
1x2 lumber (quantity determined by dimensions of credenza and length of changing pad)

HARDWARE:
Eight to ten 1½-inch wood screws

FINISHING SUPPLIES:
Builder's tape

Painter's tape

Sandpaper, 220-grit

1 gallon each primer and paint or stain

SAFETY ALERT: For maximum safety for your newborn, be sure to use only no-VOC primer, paint, or stain in this project!

MAKE THAT SPACE HAPPEN

1..
Remove any loose pieces from the credenza, tighten all the screws, and otherwise make sure it is solid and sturdy. Sand and paint or stain the dresser if necessary or desired.

2..
Place the changing pad on top of the credenza. Using a pencil, outline the exact dimensions. This will be your template for installing the safety lip.

3..
Using a handsaw or circular saw, cut four pieces of the 1x2 lumber according to your pad's dimensions—two pieces match the length and two are for the width—for the frame. The frame uses simple butt joints at the corners. For a long credenza, cut two pieces 1 inch longer than the changing pad to accommodate the pad and its cover comfortably.

4..
Sand and then either stain or prime and paint the frame to coordinate with your existing furniture. Use builder's tape to protect the existing surface prior to sanding and refinishing.

5..
Before screwing in the frame, remove any drawers, if necessary, to allow temporary access beneath the credenza top (replace the drawers when finished). If the credenza has doors, just open them; you don't need to remove them. Take the measurements you traced on top of the piece and transfer them to the underside of the top. (You may have to turn the piece upside down temporarily for ease of access and accuracy.) Drill small pilot holes in the underside of the credenza top to help the job go more smoothly; to avoid going too far, place painter's tape ¼ inch down from the tip of the bit before drilling.

6..
Turn the credenza right side up. Attach the frame pieces to the top of the credenza, driving the screws from underneath, forming tight butt joints at each corner. Placement should match the pad dimensions you traced earlier.

TIP: If your pad is extra-thick, use 1x4 lumber for full support. If your pad comes with straps, attach to the unit with screws.

NOTE: If you want to remove the lip at a later date, unscrew the pieces, fill the holes with wood putty, and then repaint or stain. Or consider keeping the trim on the piece: it will help keep objects in place on the dresser top even after baby is grown and becomes a "big kid."

SAFETY ALERT: Choose a changing pad with the two soft seat-belt type straps attached. Just in case! And, of course, never leave baby—strapped in or not—unattended when on a changing table.

The changing pad should fit snugly within the frame attached to the tabletop.

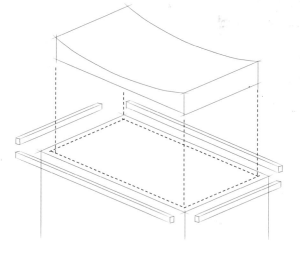

PROJECT:

COUNTER-HEIGHT BOOKCASE FOR A DUAL-USE DINING ROOM

COUNTER-HEIGHT BOOKCASE FOR A DUAL-USE DINING ROOM

If you don't often entertain on a formal scale, your dining room may represent under-used real estate. This project will make that space function better while still allowing for those four or five celebratory meals you host every year. To make the dining room into a quiet area for study, work, reading, or crafts, a set of counter-height (about 36 inches) bookshelves, 30 inches long, installed along one wall (or even around the perimeter of the room if you're ambitious and an avid reader or collector) becomes a place to store china and table linens, as well as books, hobby materials, and office supplies. Attractive baskets and boxes hide unsightly items such as staplers and paper, while also corralling linens and dishes neatly.

The instructions here are for building bookcases. You can certainly buy premade or unfinished book-shelves made to your specifications and install them following the directions, but I suggest tackling the bookcase-building project yourself. Bookcases are one of the easiest construction projects, and you'll learn a lot of basics, such as making joints and creating level shelves.

Once the shelves are done and the bookcases are installed, fill them with books and decorative (but useful) items to give the room a warm, inviting feel. A long trestle or pedestal table in the middle of the room can serve as desk and workspace as well as a dining surface. The top of the bookcases can serve as a long buffet. When not in the service of a dinner party, bookcases can be an excellent place to display artwork. A club chair or comfy reading chair (or two, if you have room) and a standing lamp create a quiet nook in the corner of the room.

TIME:

2 to 5 days, depending on the number of bookcases made

DIFFICULTY:

ΤΤΤ

TOOLS:

Tape measure

Pry bar

Utility knife

Circular saw or table saw

Orbital or palm sander

Drill/driver with bits

4-foot level

Hammer or nail gun

Framing square

Paintbrushes, or rags, for stain application

Stud finder

Sliding bevel

Coping saw

Miter saw

Framing square

Pencil

Safety glasses

Ear protection

Face mask

MATERIALS:

WOOD:

2 to 3 sheets ¾-inch birch plywood (quantity determined by size of bookcase and number of shelves)

Bead board paneling (quantity determined by dimensions of back of bookcase)

1½-inch wooden flat edge banding or trim (optional)

Baseboard trim (to match existing baseboard)

Decorative crown molding (optional)

HARDWARE:

1 box wood screws

1 box finishing nails

Wall anchors (if needed)

Shelf pins

FINISHING SUPPLIES:

Sandpaper, 120- and 220-grit

Wood putty (optional)

Wood glue

1 gallon each primer and paint or stain per bookcase

1 gallon clear water-based polyurethane per bookcase

MAKE THAT SPACE HAPPEN

1 . . . .

Use a tape measure to determine the length, height, and depth of your bookcase(s) and note the measurements. A height of 36 inches is standard for a counter, but you may want something shorter or taller depending on your needs. Likewise, a depth of 20 inches is useful in a dining room because shelves of this depth can hold a variety of items, from books to a china service, and the top surface is more functional as a buffet.

Include the number of shelves you want in your measurements; plan for at least two, spaced about 12 inches apart, with one stationary and the other adjustable. If you want three shelves, make the middle one stationary. If the overall unit (or box) is longer than 30 inches, install a vertical plywood support underneath the stationary shelf. The support should run from the base to the top and divide the interior space below the stationary shelf in half. Another option (not described here) would be to skip the trim and add doors to hide the shelves; these can be made to order from a number of online sources (see Resources & Suppliers section, page 249).

2 . . . .

Use a flat pry bar to carefully remove the baseboard molding from the area where you plan to install the bookcase(s). This allows the bookcase(s) to sit flush against the wall and be anchored properly to the wall studs. Save the molding if you can; you can use it both to trim out the bottom of the bookcase(s) once they are installed and also to carry as a sample for matching molding at the lumberyard. To avoid tearing the wall when removing trim, first score the top of the baseboard where it meets the drywall with a utility knife.

3 ....

Using your measurements, cut the ¾-inch plywood using a circular saw or a table saw. At a minimum, you need six pieces: a top, a bottom, two sides, and two shelves. Note that the top and bottom pieces will be inset within the two sides, so account for the plywood widths when measuring each piece.

SAFETY ALERT: Always wear safety glasses and ear protection when cutting wood.

4 ....

Once the pieces are cut, sand the edges and surfaces using an orbital sander. Start with 120-grit sandpaper and move to 220-grit for the final sanding. Remove dust with damp paper towels or a tack cloth.

5 ....

Build the bookcase frames or "boxes" using butt joints and wood screws. Attach the sides, top, and bottom. Once a box is built, attach the stationary shelf by driving in wood screws (with a drill) from the outer sides of the box.

6 ....

For the adjustable shelf, drill holes in the sides of the boxes and install shelf pins. It's very important that the holes are aligned and level on opposite sides of the box (or else the shelf will wobble or tilt); see the following Tip for advice on doing this. Also ensure that the holes are no larger than the pins. Fit the pins into the holes and check the shelf for level; if you make an unfixable mistake, drill a new set of holes at a different height or offset to the first set of holes and cover the old holes with wood putty.

continued

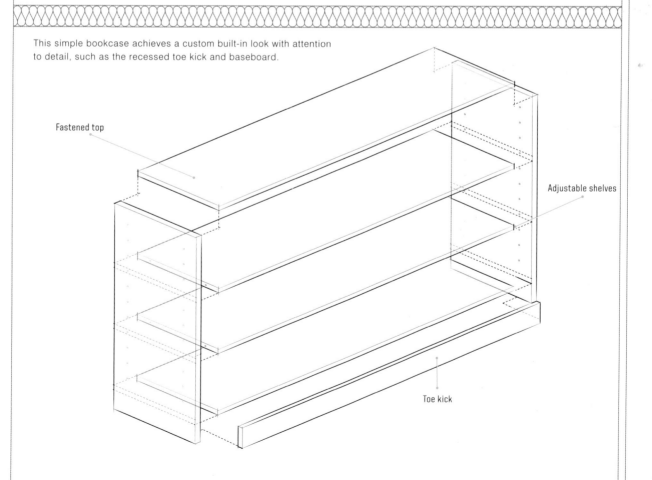

This simple bookcase achieves a custom built-in look with attention to detail, such as the recessed toe kick and baseboard.

Fastened top

Adjustable shelves

Toe kick

TIP: The best way to line up shelf support pins is to use a framing square. When you have established the height, hold the edge of the framing square against the front face and draw a very light pencil line across the width of the side leg of the square. If your sides are plumb, the line will be level. Use a tape measure to mark the same height up from the bottom on the other side and repeat the same process. Use the line as your drilling location. Use a nail or nail set to prep the hole and then use a drill bit with the same diameter as the shelf pin. Make sure you do not drill all the way through the sides! Use a drill stop or use painter's tape as a guide by wrapping a piece ¼ or ⅓ inch from the tip of the bit so you know when to stop drilling.

7 . . . .

Measure and cut the bead board paneling for the backing with a circular saw.

8 . . . .

Attach the bead board backing with wood glue and a nail gun using finishing nails. The "good" side of the bead board should face the front of the bookcase. Use your framing square to ensure that the unit is braced and square before you fasten it all around.

9 . . . .

Prime and paint or stain the bookcases and let them dry completely. Lightly sand with a 220-grit sandpaper and then apply polyurethane to the bookcases for clear protection. Allow the finish to dry completely before installing. The polyurethane will better protect the surface.

10 . . . .

Install the shelving units along the wall. Using a stud finder, locate and mark the wall studs behind the bookcases. Then drill pilot holes and screw the units into the walls, ensuring that you screw into at least one stud and use wall anchors when attaching to drywall. If you are placing two shelving units next to each other, screw together the units at the sides, two on top and two on the bottom, for a tighter fit.

11 . . . .

Once the unit is secured to the wall, attach the salvaged or matching new baseboard molding to the bottom of the unit. If your bookcase(s) extends the length of one wall, you can trim each end of the molding so it fits snugly against the molding on the walls to either side of the bookcases. You need a coping saw for this job (see Tip on crown molding below). If you plan on wrapping the molding around a bookcase that does not extend the length of the wall, use a miter saw to cut new molding, or salvaged and new matching pieces, at a 45-degree angle. If you have attached two units together, trim the seam (or face of the shelf) where the sides meet with the edge banding and glue.

Another option is to trim out the top of the bookcases with crown molding. This is not necessary, but it may fit the room's aesthetic. However, I have to be honest and say that cutting crown molding right is quite often a pain in the you-know-what for a first-timer and even for the tradesman who has not tackled it in a while. See the Tip below for advice on doing this.

TIP: Think of crown molding as a baseboard for the ceiling, except upside down. Hold your crown molding upside down against the fence of the miter saw at the same angle it will fit onto the ceiling. Then cut the crown using a 45-degree angle. Try it out, and if the joint is not perfect, slowly keep trimming it until you have a perfect fit. A sliding bevel will enable you to find the exact angle so you'll make your cut perfect the first time. If you are going to stain the base or crown, a coping cut, made with a coping saw, is the way to go to avoid a likely open joint. You can use a coping saw to cut molding so it fits against the profile of existing molding as well.

12 . . . .

Prime and paint or stain the baseboard and crown molding to match the bookcases. Then attach the trim with finishing nails and touch up the units as needed.

PROJECT:

WINDOW SEAT STORAGE

WINDOW SEAT STORAGE

A window seat has a certain romance—it's a wonderful place to perch for bird-watching, gazing at the sunset (or sunrise), reading, dreaming, or canoodling with a sweetie. Storage compartments underneath the extra seating also come in handy for all manner of items. You can build a custom window seat with storage using ready-made, off-the-rack kitchen cabinets from a favorite big box store. The seat can be adapted to any size window and any room. I like the idea of installing the space in a public room because it expands seating options. For a custom, built-in, and professional look, make sure the new trim matches your existing baseboard trim.

TIME:
A day

DIFFICULTY:

TOOLS:
Handsaw or circular saw

Clamps

Hammer or nail gun

Nail set

Tape measure

Level

Stud finder

Drill/driver with bits
(and countersink drill bit)

Miter saw

Paintbrushes, roller, and tray

Pencil

Safety glasses

Ear protection

MATERIALS

2 stock kitchen cabinets (each measuring 36 inches wide by 15 inches high by 12 inches deep; any style and finish)

One 12-by-36-inch seat cushion

WOOD:

2x4 or 2x6 lumber (quantity determined by matching it to the height of existing baseboard)

Baseboard trim (to match existing baseboard)

HARDWARE:

1 box 1½-inch finishing nails

1 box each 1¼-, 2½-, and 3-inch wood screws

FINISHING SUPPLIES:

1 quart each primer and paint or stain

Wood putty

MAKE THAT SPACE HAPPEN

1 ....
Build a simple toe kick out of 2x4 or 2x6 lumber. (Match the height of the existing baseboard.) The front, back, and sides of the toe-kick frame should be about 1 inch smaller than the cabinets, not including the doors. Using a handsaw or circular saw, cut four pieces of lumber to make the frame, using butt joints. Assemble and check level and then secure the toe-kick frame together with 3-inch screws.

2 ....
To determine where you will anchor the toe kick, first position it about 1 inch away from the wall and "dry fit" a cabinet on top of it to make sure the cabinet sits flush against the wall. If it doesn't, make adjustments to the position of the toe-kick frame. Once the positioning is correct, remove the cabinet and mark the floor lightly with a pencil to note the proper positioning of the frame.

3 ....
Next, remove the doors, then attach the cabinets to each other by driving three 2½-inch screws directly through the sides. Make sure you do not drive the screws through the other side.

4 ....
Then attach the toe-kick frame to the cabinet by screwing the bottom of the cabinet to the top of the frame, using 1¼-inch or 2½-inch wood screws, being mindful of the proper positioning.

5 ....
Attach the cabinet to the wall. Find and mark the wall studs, drill pilot holes, and then drive 3-inch screws through the back of the cabinet into the wall studs, three screws per side.

6 ....
Prepare the baseboard trim to place around the bottom of the cabinet to hide the rough toe kick. Cut three pieces of molding; use a miter saw and 45-degree-angle cuts at the front corners.

7 ....
Paint (or stain) the baseboard trim to match your existing baseboards and then attach the trim to the toe kick using finishing nails. Reattach the doors. Place a cushion fitted to the size of the two cabinets on top and have a seat!

A very easy and practical project, giving you additional storage and a place to change your shoes.

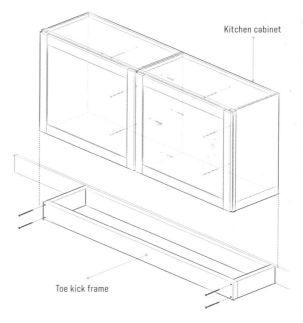

Kitchen cabinet

Toe kick frame

ADD CABINET AND SHELVING NICHE TO WINDOW SEAT

To add the cabinet and shelving niche, follow the window seat instructions through Step 4 on page 149, and then continue with the project here. The following tools and materials are what you need in addition to what's listed on page 148 for the window seat. Make sure that the cabinets and the bookshelf units are all in matching styles and finishes.

TIME:

6 to 7 hours

DIFFICULTY:

TOOLS:

Caulking gun

Thin pry bar

MATERIALS:

2 stock kitchen cabinets (each measuring 30 inches wide by 12 inches deep by 24½ inches tall)

2 intermediate cabinets (each measuring 30 inches wide by 12 inches deep by 15 inches tall)

2 bookcases (each measuring 30 inches wide by 12 inches deep by 4 feet tall)

WOOD:

Plywood skins (optional; quantity and width determined by height of cabinets and width between units, as it is used to cover seams if necessary)

Waistband molding or trim (optional; quantity and width determined by height of cabinets and width between units, as it is used to cover seams if necessary)

Crown molding (to match existing molding)

2x2 lumber

Shims

FINISHING SUPPLIES:

Latex caulk

Contact adhesive

½ gallon each primer and paint or stain

MAKE THAT SPACE HAPPEN

1 . . . .

To create the window seat surround, first remove all the doors, then install one of the 12-by-24½-by-30-inch cabinets to each end of the toe kick. Clamp and screw these end cabinets to the window seat cabinets. Make sure the face frames are perfectly flush before driving in the screws to connect the cabinets (in the same way as Step 4 on page 149). Alternatively, you can attach ready-made bookcases to either side of the window seat, anchoring them to the wall for extra support—and leave it at that!

2 . . . .

Check the level of each end cabinet and then secure it to the wall with two screws driven into wall studs. If necessary, place wood shims behind the cabinets to prevent the screws from pulling the cabinets out of alignment.

continued

If you take the cabinet up to the ceiling, wrap its crown molding to match existing molding for a built-in look.

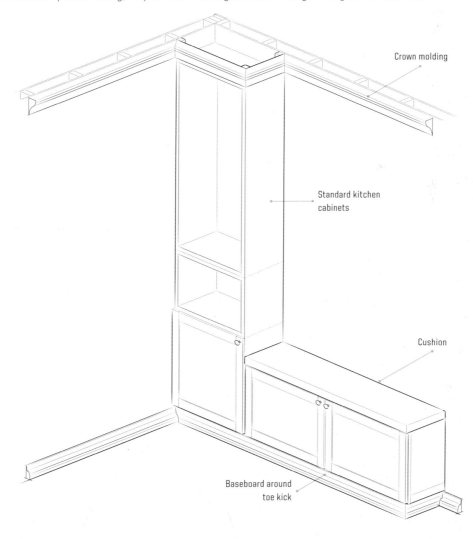

Crown molding

Standard kitchen cabinets

Cushion

Baseboard around toe kick

3 . . . .

The end cabinets can be topped with a set of 15-inch-tall intermediate cabinets and then with bookcase units. Or the cabinets can be topped with bookcases only. Either way, position the intermediate cabinets or bookcases on top of the end cabinets and screw them to the wall studs. If using intermediate cabinets, install the bookcase units by first clamping them to the intermediate cabinets and then fastening them with 2½-inch screws driven through the face frames. Once the tall unit is on, attach it into at least one wall stud ensuring that it is plumb and level.

4 . . . .

Conceal the joints between the two cabinets on each end (if necessary) by attaching trim. Another option is to adhere prefinished plywood skins with contact adhesive. These are sheets of veneer that can be adhered and cut using a utility knife or sharp chisel.

5 . . . .

As with Step 5 in the main window seat project, install baseboard molding around the bottom of all the cabinets to hide the rough toe kick. Miter the corners of the molding. Cut the molding to size, paint or stain as necessary, and attach with finishing nails. If the molding is too wide, rip it down to the proper size on a table saw.

6 . . . .

Nail crown molding along the tops of the cabinets. If there is a gap left between the top of the cabinets and the ceiling, fasten three pieces of 2x2 to make up the difference, and nail the crown molding to the 2x2. Paint or stain the molding as necessary to match your existing crown molding. Fill any small spaces that remain above the molding with caulk.

7 . . . .

Replace the cabinet doors, install adjustable shelves in the bookcases (see page 145), and set the cushion on the window seat. Have a seat!

ZONING IN

When planning a multipurpose room, think of it in terms of zones. Make a preliminary list of all the activities you want space for, in order of importance. For instance, you may decide that family movie night is the most important function of the room, followed by crafting, reading, eating light meals, working on the computer, and watching TV. Add to your list what each activity would need in terms of furniture and other items. For crafting, for example, the room might need a worktable, a good light, storage, and a chair. Light meals may be taken at this table if you have easily movable chairs. When you have the list, you can clearly see which items can easily do double duty and which zones will need to be spaced apart (i.e., you may want the crafting station to be at a distance from the computer area to reduce distraction).

Then map out the room to scale on grid paper (noting windows, doorways, and traffic patterns) and designate zones for everything on your list. A sectional or comfortable club chairs and the TV screen may take up the center of the room, with a table and storage shelves on one end for crafting and snacking, and a smaller desk with a computer or laptop on the other end of the room. Create to-scale cutouts of furniture and move them around your virtual room, experimenting with different arrangements to find out what works best so that you have to lift and shift real furniture only once, thereby saving time and your back.

PROJECT:

BUILD A PLATFORM

BUILD A PLATFORM

A 6- or 8-inch-high platform, especially in a great room or long living room, can delineate separate spaces for dining, working, or recreation. Platforms also add visual and architectural interest to expanses of space, and they can make formerly unused "dead" space quite functional. A platform also extends a great opportunity to include some hidey-holes (see page 125) for extra storage.

However, before starting, take the room height into consideration. By adding a 6- or 8-inch-high platform, you effectively "lower" the room's ceiling height by half a foot or more. This is no big deal if you have cathedral ceilings or even 9- or 10-foot ceilings, but this may look and feel tight if you have 8-foot ceilings. As well, ceilings of less than 8 feet can sometimes be in violation of local or city building codes. To check your local codes, just call your local city office to inquire about height requirements; this prevents any complications if you decide to sell the property at a later date. You may also need to raise outlets and switches to meet code.

A platform isn't structurally complicated to build, but it does require a great deal of carpentry and moderate building skills. Even though you are raising the floor by only a step, the platform must be supported by a floor joist system, which is topped by a subfloor, which is topped by a finished floor material of your choice. (Cork flooring is a nice option, as is sea grass or prefinished snap-together wood flooring.)

My instructions assume that the platform will be installed along the entire length of one wall in your room (and abut the two side walls), with only one side of the platform being open to the rest of the room. However, if you don't want your platform to go wall to wall, or if you want it open on two or three sides, follow the instructions for creating the front finished side of the platform when creating any other outfacing sides.

I'm also assuming that the floor you are building on is level. If it's not, it may be more challenging and require more maneuvering using packers or shims to get your platform level.

Finally, as with Project: Window Seat Storage on page 147, this project is easiest if the floor where the platform will go is already free and clear of obstructions. For example, if the area contains heating registers, these need to be moved or raised to the level of the platform, and the ducts need to be adjusted accordingly. If the area contains baseboard heating, consult a heating contractor for advice.

TIME:
2 days

DIFFICULTY:
↑↑↑

TOOLS:

Stud finder

Drill/driver with bits

Chalk line

Miter saw

Circular saw

4-foot level

Combination square

Tape measure

Hammer (if using nails)

Pencil

Safety glasses

Ear protection

Nail gun (framing) and nails

MATERIALS:

WOOD:

2x8 or 2x6 boards (for the joists; see Step 1 for help calculating the amount)

¾-inch tongue-and-groove plywood (enough to cover the platform)

Floor covering, such as carpet, cork, hardwood, or tile (see box, below)

HARDWARE:

2 boxes 3-inch wood screws

2 boxes 3-inch nails (optional)

2 boxes 1½-inch wood screws

FINISHING SUPPLIES:

Masking tape

Construction adhesive

CARPET, CORK, AND TILE—OH, MY!

When it comes to putting in a new floor, you have a number of options, from quick and easy to involved and long lasting. Carpet tiles are easy to install on your own, and this system has many advantages, like the ability to replace only certain tiles if they become stained. Sea grass, Berber, and sisal are interesting and practical choices as well. Cork flooring is another good option, as it coordinates with existing wood. Carpet and cork tiles are both easy to maintain. Laminate or prefinished wood flooring is also easy to install, although covering the front of the platform that faces the room can be somewhat tricky. Corner bull nose trim can be used to hide the rough edge and cover the seam in the front of the platform. Tiling is also an option, but masonry is more time-consuming—although the finished project, if done well, is very attractive and durable. Use the same technique for tiling a countertop (see Project: Storage Island, page 62). However, if you use porcelain tiles, you may need to rent a wet saw to make any necessary cuts. Be sure to ask for detailed instructions from the rental company before taking that baby home and firing it up!

MAKE THAT SPACE HAPPEN

1..
Determine your platform height and decide whether
you will be using 2x6 or 2x8 boards for the joists.
Remember, the actual width of rough lumber is
½ inch less than stated, but your layers of flooring
will add another inch or so. You need enough lumber to border all four sides of the platform, plus
enough additional boards for joists every 16 inches
of the length of the platform. Keep in mind that the
boards for the joists need to be at least as long as
the width of the room.

TIP: Choose joists yourself at a lumberyard or home improvement store so you can ensure that each one is straight. Leave
twisted or curved boards on the shelf! Check boards by running
your eye along the length of the lumber. Consider using straight
recycled wood, if it is available (you may find it at re-use centers).

2..
To begin, strip the platform area of any carpeting,
linoleum, tile, baseboards, or trim molding; remove
any other obstructions. If you think you might want
to remove the platform at a later date, you can leave
the current tile, linoleum (possible asbestos!), or
hardwood flooring in place, if you wish. In this case,
skip the use of construction adhesive in Step 4.

3..
Use a stud finder and masking tape to mark the
wall studs on the three walls where you plan to
build your platform.

4..
Build the frame. Starting at the inside corner of the
room, lay a straight 2x8 (or 2x6) next to the wall,
positioned so it is lying flat. Spread construction
adhesive (optional) along the face and stand it up
and press it to the wall, with the edge sitting on the
floor. Screw three 3-inch wood screws along the
width of the board into every second stud. Continue this way around the next two sides. Measure
and cut the boards with a miter saw or circular
saw as needed to make them fit. Use butt joints at
the corners, setting one piece along the length of
the wall and butting the next piece perpendicular

to it. For the open end of the room, snap a chalk
line to ensure this piece is straight. Using 3-inch
screws, screw the 2x8 (or 2x6) into the edges of the
perpendicular boards at each side. Glue and screw
a second board to the inside of the first one to give
it added strength.

TIP: If the existing floor is out of level, find the highest point,
measure and mark the top of your joist on the wall, and then
transfer that mark all around. This will prevent you from having
to cut many joists. Once the perimeter boards are attached to
the walls at a level height, the internal joists will just require
shims to match that height. This will save you a ton of time! This
same tip applies to the installation of any cabinetry placed on
a floor.

5..
From the back wall of the platform, measure along
the joist attached to one of the side walls toward
the front edge of the platform. Make a mark on the
board at 16 inches. From that mark, continue your
marks every 16 inches. Continue this pattern all
the way down the wall and repeat on the opposite
wall. It's fine if the gap between the last internal
joist and the front edge of the platform is less than
16 inches, but it shouldn't be more than 18 inches.
You will then center a stud on each of your marks

Front detail, Step 4.

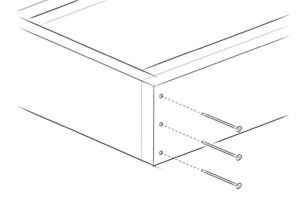

so that approximately ¾ inch of the stud is on either side of the mark. Done correctly, this marking pattern ensures that the joists are 16 inches apart from their centerlines (not from either edge).

TIP: You will notice on your measuring tape that there is a red box or marking of some sort at every 16 inches on your tape. This takes out the guesswork and enables you to run out your tape and mark these boxes every 16 inches.

6 . . . .
Measure the width of the room between your two anchor pieces and use a circular saw to cut your first joist at that measurement, to span the width of the room. Wedge the joist between the two anchor pieces so that the interior edge of the joist lines up with the first line and the width of the board is on the X side of the line. Use 3-inch wood screws, nails, or a nail gun to attach the joist to the anchor piece, putting the screws or nails in at an angle on the sides of the joist, two to a side.

MORE SPACE SEPARATION TRICKS

Turn a great room into two rooms without heavy construction using these easy techniques. Or go ahead and build a new wall (see Project: Wall Construction—Make One Room into Two, page 195).

+ Use backless or open shelving units to divide entryways from living areas, or section off a room for different functions. These widely available units (they are also easy to make; see the dining room shelving project, page 142, for the method) are terrific places to display objects that have sculptural appeal—even if they aren't sculptures. For example, your son's collection of metal trucks or your own stash of McCoy pottery could both make for interesting displays.

+ Hang panels to add color and texture to a room while dividing the space. IKEA's affordable Kvartal curtain panel track-based hanging system affixes to walls or ceilings and can hang fabric, fiberglass, bamboo, or even paper panels.

+ Hang drapery panels from the ceiling to divide a room halfway or all the way across. The great thing about drapery hung on standard poles or a hospital curtain track system (which installs on the ceiling) is that you can easily open and close them according to your mood or needs.

+ Divided or three-piece screens can be moved around according to your needs. They're also quite decorative—whether they are sleek and modern or traditional and highly ornamented. Two or three vintage doors hinged together make for a charming screenlike divider; likewise shuttered closet doors can easily be transformed into a beach-y looking screen. Shoji screens are modern looking and translucent, which allows soft filtered light to come through.

+ Create a green screen with a line of big potted plants. Bamboo, palms, ficus, yucca, and jade plants all grow large enough—yes, indoors—to provide a private nook in an open-plan room.

+ A garden trellis can be primed, painted, and then framed with 1x2s and secured to one wall with wood screws (be sure to drill into wall studs). Or, suspend the trellis from the ceiling (from the joists) with fishing wire or line and eye hooks.

+ Use furniture for a convenient divider. A buffet or credenza, for example, placed perpendicular to a wall instantly divides a space. If the back of the piece is unattractive (which is often the case!), cover it with bead board paneling (which comes in 4-by-8-foot sheets) or back it up, literally, with another similar size piece of furniture. Two matching narrow credenzas placed back to back create division, storage, and a useful surface.

TIP: If your joists are more than 10 feet long, place stag-gered 2x6- or 2x8-inch braces (otherwise known as blocking) between them. Each brace should be 14½ inches long. Secure each by sinking 3-inch screws or nails from the other side of the joist. This will reinforce it.

7 . . . .

Place the rest of the joists following this same procedure. Once all the joists are in, use the ¾-inch tongue-and-groove plywood for subfloor-ing over them. The plywood should run lengthwise in the opposite direction of (or perpendicular to) the length of the joists. As necessary, cut pieces to size with a circular saw. Spread construction adhesive over the top edges of the joists as you lay each plywood piece.

8 . . . .

Next secure the plywood with a drill driver, using 1½-inch screws going through the top of the plywood into each joist. Make sure the seams of the plywood that run in the same direction as the joists are resting directly on the tops of the joists. Plywood sheets are normally 8 feet (or 96 inches) long and 4 feet (or 48 inches) wide, which means that full sheets will always come to the centers of joists positioned at 16 inches on center.

9 . . . .

Now the platform is ready for a floor covering. See the box "Carpet, Cork, and Tile—Oh, My!" on page 155 for advice. Carpeting, which can be pro-fessionally installed in a couple of hours, is prob-ably the easiest and least expensive of all solutions.

Be creative with this project. It can be any size to suit your design choice. This is also a great opportunity to allow for extra storage like hidey holes (page 125) or toe kick drawers (page 55).

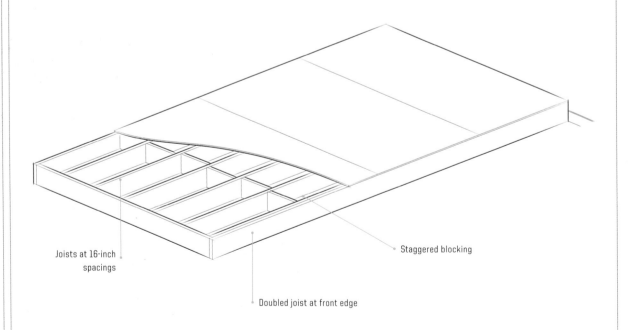

Joists at 16-inch
spacings

Staggered blocking

Doubled joist at front edge

08
ENTRYWAYS & HALLWAYS

Often forgotten or neglected, entryways, mudrooms, pass-throughs, stairways, and hallways offer a plethora of storage, display, and functional opportunities. The irony is these often tiny and awkward spaces are sometimes most in need of storage and function. These areas are hubs of activity with people moving themselves (and their pets) in and out; taking off and putting on shoes and jackets; sorting mail; and stowing keys, dog leashes, and bags. The projects in this chapter help make these too-tight spaces neater, more functional, and very welcoming—from a shelf to hold mail to a mudroom unit to stow boots, backpacks, and briefcases.

PROJECT:

MUDROOM CUBBY STORAGE

MUDROOM CUBBY STORAGE

One of the great things about working with flat-pack furniture and ready-made shelving is that all of the big issues—the designing, the cutting, the predrilling of holes for hinges, and so on—have been taken care of in the factory. The controlled conditions make the final product easy to work with and easy to customize in endless ways. A unit made from melamine, for example, works beautifully for mudroom storage because it's a strong plastic laminate that looks neat and clean, and provides a scratchproof, moisture-resistant surface that is effortlessly adjustable when your needs change. This project uses melamine shelving units and closet and storage accessories from a big box store. I sourced mine from IKEA, but home centers, big discount stores, and storage centers sell similar affordable products. If a particular material or shelf size is not available, no worries! Buy stock material and customize it to suit your tastes.

TIME:

About 8 hours

DIFFICULTY:

TOOLS:

Hammer

Tape measure

Stud finder

Screwdrivers or drill/driver with bits

4-foot level

Pencil

Safety glasses

Ear protection

MATERIALS:

Flat-pack melamine shelving unit(s), fit to your space and needs

Accessories including hanging rails, glass shelves, drawers, baskets, plastic shoe-holders, baskets, and anything else that suits your specific storage needs

HARDWARE:

1 box 2½- and 3-inch drywall screws

White screwcaps (optional)

L-brackets (optional)

MAKE THAT SPACE HAPPEN

1...
Measure your mudroom space and determine the
height and configuration of shelving that could fit.

2 ....
Make a list of what you want to store in your mudroom unit. Then, create your own design and make
an accessories list. For instance, open bins on the
bottom shelf can stow shoes and hold slippers.
Baskets for gloves, hats, and scarves may be
useful. Key and coat hooks attached to the outer
side of the unit make for easy hanging access to
these essentials, as well as dog leashes, handbags,
and jump ropes. A desktop file holder makes a
perfect mail sorter.

3 ....
Buy the appropriate shelving unit(s) and assemble
according to manufacturer's instructions—many
require an Allen wrench, which is often provided
with the shelving kit.

4 ....
Using a stud finder, locate and mark the wall studs.
Anchor the unit to the wall with drywall screws long
enough to anchor into the studs. Be sure to countersink the screw heads. If the heads are exposed, you
can place white screwcaps over them so they blend
in (these are also available with flat-pack shelving
kits). Another good trick is to position the screws in
the middle of where the shelves will sit. L-brackets
can also be used in many situations. However, the
fewer fasteners you see, the better.

SAFETY ALERT: It is very important to secure the unit to the
wall studs for safety reasons. One of the top causes of child-
hood injuries in the home is large furniture toppling over.

5 ....
Place your accessories on the shelves; add a
small bench to sit on nearby, a mat to wipe your
shoes on, and you've got yourself a mudroom.

ENTRYWAY KNEE WALL

ENTRYWAY KNEE WALL

Houses with front doors that open directly into one side of an open living space and a staircase leading to the second floor can be awkward. When there is no transition between the outside and the inside of a house, you sometimes feel a little lost. Where do you go? In what direction should you turn? Decorating the area is more challenging, too, because the entryway space is often considered "dead" or unusable space.

But entryways don't have to be either unusable or cold. A simple knee wall at the door creates a space for taking off your shoes and setting down your keys before sitting down in the living room. It also enlivens the entryway and is, psychologically, more welcoming. A small chair or side table placed adjacent to the knee wall along with a floating shelf (see page 78) or drawer (see page 169) installed opposite the wall, gives you a true entryway.

For an attractive and functional finish to the knee wall, I recommend capping it with a piece of wood or stone that's 1 inch wider and longer than the wall itself. For wood, good choices are birch, maple, oak, poplar, and cherry; these will look great with just some protective polyurethane or with a stain added. Depending on your décor, you might prefer granite or marble. Look for flat stone floor thresholds in the tile department of home stores to use as a cap; depending on the length of your knee wall, you may find one in the perfect size (they come in standard sizes of 5 by 32 inches or 5 by 36 inches) that requires no cutting.

TIME:

A weekend

DIFFICULTY:

⬥⬥⬥

TOOLS:

Tape measure

Utility knife

Circular saw

Drill/driver with bits (plus masonry bit, if necessary)

Router (optional)

Hammer or nail gun

4-foot level

Caulking gun

Putty or drywall knife

Paintbrushes, roller, and tray

Stud finder

Pencil

Safety glasses

Ear protection

MATERIALS:

½-inch or ⅝-inch drywall (quantity determined by the measurements of the wall)

Heavy cardboard for template

WOOD:

2x4 or 2x6 lumber for framing (quantity determined by desired width for wall)

1x6 or 1x8 lumber (or similar-size piece of stone or marble; quantity determined by the measurements of the wall), for cap of knee wall

Floor molding, to match existing millwork

HARDWARE:

1 box 3-inch wood screws

1 box 1¼-inch drywall screws

1 drywall metal corner bead

4 masonry anchors (optional, for concrete floor)

1 box finishing nails

FINISHING SUPPLIES:

Joint compound

Topping compound

Caulk

Paper tape

Sandpaper, 120-grit

Wood glue

1 gallon each primer and paint

1 quart stain and polyurethane (optional)

Construction adhesive

MAKE THAT SPACE HAPPEN

1 . . . .

Using some rough measurements of your entry-way space, design a flat or one-dimensional template for the project on cardboard. Cut it out using a utility knife. This template will help you visualize how much space you want the knee wall to take up. Is this how long you want it? Is it tall enough? Decide whether you want the new wall to blend in so it looks as if it has always been there, or if you want it to stand out. It's your place—you can do whatever you like.

2 . . . .

Once you have determined the dimensions of the wall, measure and cut five pieces of straight 2x4 or 2x6 to make the frame for the knee wall. When assembling, have the top and bottom pieces overlay the sidepieces (using butt joints), and join the pieces using the drill and three 3-inch wood screws on the top and bottom.

3 . . . .

Use the stud finder to locate the stud in the existing wall closest to your desired location and mark it with a pencil. Attach the wall frame to the studs in the existing wall using two or more 3-inch wood screws and then attach to the floor with four 3-inch wood screws; if the floor is concrete, use masonry anchors.

4 . . . .

Measure and cut three pieces of ½-inch or ⅝-inch drywall to cover the three exposed sides of the wall frame (but not the top, where the cap will go). Score the paper on the face of the drywall with a sharp utility knife. Stand the panel on edge and break it along the score line. Cut the paper on the back with the utility knife and snap it back the other way to make a clean break. You will be surprised how easy this is—just keep that blade away from your fingers!

NOTE: If you are going to use a wood cap and want to install it so no fasteners are visible, skip ahead to the Tip after Step 10 before proceeding to the next step and installing the drywall.

continued

Knee-wall construction is no more complicated than building a box; note that six screws per stud makes your project sturdy and up to the wear and tear of an entryway.

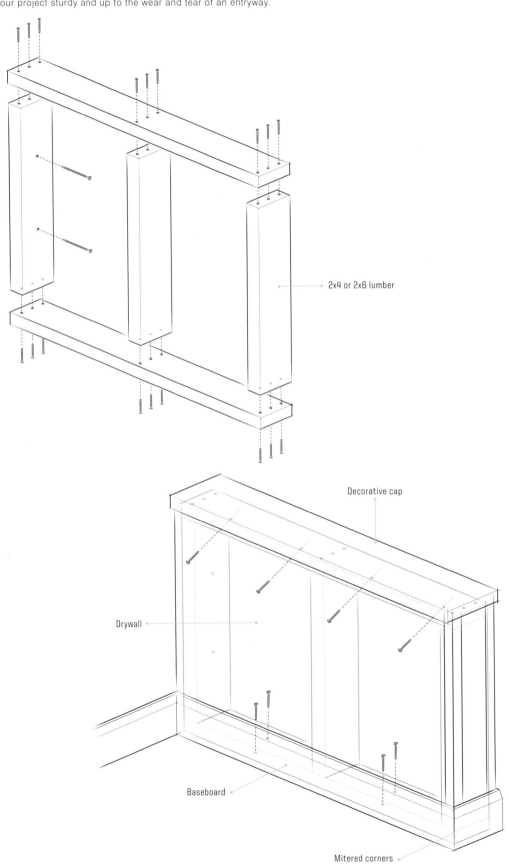

2x4 or 2x6 lumber

Decorative cap

Drywall

Baseboard

Mitered corners

5 ....
Use a drill/driver and drywall screws to attach the drywall to both sides and front edge of the frame. Attach a drywall metal corner bead with finishing nails to protect the fragile front edges of the drywall and to give the wall clean, sharp lines.

TIP: As you attach the metal beads to the exposed edges, make sure to keep them plumb and level. Go slow and easy so as not to hit the corner, as it can dent. These dents are difficult to conceal.

6 ....
Lay a coat of joint compound along the seam between the new and existing wall and cover the joint with moistened paper tape folded at 90 degrees. Dip the paper in water, and then squeegee it between your fingers to remove any excess. Center the tape on the corner seam. Keep it flat and smooth as you press it into the compound using your putty or drywall knife.

7 ....
Use joint compound to conceal the flanges on the metal corner bead and blend it into the wall. Allow it to dry completely according to the manufacturer's instructions. Once dry, apply a second coat of joint compound.

8 ....
When the second coat is dry, use 120-grit or finer sandpaper to smooth the walls.

9 ....
Next install the knee wall's cap. If using wood, use a circular saw to cut the cap to size, making sure it is 1 inch wider and longer than the knee wall. If you like, sand the edges round, or use a router to make a decorative edge; you can also add rope or other decorative trim. Finally, stain the wood if you wish and then apply two coats of polyurethane. If you are using stone, buy the piece to size or have the home center or lumberyard cut it for you.

10 ....
Attach the wood cap or stone ledge using construction adhesive (follow manufacturer's instructions for best results).

TIP: Consider screwing the wood cap diagonally from the underside of the frame with the addition of construction adhesive. This will keep the fasteners secret, giving you a better finish while saving you time. Do this before you attach the drywall.

continued

OTHER PROJECTS PERFECT FOR HALLWAYS

+ Recessed wall niches (see page 120) can go between wall studs on a stairway to hold art or other sculptural objects; around doorways they can hold books and baskets. When making a niche around an exterior door, place insulation in the back before putting the new drywall niche in place and do use waterproof drywall, known as greenboard in the industry. If the depth is not enough, consider building your niche or shelves so they protrude a little to give you the desired depth you need.

+ A floating shelf (see page 78) can be placed in even the smallest entryway. A few cup hooks screwed into the front serve as a place to keep keys. A small basket on top holds mail and other odds and ends.

+ A window seat (see page 147) made with two over-the-fridge cabinets becomes a hallway storage bench when attached to an entryway wall.

+ Under-the-bed rolling storage boxes (see page 112) can serve as movable storage for boots and shoes, backpacks, and book bags in a mudroom.

+ A floorboard hidey-hole (see page 125) is useful in a mudroom for stashing extra sets of keys, "petty cash," and valuables. It's out of the way and entirely unexpected.

11 ....
Attach floor molding with a hammer and finishing nails around the base of the wall to give it a
finished, professional look.

12 ....
Caulk, prime, and paint the wall and base molding. It will blend in seamlessly with your room.

KEEPING ENTRYWAYS CLEAR, BEAUTIFUL, AND SAFE

There are many no-construction-needed ways to make the most of entryways and hallways. Take
stock of these spaces in your home to see which of these easy options would work for your needs.

+ Reuse small furniture you may have. A student desk's kneehole is too small to function as an
  adult desk, but it's the perfect size to nestle a basket underneath to hold umbrellas, slippers,
  or mittens. A plant stand or small side table can hold a porcelain bowl for keys. A garden bench
  brings the outdoors in while providing a place to sit. One small side chair can double as a seat
  and a surface.

+ Place a large mirror or group a collection of smaller mirrors over a hall table, desk, or chair to
  expand space and help a narrow entryway feel larger.

+ An ottoman can stand in for bench seating in a compact space.

+ Letterboxes and desktop organizers work wonders on a hall table as a place to sort mail, leave
  notes, and keep items you often need when rushing out the door, such as keys, stamps, subway
  tokens, and train tickets.

+ A tall vase, large flowerpot, or traditional umbrella stand is handy for keeping umbrellas neat
  and accessible.

+ A vintage wooden medicine cabinet hung on the wall has everything you need to keep a small
  hallway organized—a mirror to check yourself in before leaving the house, a cabinet to keep miscellaneous items in, a drawer to hold mail, and a dowel for hanging keys and leashes (or remove
  the dowel and replace with hooks). A lineup of different vintage medicine cabinets works well in
  a back hallway or mudroom—install one for each member of the household.

+ A narrow console table with its back legs removed, then attached to the wall through its back
  skirt, takes up very little room, but provides a broad surface for containers, a vase of fresh
  flowers, and artwork.

FLOATING DRAWER AND MIRROR

FLOATING DRAWER AND MIRROR

Oftentimes apartments and bungalows have no formal entryway—open the front door and you fall right into the living area. Although a strategically placed knee wall can help define an entrance (see Project: Entryway Knee Wall, page 163), many spaces are too small even for that solution. Painting the area around the doorway a different color from the rest of the room also helps create a feeling of a separate area, but this floating drawer topped by a mirror gives the space identity. Sitting flush with its box, the single drawer slides in and out with the help of a knob or pull—and it's probably the simplest kind of drawer you can build.

TIME:

3 to 5 hours

DIFFICULTY:

⌐⌐⌐

TOOLS:

Tape measure

Carpenter's pencil

Table saw with dado blade set

Router with ½-inch straight cut bit (optional)

Framing square

Combination square

Drill/driver with bits

Hammer

Nail set

Clamps

Orbital or palm sander

Paintbrushes, roller, and tray

Stud finder

Long-necked screwdriver

Level

Safety glasses

Ear protection

MATERIALS:

Mirror of choice

WOOD:

Quarter of a sheet ¾-inch birch or oak veneer plywood

¼-inch hardboard (slightly larger than dimensions of drawer)

One 1-inch long ¼-inch-diameter wooden dowel

HARDWARE:

Eight 2-inch wood screws

2 or more 3-inch wood screws and washers

1 box finishing nails

1 decorative knob or pull

2 L-brackets or 2 decorative brackets (optional)

FINISHING SUPPLIES:

Wood glue

Wood putty

Sandpaper, 120- and 220-grit

Lubricant: wax or soap

1 quart each primer and paint, or 1 small can of stain and polyurethane

MAKE THAT SPACE HAPPEN

1 ....

Be sure to measure the space where you plan to install the drawer and determine how far the drawer and its box can protrude from the wall into the space. Then determine the size of the drawer by making it 1 inch smaller in width and height than the overall size of the piece you want. You will determine the exact dimensions of the box once the drawer is constructed.

2 ....

Look at the plywood before cutting to determine the direction of the grain you want, keeping in mind what part of the plywood veneer you'd like to have as the drawer front. Mark all four drawer side parts with a carpenter's pencil and rip all the drawer parts to size with a table saw. You need two sides of the same dimensions, and front and back pieces of the same dimensions.

3 ....

Set the fence of the table saw at about ½ inch from the blade. Fit the saw with a dado blade set (see "Get in the Groove," page 172) and cut a ¼-inch groove, or dado, for the drawer bottom into each piece.

If you don't want to attempt a dado, an alternative is simply to do without it. Just glue and nail the ¼-inch hardboard to the bottom of the drawer frame. Just make sure you allow for this extra height when building the surrounding box.

4 ....

Cut the drawer bottom from ¼-inch hardboard: measure the interior dimensions of the drawer frame and add ⅞ inch to both the length and width. This adds enough hardboard to fit into the ½-inch dado cut on all sides, while allowing for ¹⁄₁₆ inch of space on each side to accommodate any expansion and contraction of the wood.

5 ....

Clamp together one drawer sidepiece and the back piece to stabilize them. Then attach them with a butt joint using two 2-inch wood screws and glue. Predrill the screw holes and ensure

they are screwed in flush and the dado grooves are aligned. Repeat the process with the other sidepiece.

6 ....

Once the sides are secure, insert the drawer bottom in the drawer grooves. Then hold the front piece in place and check for square. Secure the front the same way as you did the back, using two 2-inch wood screws and glue to attach it to the sides.

7 ....

Next, make the box the drawer will sit in. Measure the drawer again for exact dimensions. You want the drawer to sit flush inside the box and still be able to move in and out easily, so add ¼ inch to the overall width and height of the opening while keeping the box's interior depth exactly the same dimension as the drawer.

8 ....

Measure and cut the plywood into five pieces to make the drawer box with a circular or table saw: two sidepieces, a top and a bottom, and a back piece that will be inset within the others. The top and bottom pieces will match the width of the opening, but to allow for the thickness of the plywood on both sides, add 1½ inches to the width of the top and bottom piece. The height of the side pieces is the same as the drawer height, however an extra ¼ inch is needed all around for the drawer to glide in and out easily.

9 ....

Assemble the box by first attaching one side to the top and bottom pieces, then attaching the other side, and finally insetting the back. For each piece, apply a thin bead of wood glue along the cut edge, using your finger to spread it evenly, and then hammer finishing nails along the joint about 1½ to 2 inches apart. Ensure the boards are flush; it helps to clamp them in place first, as you did with the drawer above.

continued

10

Next, mark the location for your knob or pull on the drawer front. Predrill a hole for the knob's screw and attach the knob.

11

Place the drawer in the box and make sure it fits and slides smoothly. An orbital or palm sander fitted with coarse sandpaper can remove any excess wood—slow and easy does it; you don't want to take off too much! Rub a candle or a bar of soap along the bottom edges of the drawer to make pulling and pushing the drawer easier.

12

Next, drill a ¼-inch hole into the underside of the top of the box, centered along the front-side of the box, about the thickness of the drawer face away from the front. This way the drawer finishes flush with the box. When everything else is complete, this hole is where you will attach the wooden dowel that acts as the drawer stop.

13

Finish the exterior of the box and the drawer any way you want—with primer and paint or with a stain and a polyurethane finish. Remember to sand lightly between coats for a smooth finish. No need to finish the interior of the box.

GET IN THE GROOVE

A dado is a groove cut into a piece of wood into which you slide another piece of wood; a dado forms a stronger connection between the two. The most common way to create the groove is to use a dado blade set on a table saw (you can rent both saw and blades if you do not own them). This usually consists of two 8-inch-diameter, ⅛-inch kerf saw blades with extra ⅛-inch and ¹⁄₁₆-inch chipper blades in between. Customize the width of the groove between ¼ inch and ¾ inch by removing or adding chippers (wider dadoes can be cut by making several passes through the wood).

SAFETY ALERT: Never use a stacked dado head cutting set on a circular saw—it's very dangerous.

Alternatively, a router fitted with a straight cutting bit will create a dado. Go slowly when using a router so as not to overcut. Better to make two or three slow, shallow passes with a small bit for a perfect fit. For instance, if you are making a ¾-inch dado, use a ½-inch bit and make two passes. A ¾-inch bit will result in a wider cut, since router bits are always slightly wider than indicated. Whatever method you use, cut no more than a third of the way through the lumber to maintain its integrity.

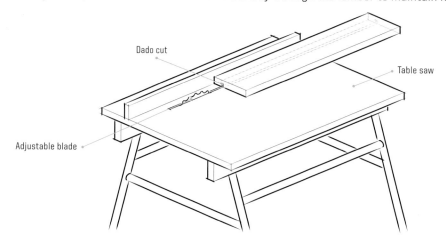

Dado cut

Table saw

Adjustable blade

Use extreme caution when making this kind of cut!

14 ....

Once the pieces are completely dry, attach the box to the wall, securing it to at least one wall stud. Using a stud finder, find and mark the stud(s) and then predrill two holes into the stud(s) and separately into corresponding holes in the back of the box. I suggest this because it is likely that your power drill may not fit into the box to predrill and drive the screws from the inside. Then, using a long screwdriver, use 3-inch wood screws to attach the box to the wall by hand.

TIP: If you are unable to attach the shelf box securely to the wall studs, consider using brackets in addition to screws. Choose either decorative brackets that will show or "hidden" brackets. To create hidden brackets, measure and mark a level line where the drawer box bottom should go on the wall. On this line, first fasten two L-brackets to the wall, with the protruding legs at the bottom. Place the box onto the brackets and fasten it with a couple of short screws from below; then screw the box into the wall through the box's back wall.

15 ....

Once the box is attached to the wall, slide the drawer partway in. Then insert and glue the wooden dowel in the hole you predrilled in Step 12. This drawer stop will keep the drawer from pulling out completely. Hang a separate mirror above the drawer on the wall to complete the entry unit. You will now know where your keys and cell phone are at all times. Add a bunch of flowers and—welcome home!

TIP: If you plan on painting the area or adjacent hallways, it's best to paint a light color (if there is a chair rail, paint the top part of the chair rail all the way up to the ceiling a lighter shade than the bottom) to make the space feel taller. When selecting paint, pay attention to the light reflective value (LRV). Black is 0 percent, and the lighter you go, the more illusion of space you'll create.

Exploded view of drawer box top and middle (left) and drawer (bottom left). L-brackets or decorative brackets provide support for drawers that cannot be attached to wall studs (right).

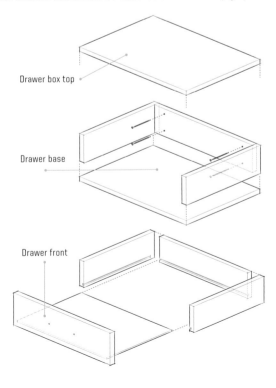

Drawer box top

Drawer base

Drawer front

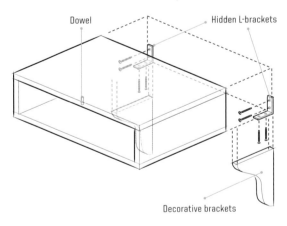

Dowel

Hidden L-brackets

Decorative brackets

PROJECT:

CLOSET UNDER THE STAIRS

CLOSET UNDER THE STAIRS

The area under staircases is a prime spot to find extra room. Creating a usable storage space can prevent you from tripping over your items that are used on a day-to-day basis, and it can be incredibly handy for items that you need at a moment's notice. (Imagine having a real home for your cell phone and keys.) This is prime real estate as a staircase is generally supported at the top and bottom, which means that this project is not going to affect the structural stability of the staircase. There are some unique situations where a previous builder has done some modification to the staircase, so always have a professional check it out if in doubt.

TIME:

1 day

DIFFICULTY:

ꝛꝛꝛꝛ

TOOLS:

Reciprocating saw (optional)

Handsaw

Flat pry bar

Hammer

Rubber mallet

Sledgehammer (optional)

Utility knife

Dust mask

Caulking gun

Work gloves

Measuring tape

Table saw or circular saw

Miter saw

Drill/driver with bits

Nail gun

Nail set

4-foot level

Painbrushes, roller, and tray

Carpenter's pencil

Safety glasses

Ear protection

MATERIALS:

1 pre-hung interior door unit and trim to fit your space

Storage bins that fit the size of your area

WOOD:

2 or 3 sheets ½-inch birch veneer plywood (wall panels), depending on enclosure size

1 sheet ⅝-inch birch plywood (shelves)

2x4 lumber, for framing (amount determined by enclosure size)

1x2 lumber, for ledger strips (amount determined by size of space)

Baseboard molding (to match existing; amount determined by size of space)

HARDWARE:

1 box 2½-inch wood screws

1 box 3-inch nails

1 box 3-inch wood screws

Finishing nails

1 doorknob

FINISHING SUPPLIES:

Drywall tape

Drywall compound

Topping compound

1 gallon each primer and paint

Caulk

Sandpaper, 120- and 220-grit

MAKE THAT SPACE HAPPEN

Before you start!

Cut out an inspection hole first. Make it big enough to get a flashlight into so you can inspect the area. Make sure this inspection hole is where the door location will be!

1 . . . .

Once you have an inspection opening, review your staircase's construction to make sure there are no heavy supporting posts midway on your staircase. If you are good to go, cut out a small opening at your door location to access and then clean out the space and remove any debris.

2 . . . .

Measure the height, width, and depth of the area beneath the stairs and transfer the measurements onto a piece of paper. This will help you to determine what size pre-hung (or custom) door you need, as well as how you want to organize the closet's interior space (number of shelves, open

floor space, etc.). Be creative and flexible; the space isn't going to be a typical rectangular closet box since the space under staircases has an angular ceiling.

3 . . . .

Open a small access area in the wall under the stairs by cutting away drywall following directions for Project: Wall Demolition—Transforming Two Rooms into One (page 190). Frame out the door with 2x4 lumber and try to use an existing stud for the hinge side of the door frame. Base the frame dimensions on the size of the pre-hung door (many pre-hung door kits come with instructions outlining frame size, which you can use as a guide). Assuming you can use an existing stud for one side, you will need to remove an additional existing stud and relocate it (or use an additional 2x4) away from the stud you're using for the hinge side

continued

Stair construction is fairly standard—even in older homes.

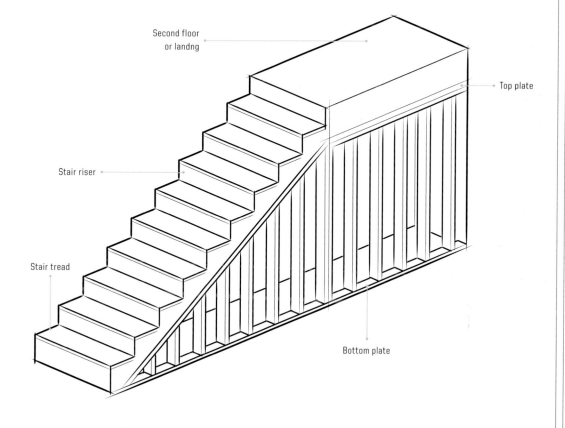

Adding a door is usually a straightforward alteration to an existing wall.

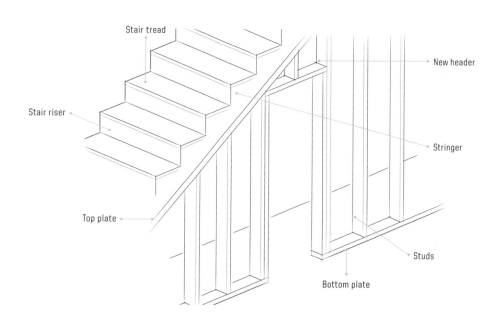

of the door frame, by the distance of the width of the door frame. Using 3-inch nails or wood screws, fasten the removed stud first to the existing bottom plate and then to the top plate. Fasten the second 2x4 horizontally, spanning the distance between this stud and the stud being used for the hinge side of the door frame, at the height of the door frame. Allow an additional ½ inch around the opening size to enable ease of pre-hung door installation!

4 . . . .

Install the pre-hung door by sliding it into the framed opening and securing the hinged side. Remove one screw from each door hinge and replace it with a longer wood screw that extends into the wall stud; then attach the latch side of the door casing. It is best that the door swings out, so make sure the new door clears your floor covering. If it does make contact, use your circular saw to remove a small sliver from the bottom of the door, and test again. Repeat until the door swings open smoothly without touching the ground. Then sand and prime the door.

SAFETY ALERT: Always wear safety glasses when using a circular saw, a nail gun, or any other power tool.

5 . . . .

Using a table saw or circular saw, measure and cut the plywood for the closet walls. Install by nailing the cut panels to the studs. Mark the stud locations on the floor and ceiling so you will know where the studs are located once you begin attaching the sheets. I like to use ½- or ⅝-inch birch-veneered plywood, which I often prime and paint white to make these deep closets seem brighter. Plywood walls also make life easier than drywall, as you can attach anything to them at any location.

TIP: Make life easier for yourself and prime and paint the plywood outside or in a roomy, well-ventilated area before installing it. Once the walls are installed, the nail heads can be filled with putty, sanded, and touched up.

6 . . . .

Repair the drywall on the outside wall around the door (and the inside wall if necessary). Apply drywall tape, cover the area with drywall compound,

and let dry. Add a second coat of topping compound and sand the repaired area until the surface texture matches that of the existing wall. Prime and paint the wall to finish covering up the repair work.

7 . . . .

Finalize your design for the closet interior, starting by measuring the finished space to confirm dimensions. Design and measure for the shelves you plan to include; remember to space shelves with some extra height to make it easier to remove containers. For instance, if you want the shelves to accommodate 12-inch storage bins, space the shelves 13 or 14 inches apart.

8 . . . .

Next build and install shelves. This can be done the same way as the "side shelves" in Project: Closet Makeover (page 102). Cut 1x2 ledger strips for the shelf brackets (or use metal brackets). Measure and mark a level line for ledger or bracket placement and use a nail gun to tack ledger strips as needed. Then secure the strips with screws.

9 . . . .

Cut the shelves with a table saw from ⅝-inch plywood. Sand, prime, and paint the shelves; let dry; and slide into place. Since the shelves are a tight fit, slip them in at an angle, flatten them down over the ledger strips, and secure them with screws.

10 . . . .

Add the door hardware and trim around your door frame. If they are included in your pre-hung door kit, follow the manufacturer's instructions. If they are not included in your pre-hung kit, or do not match your existing trim, purchase trim that matches your house. Use your miter saw to cut corners at 45 degrees and build as you would a picture frame. Cut and fix the baseboards inside and out. Caulk all seams and touch up.

11 . . . .

Lay down a new floor covering that is similar to your existing covering or use carpet tiles or strip flooring that suits your needs. Now, put away all your stuff!

ENTRYWAY HOME OFFICE

ENTRYWAY HOME OFFICE

The space under your hallway staircase is the perfect place to tuck in an office, complete with work surface, shelves, and, yes, storage.

You will be amazed by how much space you can find in this nook. Plus these tucked away offices offer lots of privacy—a good thing when you have your little ones running around.

TIME:

3 to 5 days

DIFFICULTY:

ᚚ ᚚ ᚚ ᚚ

TOOLS:

Reciprocating saw (optional)

Handsaw

Flat pry bar

Hammer

Nail set

Rubber mallet

Sledgehammer (optional)

Utility knife

Dust mask

Work gloves

Tape measure

Table or circular saw

Drill/driver with bits, including countersink bit

Miter saw

Orbital sander

4-foot level

Framing square

Stud finder

Nail gun

Paintbrushes, roller, and tray

Pencil

Caulking gun

Safety glasses

Ear protection

MATERIALS:

1 pre-hung interior door (to match existing decor)

Flooring

WOOD:

3 sheets ¾-inch birch veneer plywood

2x4 lumber (amount determined by size of enclosure)

1x2 lumber, for ledger strips (amount determined by size of enclosure)

¾-inch decorative wood trim (amount determined by size of enclosure)

3- to 4-inch flat or decorative molding (amount determined by size of enclosure)

Baseboards (amount determined by size of enclosure)

HARDWARE:

1 box 3-inch wood screws

1 box 2-inch wood screws

1 box finishing nails

FINISHING SUPPLIES:

Sandpaper, 220-grit

Subfloor adhesive (optional)

Wood putty

Caulk

Wood glue

Spackle

1 gallon paint to match existing hallway walls

1 gallon each stain and polyurethane sealer or primer and paint

MAKE THAT SPACE HAPPEN

1
Open a small access area in the wall under the stairs by cutting away the drywall following directions for Project: Wall Demolition—Transforming Two Rooms into One (page 190). Sweep out the space under the stairs and remove all debris from the work area. Measure the open area and use the measurements to sketch a design for the home office. I like to design an office inside a large box because it makes installation and construction easier. I also like to do minimal demolition at this stage until all building materials are on site to avoid disrupting the surrounding areas.

2
Design and measure for the office opening. Cut away drywall and wall studs to open up the space. Make sure the opening is big enough to accommodate the "box" for the office you will preassemble below. See the demo a wall project (page 190) for instructions and tips on doing this correctly and safely.

3
Cut out the four pieces for the office box (3 sides and ceiling) from the ¾-inch birch plywood. You will find that one side of the box needs to be angled to fit the space where the interior wall of the opening

is angled. Cut all the pieces (outside), including the supporting 1x2 ledger strips, for the office desk and shelves, according to your design.

SAFETY ALERT: Remember to don your safety glasses and ear protection when working with a power saw or any power tool—especially when working in a small space.

4
Preassemble the office box using 2-inch wood screws. Drill pilot holes using a countersink bit before driving the screws flush into the wood. This step ensures that all the joints fit properly before you stain (or paint) the wood and assemble it permanently. Don't skip this step even if you're tempted to because it seems redundant. It saves time (and headaches) later if something is off. If certain joints or seams need fixing, disassemble them, re-cut, and reassemble correctly.

5
Mark the back of the connecting sides with A-A, 1-1, or a similar system, using a pencil. This is to help you keep track of what piece goes where, which isn't easy to do once the pieces are painted and finished. Carefully unscrew and disassemble the office box.

continued

6 ....

Sand all the plywood fronts. Then stain or prime and paint the box pieces and apply several coats of polyurethane sealer to protect the finish. Stain or paint and polyurethane the pieces for the desk and shelves, along with the ¾-inch decorative trim and the wider molding that will be installed around the office opening. You may want to stain or paint this opening trim the same color as the floor molding in your hallway.

7 ....

If necessary, cut a piece of ¾-inch plywood to fit the floor under the office. Use subfloor adhesive to adhere it to the floor to bring the floor under the stairs level with the rest of the room.

NOTE: If you are creating an office over a slab or concrete subfloor and the wood comes in direct contact with concrete subfloor, moisture from the earth below can leach up through the concrete, rot the wood, and cause permanent water damage and, potentially, mold. If this is the case, use pressure-treated wood to prevent water damage.

8 ....

Reassemble the office box components in the hallway, this time using both 2-inch wood screws and wood glue—and give yourself a pat on the back for predrilling the holes outside. For even easier assembly, place lengths of 2x4 under the bottom of the office box. These lengths (skids) will also make the box easier to move into place.

TIP: Lights, power, action? Before installing the office box in the space, consider your lighting needs. Don't worry; it's easy. Add an additional receptacle and a light if need be. If you don't have electrical skills, hire a licensed electrician or install a battery-operated LED touch light or lamp.

9 ....

Find studs in the back wall and record where they are located from either end because the box will hide them. Slide the box into the cavity under the stairs, lining it up with the angle made in step two in the opening. Use 3-inch wood screws to secure it to the studs in the back wall.

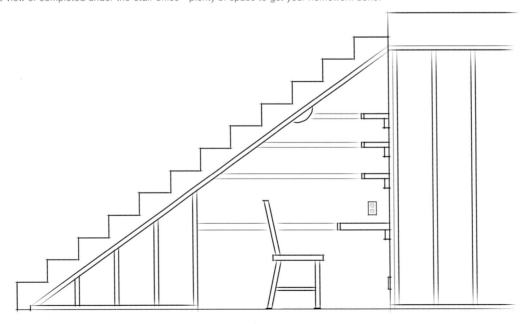

Side view of completed under-the-stair office—plenty of space to get your homework done!

10

On the walls, use 2-inch wood screws to install the finished ledger strips that will support your desk and the shelves. I recommend that you sit in the chair you intend to use at your desk to determine the exact height you want the desk and shelves to be. This is a custom project, so take every opportunity to make this office truly your own.

11

The desktop and shelves are supported by the ledger strips; if necessary, add a vertical support underneath for added support. Attach the desktop and shelf to the vertical support and then attach the entire structure to the office box and ledger strips. Tack these pieces in place with a nail gun to hold them steady while you install the 2-inch wood screws for lasting support.

12

Frame out the door opening and wall using 2x4s. You will build the frame to match the structure and studs that were removed in Step 2 (top plate, bottom plate, and studs every 16 inches). This framing will replace the (non-load bearing) support of the studs you have removed.

13

Install the door and frame (see Step 3 of Project: Closet Under the Stairs on page 176).

14

Use finishing nails and a bead of glue to attach ¾-inch decorative trim to finish the edges of the desk. Cut and install wider wood molding or flat trim (depending on your taste and the style of your home) around the office opening to give a finished look and cover any gaps between the office box and the surrounding wall.

15

Install the baseboards, trim around the door, and door hardware (see Step 10 of Project: Closet Under the Stairs on page 178).

16

Spackle all seams (if painting); touch up or re-coat with paint.

17

Install your choice of floor covering. Get to work!

Building the box is simpler if done outside, disassembled, and then reassembled in the hallway.

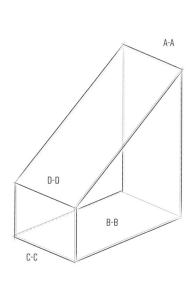

A-A

D-D

B-B

C-C

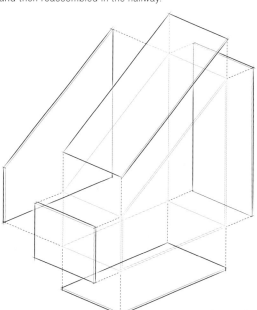

PART

CREATE
NEW SPACES

This section tackles more ambitious building projects. The first three chapters show how you can actually create more rooms within the footprint of your house, while Chapter 12 tackles the outside. More so than in Part 2, these projects may require the help of a buddy or two who is super-skilled in DIY; you may even want to bring in a few specialists and tradespeople, such as a general contractor, a structural engineer, electricians, and so on. However, if you are DIY savvy—and confident of your "3 or 4 hammer" skill level—all can be done either on your own or under your supervision. Whichever way you go, the following pages will inspire you to see the possibilities your home offers.

09
SHIFTING
SPACES

The arrangement of rooms in your place isn't set in stone—walls can be moved, removed, or added. My wife and I own a small two-bedroom flat in our homeland of Sydney, Australia. Originally, the kitchen was located at the back end of the apartment—wrong in terms of both the flow of living and the way daylight moved through the space. We moved the kitchen to the front of the flat to take advantage of the views and put the bedroom in the back, where it was quiet at night and light and bright in the morning. Obviously, plumbing work was involved in this job, but because the apartment isn't large, it was not that costly to do—and, fortunately, we were able to do a lot of the work ourselves. The three projects in this chapter provide you with the basics for making similar changes. Working within your home's existing "footprint" can be as simple as opening up a wall or adding one. Even major changes (adding a bath by making a closet smaller, enlarging a kitchen by taking over a dining room) are still about 50 percent less expensive than adding on. Let's get cracking.

PROJECT:

REARRANGE YOUR
FLOOR PLAN

REARRANGE YOUR FLOOR PLAN

This project shows you how to draw plans in order to rearrange the rooms in your home. As I said in the introduction to this chapter, the arrangement of rooms and walls in a house is never set in stone—even stone walls can be moved if you have the resources (and strength) to make it happen. Many homes have adequate square footage, but because they circulate poorly, they seem to "live small." When rooms are cut off from each other or if a home is chopped up into a lot of tiny rooms, it can feel cramped. Changing the flow of your home can make a huge difference. For instance, creating one large kitchen-living-dining area by removing walls and adding beams can open up a 1920s bungalow characterized by a warren of tiny rooms. A narrow townhouse can be made airier and wider by removing the hallway wall.

If you plan on taking down all or a significant portion of a wall, I recommend hiring a structural engineer to ensure that you aren't removing a load-bearing wall; when moving walls around, you don't want to compromise the structural integrity of your home. If your plans become extensive, you also might consider hiring an architect or interior designer to help you space plan (see Chapters 10 and 11 for more advice on hiring and working with architects and general contractors).

First, however, you need a floor plan for your home. If you already have one, make a copy of those plans. Otherwise this project guides you in how to make an accurate floor plan of your home (for more guidance in doing this, see also "Make an Accurate Floor Plan," page 15). Once you have the layout of your home on paper, it is much easier to experiment, on paper, with new layouts. Try to be as accurate as you can be without losing your mind. This floor plan is not (and cannot be) an official document that can be used to apply for permits. This is for your own use. Then, if permits are necessary, and an architect or designer is brought on board, they have a good, accurate map of what you want.

TIME:
2 to 3 hours

DIFFICULTY:
↗

TOOLS:
25- and 50-foot tape measures

Scale ruler

Pad and pencil

MATERIALS:
¼-inch graph paper

MAKE THAT SPACE HAPPEN

1..

Make a list of all the rooms in your house. Include the hallways, foyers or entryways, porches, decks, and balconies. Without measuring, sketch out a rough layout of your floor plan, making separate drawings for each floor or level in your house.

2..

Measure the dimensions of your entire property, the length from the street or sidewalk to the end of the backyard, and the width between the houses on either side. Also measure the distance from your house to the property line on all four sides. Capture these measurements both in a list and on your rough sketch. If you do plan on building an addition at a later date, or if you add any outdoor features, you need to conform to your community's setback rules (how far a structure needs to be from the street, utilities, other houses, and existing waterways).

3..

Next, measure each interior space and add those figures to your list and rough sketch. Be sure to measure and note all window and door placements; if certain areas or rooms are particularly complicated, make new rough sketches to show the detail. It's important to note accurately all structural elements and their relation to each other; in bathrooms and kitchens, be sure to measure and mark all fixed structures and appliances, including toilets, tubs, sinks, stoves/ovens, and so on. Sometimes, this is easier to describe, as in, "36-inch-wide door, 3 feet in from front wall of living room." Or, abbreviated, it might look like this, "36" w door, 3' in from fr wall of LR."

4..

Once you have completed all the measurements, transfer them to ¼-inch graph paper, so that the rough sketch is turned into an accurate scale drawing of your house's actual dimensions. In this case, ¼ inch represents 1 foot, so that an 8-foot wall would be drawn with a 2-inch line. Mark and

draw the basic room measurements. Then add the windows, doors, and other openings in each area. Also add all fixed items within a room. As you do, use the following symbols, which are standard in the building industry:

North arrow	
Solid wall	
Partial wall	
Door swing	
Window	
Toilet	
Bathtub	
Built-in kitchen cabinets	Upper Cabinet / Base Cabinet
Sink	
Stairs	

5..

Note where outlets and switches are in each room so you have an idea of electrical runs. Likewise, note where plumbing and other utilities are located.

6..

Make copies of your plans, make to-scale cutouts of your furniture, and start redesigning your space. Where might walls be opened, removed, or added? If you want to add or move sinks, toilets, or baths, can you do so adjacent to where plumbing currently exists?

PROJECT:

WALL DEMOLITION– TRANSFORM TWO ROOMS INTO ONE

WALL DEMOLITION—TRANSFORM TWO ROOMS INTO ONE

Whenever I'm filming a DIY show, the producers love it when a homeowner gets a chance to pick up a big sledgehammer and swing it into some drywall. All the better if the homeowner dons a pair of mean-looking work boots and kicks a hole in the wall with his or her foot. Great TV; bad reality. Removing an interior wall is a serious remodeling task that should be undertaken with care and safety in mind, along with an understanding of how your house is built. In many situations, opening up a space and making two cramped rooms into one spacious area is fairly easy to do. And what a difference it makes, especially in an older home that is a warren of little rooms and awkward doorways.

The most important—vital—part of demolishing an interior wall is knowing, before the wrecking ball comes through, whether or not the wall in question is load bearing. A load-bearing wall supports several tons of weight above it, whether it is a second floor or a roof. Determining whether a wall is load bearing is not always an easy process. If you have the original plans for your house, you can check to see if it indicates this information. But plans can change, and notations can be forgotten, so it's best to consult a structural engineer to find out exactly what you are dealing with.

TIME:
4 to 6 hours (for demolition only)

DIFFICULTY:
⌁⌁⌁

TOOLS:
Reciprocating saw (optional)

Handsaw

Utility knife

Flat pry bar

Hammer

Sledgehammer (optional)

Pencil

Dust mask

Work gloves

Safety glasses

MATERIALS:
Plastic sheeting

Drop cloths

Painter's tape

MAKE THAT SPACE HAPPEN

1 . . . .

Identify whether or not the wall is load bearing. In almost all cases, it's prudent to hire a structural engineer to confirm this. If it's not load bearing, skip to Step 3.

2 . . . .

To remove a load-bearing wall, you must support the opening (and the house above) with a beam or structural columns; I do not have room in this book to describe this. An alternative is to remove only part of the wall to create a 6-to-8-foot opening, which will make two rooms appear as one flowing space. In this case, you must install a header across the opening that's supported by studs at either end. Installing a header properly requires advanced carpentry skills; if you are an experienced carpenter, see Project: Install a Pocket Door (page 96), for basic instructions for how to do this. In either case, I highly recommend that you work with a pro to ensure the integrity of your house. Altering or removing a load-bearing wall is a relatively straightforward job for a pro and would not be that costly, especially if you help as the laborer and then complete all the finish work yourself.

3 . . . .

Next, determine if the wall is made of drywall or if it's a plaster lath wall. These instructions only address removing a non-load-bearing framed drywall wall. Removing a plaster wall is a bigger, messier job that requires brute strength and heavy lifting. If you have a plaster lath wall, consider enlisting another pair (or two) of helping hands and take demolition very slowly. With plaster and lath, it's much harder to confirm whether services are running behind the walls because the lathing system is made from wood in older homes—often hardwood like oak—and it has hardened over time. This is common in Victorian-era houses. Just by virtue of this fact, you must remove the plaster coating and lathing strips to see behind the wall. This is more laborious and messier than removing modern drywall.

4 . . . .

Once you have definitively determined that you have a non-load-bearing drywall wall, make exploratory openings between every stud to see if there are any services (like electrical wires or plumbing) running through the walls; see Project: Maximize the Medicine Cabinet (page 82), for instructions on doing this. If you find any service lines, they will need to be rerouted once all the drywall has been removed; if you don't have the skills to reroute the services, hire a pro. Note that chimneys and flues cannot be rerouted easily; you may wish to skip any wall that has these, unless you want them to be a feature in your new room.

5 . . . .

Don't break out your hammer just yet. First turn off the electricity for the room at the breaker whether or not you see an outlet or switch on the wall you are removing; there could still be wires in the wall that you don't see.

6 . . . .

Seal off the area with plastic sheeting and painter's tape to keep airborne drywall or insulation particles from entering other areas of the house. Using painter's tape around a door, sealing the sides and bottom, also works well. It won't keep absolutely everything contained in the work area, but you will appreciate all that it does keep out of the rest of your living space.

7 . . . .

Protect your floor coverings. Painter's drop cloths are great for this type of work, as they will protect the floor and then can be rolled up and shaken outside. Go to the trouble of taping down drop cloths all around. Trust me: that 10 minutes of prep now will save you at least two hours or more later.

8 ....
Next, remove any receptacle and switch covers.
Use a sharp utility knife to score molding and trim
where they meet ceilings and adjoining walls, so
these adjacent areas are not damaged. Also score
the corners where two walls meet, to avoid tearing
up the adjacent walls. Remember a slow demo is a
smart demo because it creates less work later on.

9 ....
Put on your safety glasses and use the claw end
of a hammer and a flat pry bar to pry off any baseboard, trim, and crown molding from the wall you
plan to remove. Set it aside in case you need to
reuse it.

continued

Take your time when demolishing, as you will do less damage to surrounding areas.

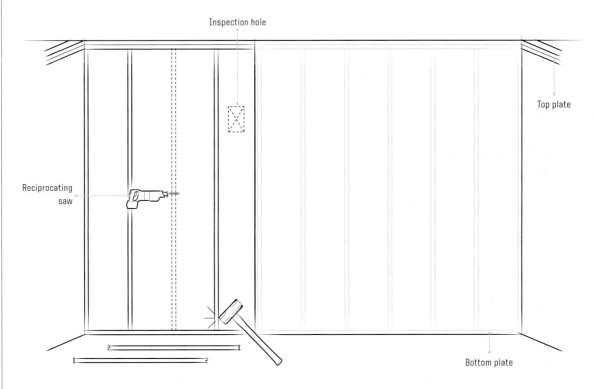

Inspection hole

Top plate

Reciprocating
saw

Bottom plate

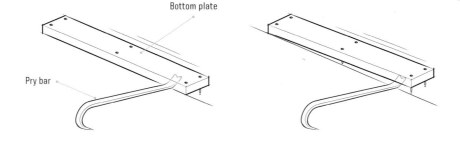

Bottom plate

Pry bar

10

Don your mask and work gloves and use the utility knife to make an X between two studs. Give it a slight whack with a hammer to create a hole big enough to fit your hand through. Reach in with a gloved hand and pull off the drywall. Use a flat pry bar and nail hammer to remove one side of the drywall to expose the studs. Go slow, working carefully around any wires or pipes and looking out for any you may have missed when looking before. Continue until all the drywall is down from both sides of the wall and the studs are exposed. Make another pass through the room to remove any remaining nails, drywall scraps, or other debris from the studs and surrounding area. Haul out debris regularly to keep your work area safe. Remember that your closest window may be the best way to remove debris. If so, back your trailer, truck, or bin directly under it.

11

If there is any wiring or plumbing, reroute it, with the help of a pro, before proceeding.

12

Once you have rerouted any existing utilities, or if there are none, remove the studs. There are two ways to do this: either knock studs loose from the bottom plate with a sledgehammer and twist them loose from the top; or saw through the middle of each stud with a reciprocating saw and then knock out the top and bottom halves with your persuader (i.e., your hammer). Use a reciprocating saw or oscillating cutting tool to cut out the bottom plate flush with the opening.

13

Do a final clean up of all materials, debris, and any remaining protruding nails in the top plates and adjacent studs.

TIP: This is a beauty! A box fan placed facing out in a window will extract the dust from the room. Also keep your work area as clean as possible when working. An inexpensive shop vac is your best tool for cleaning up because it sucks up everything from dust to debris to water.

PROJECT:

WALL CONSTRUCTION—
MAKE ONE ROOM INTO TWO

WALL CONSTRUCTION—MAKE ONE ROOM INTO TWO

Sometimes a private space, even if it's a small one, can go a long way to bringing peace and contentment to a household. A new baby needs a nursery, an elderly parent may need a space of his or her own, or you may want or need a roommate. Whatever reason you have, building what I call a simple Z-wall—which allows for a closet on either side—is the easiest way to add another room to your house without adding on. Even better: You can probably do this project on your own for less than $2,000—and, in the process, increase your home's value by more than $20,000 by virtue of adding another bedroom. Telescopic coat racks eliminate the need for a deep closet (a foot is all you need to provide ample wardrobe storage). You can also divide the room without adding closets, by installing a straight wall. For other less permanent or less construction-intensive ways to divide a room, see the box "More Space Separation Tricks" (page 157), in Chapter 7.

TIME:

2 to 3 days

DIFFICULTY:

ϓϓϓ

TOOLS:

Scale rule

Tape measure

Grid paper

Chalk line

Circular saw

Framing nail gun (optional)

Drill/driver with bits (plus masonry bit, if necessary)

Hammer

Miter saw

Handsaw (if using a wood dowel; optional)

Hacksaw (if using a pipe; optional)

2 clamps

4-foot level

Stud finder

Plumb bob

Utility knife

Putty knife

Drywall knives

Ladder

Drop cloths

Paintbrushes, roller, and tray

Pencil

Safety glasses

Ear protection

MATERIALS:

1 pre-hung interior door (to match existing doors)

1 louvered closet door kit for closet in "new" room

Your choice of insulation/batting (recycled denim is a good choice as it has great soundproofing qualities)

One 1¼-inch-diameter wooden or chrome metal pipe closet dowel

WOOD:

2x4 lumber (quantity determined by width of room; studs placed every 16 inches)

½- or ⅝-inch drywall (quantity determined by width and height of room)

1 sheet ¾-inch birch plywood or melamine

Baseboard trim (quantity determined by width of wall)

Crown molding (optional, quantity determined by width of room)

HARDWARE:

1 box 3-inch nails

1 box 3-inch drywall screws

1 box 1½-inch wood screws

Two 5-lb boxes of 1¼-inch drywall screws

1 box 3-inch wood screws

1 box concrete anchors

1 box finishing nails

2 dowel brackets

Four 1½-inch screws (with anchors if necessary)

FINISHING SUPPLIES:

Painter's tape

Drywall tape

Drywall compound

Topping compound

Sandpaper, 120-grit

2 gallons each primer and paint

Wood putty

MAKE THAT SPACE HAPPEN

1 ....
Determine where to erect your new wall and access to the new room. Decide whether you will install a straight wall or a Z-wall. Map out a plan before you start. If you haven't already made a scale model of your house's floor plan (see Project: Rearrange Your Floor Plan, page 187), make one for at least this room using grid paper and a scale ruler. Looking at the plan, do you see room along the hallway to install another door to give the new room its own entrance? Mark where a pre-hung door would be installed along the hallway.

2 ....
Next, position all of your potential furniture on the graph paper: Where will the bed, side tables, and chairs go? Take note of your window locations; each room needs natural ventilation, and windows are very important as a fire escape. Also take into account light fixtures, receptacles, air-conditioning

registers, and so on. All of this information will help determine the best wall location and size (or depth).

3 ....
Mark out the location of the Z-wall (or straight wall) on the floor, outlining it exactly as you want it with painter's tape. In addition, mark out an area for a second door on the hallway side of the room to create a separate entrance. If you want a simple flat or straight wall, follow the instructions below and simply skip making the closets. If you have ample space, mark out the wall using full-depth wardrobes. This determines the depth of the Z.

TIP: You may fasten your new wall directly over the existing floor covering. However, if it's carpet, make sure you cut either side of the drilling location to keep the drill bit from pulling up carpet strands before your very eyes!

continued

4 ....

The placement of your new doorway location is important. This is where a plan comes in handy. You will need to take certain items into account. For example, which way will the door swing? This will affect furniture placement, but aside from that, it's never a good idea to swing a door into a narrow hallway (or it will be nicknamed the "headache door"). Because a door is relatively narrow, you are generally safe with removing this portion of wall. However, it is always wise to check to see if the wall is load bearing, as some walls contain posts that support a heavier load above. If you have the original blueprints, you are in great shape, but even with them, be cautious. If you are not the original owner, details may have changed.

Framing a doorway is easy: you simply create a 2x4 or 2x6 wooden frame to fasten the door jamb to. Always try to use the existing stud on the hinge side of the door for strength. A header is required for even a non-load-bearing wall, and your new trim should match the existing trim so it will look as if the door has always been there.

Remove the area of the existing wall where the new door will go, following the directions for Project: Wall Demolition—Transform Two Rooms into One (page 190). Frame out the new doorway and install the pre-hung door, which should match your existing doors. Try to match your door hardware as well.

NOTE: If a swinging door is out of the question, consider bifolding doors, a pocket door, or a barn type door.

5 ....

Use a circular saw to cut 2x4s to make the Z-wall's or straight wall's top and bottom plates. Each plate should be one piece of lumber the full length of each section of the Z-wall (or of the width of the room if you are constructing a straight wall). Once you have cut the bottom plate, use this to measure and cut the top plate. However, double check the dimensions as the top may vary if the walls are not plumb. Line the two plates side-by-side and flush at the ends: from one end, measure 16 inches and use a square to mark a line across both plates. From this line, measure 16 inches again and mark both studs, and continue this way to the end of the plates. These are the stud locations. See Step 5 of Project: Build a Platform on page 153 for more information on this process.

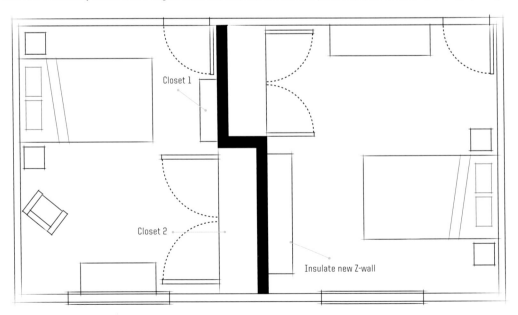

Aerial view of Z-wall clearly shows how a largish room can become two efficient private spaces for feuding siblings (or anyone else).

Closet 1

Closet 2

Insulate new Z-wall

Note exterior windows for fire escape requirements.

6

There are two ways to build the wall frame: either build the wall (three walls for the Z) flat on the floor and raise it up to attach, or assemble the wall piece by piece as you go. I'll describe both methods. For the piece-by-piece method, skip to Step 13.

7

DIRECTIONS FOR STRAIGHT WALL: First, cut the studs. Measure the room's height from floor to ceiling. From this measurement, deduct the thickness of the two plates (generally 3 inches), plus an additional inch. Using a circular saw, cut 2x4s to this length—as many as you need to match the 16-inch markings on the plates.

8

Attach the studs to the top and bottom plates at each 16-inch mark, aligning the center of the stud with the mark. Using 3-inch screws or nails (or best of all, a framing nailer if you have one), drive the fasteners from the underside of the plates into the ends of the studs, ensuring they are lined up with your spacing as you go.

9

Lift the wall frame slowly without scratching the ceiling; this is why it's good to deduct an additional inch from your stud height. When the frame is up, use your 4-foot level to make it plumb and then drive in a couple of screws into one adjacent wall. This will hold the frame up while you line it up with your floor line.

10

Fasten the bottom plate to the floor, using 3-inch wood screws for a wood floor. Or if you have a concrete floor, use a hammer drill equipped with a masonry drill bit and install concrete anchors approximately every 32 inches.

NOTE: If you have a concrete floor, your bottom plate needs to be treated to avoid deterioration. See note on page 182.

11

Cut some packers, like strips of plywood, or use shims to make up the difference between the top of the plate and the ceiling. Place them approximately every 12 inches. Use your level to check for plumb.

continued

While Z-wall construction uses basic carpentry skills, getting measurements right and ensuring your wall is plumb may be challenging for a beginner.

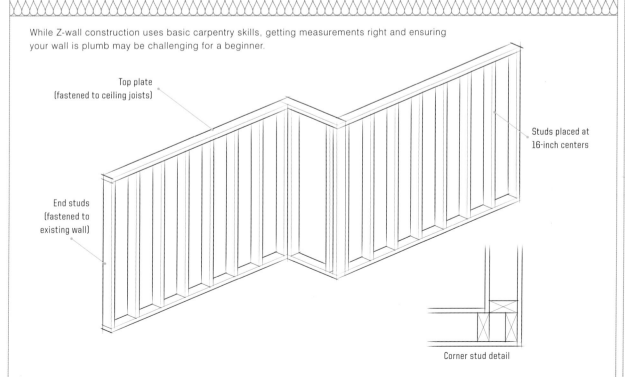

Top plate
(fastened to ceiling joists)

Studs placed at
16-inch centers

End studs
(fastened to
existing wall)

Corner stud detail

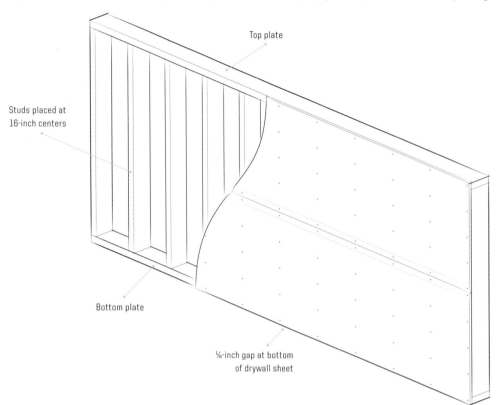

Drywall is attached to studs with drywall screws; seams must be taped, spackled, and sanded before painting.

Top plate

Studs placed at
16-inch centers

Bottom plate

¼-inch gap at bottom
of drywall sheet

12

Locate the ceiling joists with a stud finder, or, if your
ceiling leads directly to an attic, get up there first
and check for the joist locations as well as for any
services that may be notched into the joists. Use
2-inch wood screws to fasten the top plate into the
ceiling, driving the screws through the plate, the
shims, and into the ceiling joists. This is important!
If the ceiling joist runs parallel to your wall, hop
up into the attic, provide some blocking (every
32 inches) between the joists, and fasten the top
plate of your new wall to these. At this point, the
wall frame is attached, and you can skip to Step 16.

13

The second way to build the wall frame is as
follows: Using 3-inch wood screws or concrete
anchors, screw the bottom plate along the floor
line you marked in Step 3.

14

Mark the ceiling with the location for the top plate.
To do this, hold a plumb bob to the ceiling and
mark when the plumb bob is lined up to the edge

of the bottom plate. Locate the ceiling joists with
a stud finder, or, if your ceiling leads directly to
an attic, get up there first and check for the joist
locations as well as for any services that may be
notched into the joists. Using 3-inch wood screws
or concrete anchors, screw the top plate into the
ceiling along the line, making sure to screw into
a couple of ceiling joists.

15

Measure the height for each stud between the two
plates. Add ⅛ inch to this length and cut as many
2x4 studs as you need to match the 16-inch markings on the plates. It is often a good idea to cut your
stud (not your husband) slightly longer (only ⅛ inch)
for a tight fit; doing this enables the top plate to stay
in place while you nail it. Then use 3-inch nails to
toe nail the studs into the top and bottom plates at
the stud markings.

16

Once the wall frame is up, this is the time to run
any services in the walls—phone, cable, electric
wires, or even wires for speakers. Do you want any

outlets or light switches on this wall? If you're not up to adding these, grab a sparky (that's Australian for "electrician") to do this for you and make sure that it is done to code. You can check this out with your local city office.

17 ....
Insulate the walls with a good soundproof batting. Recycled denim has better soundproofing qualities than fiberglass.

18 ....
DIRECTIONS FOR A Z-WALL: The construction method is the same as for the straight wall. However, you are building three individual walls and standing them up as per the markings on your floor. The only difference here is the corner details. You will need to add additional studs at the corners so that the internal corners have adequate support for the drywall to be nailed to (see the illustration on page 199). A Z-wall is very strong, as the Z shape reinforces itself.

TIP: Before you drywall, transfer your stud locations to the floor or ceiling, so you will later know where the studs are hiding. This makes it easier to screw and nail the sheets to the studs.

19 ....
Start by standing up the first sheet of drywall you'll use on the bottom half of the wall on the floor. I also recommend that when attaching the bottom sheets of drywall, you lift them up off the floor a bit (¼ inch) to avoid future moisture issues. Line both sides of the Z-wall with ½- or ⅝-inch drywall (the thicker the better for strength and sound). The finished edges of drywall are slightly recessed to account for the tape and compound used to hide the seam between sheets. The recessed edges are on the face of the drywall sheet. Fasten the sheet of drywall into the studs using at least a dozen drywall screws. Drive screws so that the screw heads are just below the drywall face. However, it is important not to sink the screw past the paper face as this reduces the holding strength. Measure the length needed for the drywall sheet for the top half of the wall and cut it to size using a straightedge (4-foot level or straight 1x4) and your utility knife: first cut one side, fold over (or snap) the piece away from the cut, and then use your utility knife to cut the inside fold to separate

it. (Hold both pieces as you fold and cut it.) Lift the sheet and rest it upon the top edge of the attached bottom sheet; a friend comes in handy with this. Two horizontal sheets make up 8 feet, as they are 4 feet wide. Note that drywall comes in a variety of lengths—the longer the better, as this saves you a lot of work with less mudding and sanding. If you need to cut the top sheet so it's less than 4 feet, make sure the cut edge is against the ceiling. With the horizontal sheet flat against the wall studs, adjust it into place and then quickly drive in a few screws to hold it up. Use your 4-foot level to create vertical or plumb lines from your previous stud markings on the floor and ceiling. Continue like this till the wall is covered. Then add more screws at regular spacing, approximately every 16 inches along the top and bottom plates and along the markings you made up every stud.

20 ....
Fasten metal corner beads to all external corners with drywall screws, ensure they are plumb by using your level, and then tape internal corners. Apply compound and tape to all joints and compound alone to screw holes. Lightly sand when dry and apply a topping compound using a wider blade.

21 ....
Fit out your closet space with ¾-inch birch plywood (or melamine), and some hanging rods (as per Project: Closet Makeover, page 102).

22 ....
Install louvered closet doors following the manufacturer's instructions in the new "Z" formed closets. Louvered door kits generally come with all necessary hardware, tracks, and other materials. If you have an existing closet that is in the form of a niche, it can be used for a second closet, shelving, a desk, or a bed, depending on its size.

23 ....
Install baseboard, crown molding, and receptacle plates to walls to suit the existing rooms.

24 ....
Sand, prime, and paint the rooms, the exterior hallway, and the trim around the new door. Voilà—two rooms!

10

ABOVE & BELOW: ATTICS & BASEMENTS

Finishing attics and basements are major undertakings, and many of you will need helping hands and expert counsel to proceed with one of these projects. Unless you are a highly skilled DIYer who knows how to frame, run electrical wires, and tackle advanced plumbing projects, at a minimum you'll need licensed pros to handle some phases of construction. That being said, these two areas are exciting parts of the home because they are ripe with possibilities: by making them livable, you can double the footprint of your house without adding on. It's an investment worth making if you can—a finished attic or basement, if well done, can add up to $60,000 (or more, depending on where you live) to the value of your investment.

Even small crawl-space attics can be used for sensible storage—but that doesn't mean regularly fighting your way through that little opening to store or to retrieve holiday decorations or out-of-season clothing. Products like pull-down ladders and hinged doors make it easy to create an accessible storage space out of a low-hung attic.

I built a closet for some young children using the crawl space in a trussed attic. Please note that modern truss roofs are very different from those in older homes, in that none of these roof members can be cut or altered. That's because engineered trusses span from exterior wall to exterior wall, eliminating interior bearing walls. Cut one of these babies, and your roof could sag.

In this instance, I built a closet (4 feet wide by 3 feet deep by 6 feet high) in the attic above their room and installed a garage door opener. Just hit a button and down came the closet of clothes, shoes, and toys that previously had taken up so much room down under. The closet was built of plywood and had a few battery-operated lights so their wardrobe would be visible. (Did I mention that the family loved this novel approach to their clothing storage?)

In another house, I transformed a basement into two bedrooms and closets, a lounge area, and a laundry room for two boys who had come home to live after college. There was no tricky construction involved—just basic building skills and stock materials. As a result, a three-bedroom house became a five-bedroom dwelling.

Keep in mind that even if you don't have the funds to do a complete remodel today, you can begin work and finish it as your budget allows. For example, frame out your basement and drywall it, or insulate and place a subfloor in the attic, and you've made these rooms more usable than they would be otherwise. Over time, you can hire tradespeople to do specific jobs when you can. The point is that big jobs like these don't have to happen overnight. I'm a big fan of DIY shows (I host two, after all), but they tend to convey an idea of speed, which is neither necessary nor even recommended in real life.

So let's get started.

INSTALL ATTIC ACCESS

INSTALL ATTIC ACCESS

If you can't access your attic, you can't use it. A drop-down staircase is just the thing you need. You can find kits for these staircases at large home centers and on the Internet. They are normally available in widths of 25 to 30 inches and lengths of 54 to 60 inches, and account for different ceiling heights. They generally come preassembled, are ready to install in a rough opening in your ceiling, and are then easily finished with a casing around the edges and a few coats of paint.

TIME:
6 to 8 hours

DIFFICULTY:
ʏʏʏʏ

TOOLS:
Tape measure
Combination square
Reciprocating saw
Circular saw
Framing square
Drill/driver with bits
Wrench
Drywall saw
Utility knife
Hammer
Nail set
Portable light
Paintbrushes, roller, and tray
Ladder
Pencil
Safety glasses
Ear protection
Face mask
Work gloves

MATERIALS:
1 folding stair kit

WOOD:
2 pieces 2x6 or 2x8 lumber (to match size of existing ceiling joists), cut to 8-foot lengths
1x4 lumber (amount determined by size of attic)
Shims
Wood trim to finish around outside dimensions of staircase

HARDWARE:
1 box 3½-inch wood screws
1 box 1¼-inch drywall screws
Six 5-inch lag bolts
1 box finishing nails

FINISHING SUPPLIES:
1 quart each primer and paint
Wood putty
Lubricant: dishwashing liquid or soap

MAKE THAT SPACE HAPPEN

SAFETY ALERT: When embarking on a DIY project that could potentially kick up a great deal of dust (as in attic and basement projects), a thin paper face mask may not be enough protection—especially if you are sensitive or have asthma or allergies. Choose a mask that is specifically designed to provide comfortable protection and is suited for work that involves grinding, sanding, sweeping, bagging, and other dusty, hot operations. For instance, 3M's Particulate Respirator with Cool Flow Exhalation Valve comes in packs of ten, and a pack costs less than $20.

1 ....

Identify the best location for your stairway and make sure there is enough room for the stairs to unfold easily. You may already have a trapdoor to your attic in a closet or hallway. If so, see if there is enough room for the stairs to fold down in that space; if not, you will have to create another opening. The new stairway will be installed parallel with ceiling joists, therefore you need cut only one joist length to create a rough opening. Check for any other services (electric, plumbing, gas, air ducts, and so on) that may need to be rerouted; if you're unsure how to reroute services yourself, call an appropriate tradesperson to consult with and do it for you.

SAFETY ALERT: Whenever you use a ladder, always make sure it is tall enough so you do not have to use the top step. Never use a ladder when you're alone; practice the buddy system, so that in case you do fall, someone is there to help.

2 ....

In your attic, pull back the insulation in the floor to expose the area for the rough opening. Be sure to wear your face mask to avoid inhaling insulation fibers, which are prone to fly around. You will build the entire rough-in frame before cutting the ceiling drywall. Based on the dimensions of your stair kit, determine the final rough opening size you will need. This should be about ½ inch longer and ½ inch wider than the stair frame so that you will have an extra ¼ inch all the way around the stair frame. Add the thickness of four ceiling joists (which will form the blocking or framing pieces)

to your length dimension. "Two-by" boards are usually 1½ inches thick, so you will probably be adding 6 inches to your length dimension (4 times 1½ inches equals 6 inches).

SAFETY ALERT: Provide temporary support to the ceiling joist prior to cutting it by making a floor-to-ceiling T: attach a short length of 2x4 as the horizontal top to a long length of vertical 2x4 with 3 or 4 nails. Now you have a T support. Then, use two scrap pieces of plywood to brace the two pieces together where the "T" forms. This simple structure will function like a second set of hands. You can also use this method to help support the staircase as you install it.

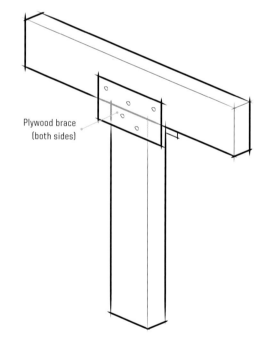

A T made from 2x4s helps support the ceiling when the ceiling joist is cut.

Plywood brace (both sides)

3 ....

Using this dimension, mark the joist you need to cut in the position you want the stairway opening. Use a square to mark the plumb/vertical line of the joist for cutting. Using a reciprocating saw, cut through the joist on both ends. Pull out the joist piece you have cut free. **Do not stand on the cut joists.**

4

Measure the width between the two joists on either side of the joist you cut. Cut four pieces of 2x6 (or 2x8, depending on your joists) to this length. These are your blocking or framing pieces. One at a time, position the blocking at each end of your opening perpendicular to the joists and flush against the end of the joist you cut. Use a square to make sure all corners are 90 degrees. Using a drill/driver, screw a minimum of four 3½-inch screws through each side of the existing joists into the new blocking pieces.

5

On each end, place the second joist block flat against the first you just installed. Screw these to the perpendicular joists in the same way. Then put a few screws through the second blocking into the first blocking.

TIP: Lubricate the screws with a bit of dishwashing liquid or soap, as the existing joists are 100 percent dry and often very hard. Drilling a pilot hole slightly smaller than the nail, screw, or lag bolt makes inserting it easy.

6

Typically, staircases from kits are narrower than the full width between three joists, so you must install a new joist parallel to the existing joists between the newly installed blocking. Measure the width required for your final rough opening, using one of the existing joists as one side of the opening. Cut a 2x6 (or 2x8) to form the other side of the opening. Again, use a square to make sure all corners are 90 degrees. Use 5-inch lag bolts and a wrench to install this short joist in place, placing three lag bolts into each end of the joist. A lag bolt is a heavy wood screw with a hexagonal head. It is driven in with a wrench and offers strong support, which is necessary in this instance.

7

From the attic above, using the rough-in frame as a guide, cut the drywall out of the rough opening with a reciprocating saw or drywall saw. Then, from the room underneath, use 1¼-inch drywall screws to fasten all edges of the drywall around the area you just cut out as the rough opening frame.

continued

Fasten all framing members together to ensure construction is stable.

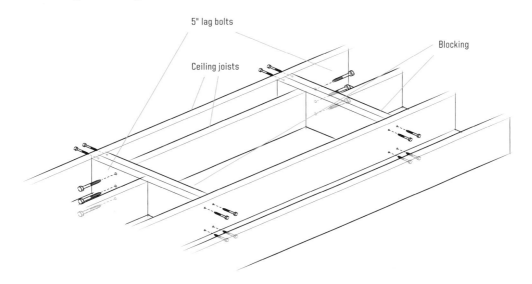

5" lag bolts

Blocking

Ceiling joists

8 ....

Measure two lengths of 1x4, making them several inches longer than the width of the opening. From below, drive these ledgers into the face of the ceiling with 3½-inch wood screws so they span the opening at both ends. These will support the staircase while you screw it in place. Add a T support (see page 206) as an extra precaution. Get a helper and lift the stair assembly through the opening and rest it on the supports.

TIP: Note that when it's time to install the drop-down staircase, you will need another pair of strong hands to help lift the staircase and hold it in place while you attach it. You may also need to consult a professional tradesperson if you need to reroute any services to accommodate the new staircase.

9 ....

Using shims to help wedge and support the stair assembly, position it in the middle of the opening and, uisng 3½-inch wood screws, screw it to your rough-in frame (per the manufacturer's instructions). Once the staircase is securely fastened, remove the 1x4 ledger strips from the ceiling (and the 2x4 support T, if used).

10 ....

Finish the new opening by using finishing nails to attach minimal-size trim that's not too obtrusive and that matches the trim of your windows and doors. Finish, prime, and paint the new surfaces the same color as the existing ceiling to avoid standing out.

WHY ARE ATTICS POPULAR? THEY ALWAYS HAVE FANS

You can't store just anything in an attic unless you have either good cross-air ventilation or a completely renovated space that is cooled and heated in the same way as the rest of the house. New homes usually have a variety of venting systems built into the attic and soffits. Older homes may not be properly ventilated. If that's the case in your crib, be sure to install a simple whirly bird, a circular wall fan that operates on its own steam. The rising hot air makes the fan spin and, in the process, it sucks the hot air out and brings cool air in. Most fan kits come with installation directions, and placement depends on your roofline, the size of vent you buy, and other considerations. If you are replacing an old fan, you may not have to make additional cuts in the siding or roof of your house. If not, you may need to make cuts from inside the attic.

But it's worth the effort. Otherwise, an attic crawl space can't hold valuable photos, for example; they'll stick together and ruin a lot of precious memories. And don't put that case of Châteauneuf-du-Pape up there either. Our apartment in Sydney had a loft that was basically an attic, and I had placed a nice bottle of red on one of the shelves up there. Flash forward a year or so: I was in the loft looking for some documents and just happened to notice the wine. "Great," I thought. "We should drink that tonight." Then I took a closer look—the bottle was about to pop its cork. There was about ¼ inch of cork left in the neck of the bottle; the rest had forced its way out because of the attic's heat. And the wine, obviously, was ruined.

ATTIC STORAGE

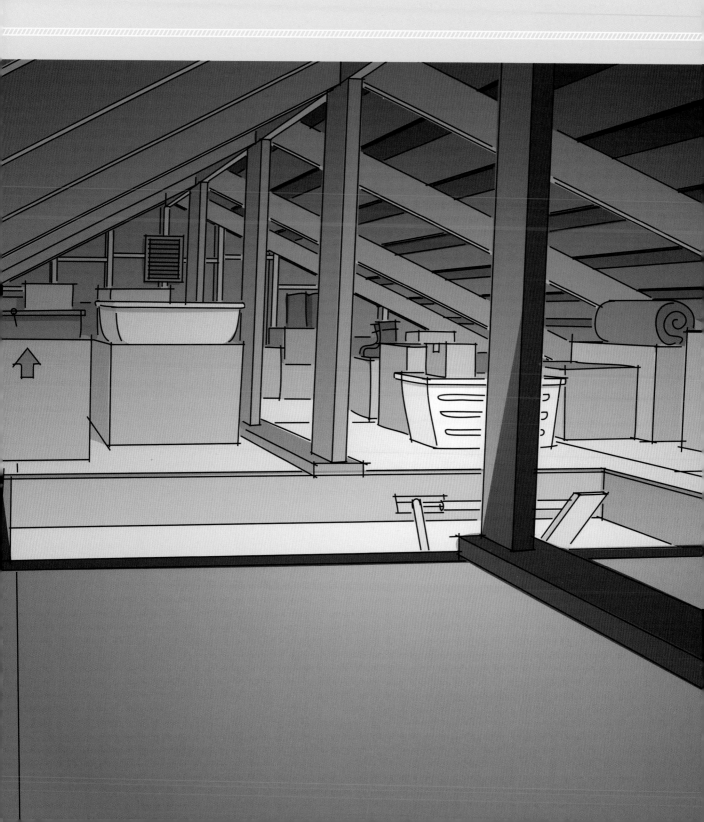

ATTIC STORAGE

Once you've installed a drop-down staircase, it's time to put your attic to good use. Let's put stuff up there! If the attic has no floor but is simply a row of joists, this project is for you. You'll create a floor by covering the joists with sheets of ¾-inch tongue-and-groove plywood. Thinner plywood isn't strong enough to carry the weight of objects placed on top of the floor—including your weight when you're scrounging around up there looking for holiday decorations.

TIME:

8 hours

DIFFICULTY:

TOOLS:

Tape measure

Pencil

Circular saw (optional)

Chalk line (optional)

Drill/driver with bits

Pnuematic floor nailer (optional)

Portable light

Hammer

Face mask

Safety glasses

Ear protection

MATERIALS:

WOOD:

4x8 tongue-in-groove plywood sheets (¾ inch), (enough full sheets to cover the attic floor)

2x6 framing lumber (quantity determined by project)

HARDWARE:

1 box 1½-inch wood screws

1 box 3-inch nails or screws

SAFETY ALERT: When storing items in the attic, be mindful of what's below. You can do structural damage to your home if you pile heavy items in the middle of the attic. Play it safe and concentrate heaviest loads over support walls underneath. You can also install support beams where you plan to place heavy items, laying joists alongside existing joists and in conjunction with the load-bearing walls on each end. This way, all the joists will be parallel to each other so that larger objects can be placed across them. Balance storage weight by spreading items all around the room, including the corners. If you are unsure about your attic structure, seek advice from a structural engineer or contractor.

MAKE THAT SPACE HAPPEN

1 . . . .
Measure the width and length of your attic, being very careful to stay on joists, and calculate the number of plywood sheets you'll need.

TIP: Before you begin, measure your doorways and ceiling access to make sure you can fit 4x8 plywood sheets through them. If access is tight, cut the sheets into smaller pieces (or ask the lumberyard to do this for you), using a chalk line and circular saw. If you have really tight attic access, consider using tongue-and-groove strip flooring to make the project easier.

2 . . . .
Lay the plywood sheets down on the joists one at a time without screwing them in, beginning at the nearest corner and working your way around the space until you end up on the opposite side of the same end where you started (the entrance to the attic). As you lay the sheets, make sure the edges meet halfway on a joist. Everything is a standard size in framing, so the sheets should match the joist spacing. However, if the sheets don't meet properly, you can avoid cutting a sheet by adding an additional piece of lumber (minimum 2x6) between the joists to support the end of the sheet. Fasten this lumber the same way as you

do in blocking using 3-inch nails or screws (see Step 4 of Project: Install Attic Access on page 204). Or you may find that you need to add a long piece fastened directly against the side of a joist. Easy.

3 . . . .
Fasten the plywood sheets to the joists one at a time with 1½-inch wood screws. Beginning on one long side, screw into the top of the joists—at least one screw in each corner and one in the middle of all four sides. Set another board flush next to it and screw it in the same way. Once all sheets are in place use a chalk line to mark the center of all joists and screw the plywood sheets down approximately every 12 inches using 1½-inch wood screws. Be careful not to screw into any pipe or wire that may be notched into the joists.

If using strip flooring ensure that you nail the first board with the groove against the wall. This will enable you to use a pnuematic floor nailer so as to secretly hide the nails. Most strip end joints connect easily and do not require blocking. You can also simply nail the boards through the face.

continued

BOXED IN

If you have ductwork running over the top of the joists that cannot be rerouted, consider boxing them in as protection; these raised boxes will also function as seats or even additional storage at a more comfortable height. See Project: Modular Storage and Floating Cube Nightstands (page 116) for the method. The boxing process is easily done. After the flooring is installed, you need to cut three strips of plywood for each box. Two are for the sides, and one is for the top. Make this three-sided box large enough to cover the ductwork. Nail or screw down lengths of 2x2 pine a little shorter than the length of the box, so that the three-sided box sides fit over them, and then screw the sides into the 2x2s.

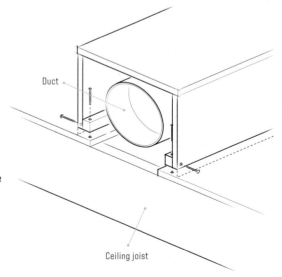

Duct

Ceiling joist

Stagger the plywood sheets for structural soundness.

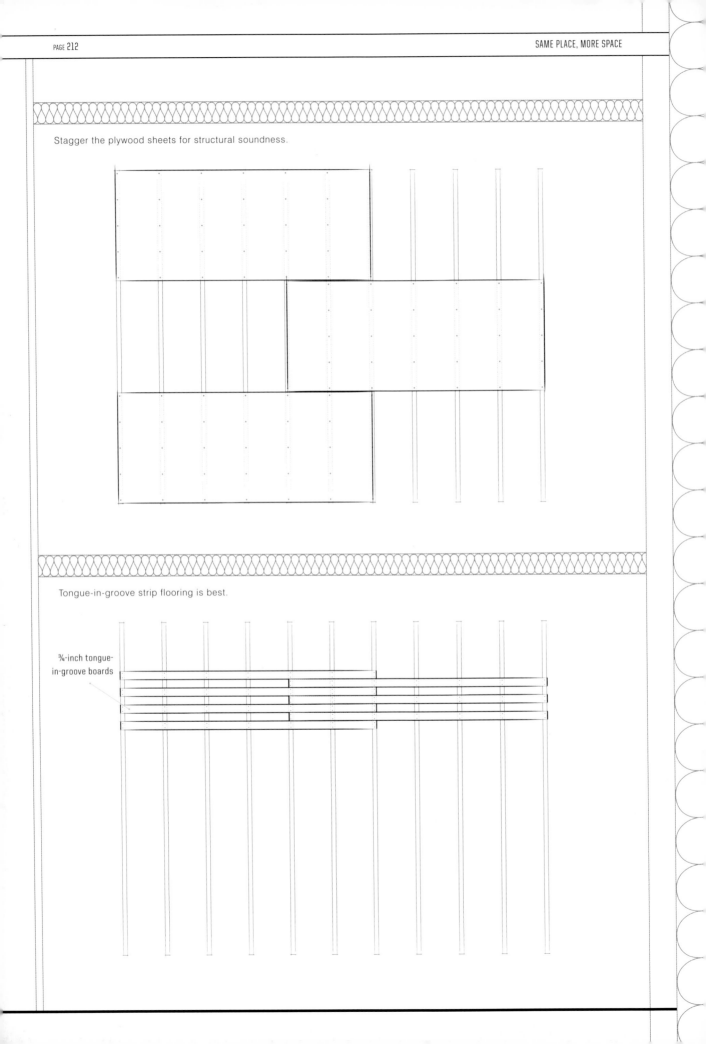

Tongue-in-groove strip flooring is best.

¾-inch tongue-
in-groove boards

PROJECT:

ATTIC REMODEL AS AN "OWNER BUILDER"

ATTIC REMODEL AS AN "OWNER BUILDER"

Creating attic access and storage is one thing. Remodeling an attic into a living space is quite another, and it presents its own specific lighting, heating, and cooling challenges. In addition, attic dimensions are usually completely different from those on the other floors of your house. Depending on how ambitious your plans are, finishing an attic may require the help of several tradespeople: plumbers, carpenters, electricians, HVAC (heating, ventilation, and air-conditioning) specialists, and others, such as flooring or tile specialists.

But I'm getting ahead of myself. Very few of us are skilled enough to do all of these jobs with our own two hands. So instead of describing how to completely remodel an attic, this project guides you in successfully managing this or any similarly complex project (such as remodeling a basement, page 219) by acting as the general contractor. In contractor jargon, you will become the "owner builder." Note that legally, you can act as "owner builder" only if you own the home—so don't remodel the basement of your summer rental!

TIME:

Depends on the remodel; anticipate spending several hours daily for the project duration

DIFFICULTY:

ⵣⵣⵣⵣ

TOOLS:

Budget with estimates and actual columns to keep track of costs (see "Create a Budget Book," page 217)

Calendar

25-foot-long blade tape measure

Folder for keeping notes

Clipboard and pen

Cell phone

Digital camera

Patience and understanding

MATERIALS:

Depends on the remodel

PERMIT, PLEASE! MAKE YOUR EFFORTS AN ASSET, NOT A LIABILITY

When planning to transform an attic into livable space, you must get the necessary permits from your local city or county agency. Do not skip this step or assume it does not matter because you are doing interior work. Of course, filing for permits means you'll get inspections. But these are actually a benefit because they ensure that the end result of all your work is safe and up to code. They also protect your investment: if you ever sell your home, having the proper permits for any alterations or additions you've made shows potential buyers that the work has been done correctly and conforms to local building codes.

MAKE THAT SPACE HAPPEN

Plan the Attic Remodel

1
Decide how you want to use the space—if the attic has ample headroom, your options are many. If your home's roof has a low pitch, you may be limited in the ways you can use the space. Do you want an extra bedroom for a teenager, a home office for occasional bill paying, a children's play-room, or just climate-controlled storage for clothes, linens, and family heirlooms? Decisions on function will inform your needs and choices, such as the finishes. For example, a children's playroom might be covered in affordable and durable linoleum tiles or by a large carpet or carpet tiles. A basic storage area can be more roughly finished.

2
Determine your budget. Developing a realistic budget takes research (and time), and sticking to a budget often involves trade-offs. Research the costs of different types of materials for every aspect of the job—lighting fixtures, floor coverings, and so on—and get multiple bids from a variety of subcontractors (for advice, see "Best Bets for Bids," page 226). You can also buy your own materials, such as fixtures and finishes, to save money on the markup plumbers, electricians, and carpenters may charge. Ask tradespeople if they mind working this way. If they do—find another pro. Compare and contrast your options to get what you need for the money you have. This will also help you to be prepared to adjust when unex-pected costs arise. (And they will.)

3
Assess which aspects of the job need professional tradespeople and which you can accomplish (or learn to accomplish) on your own. Whom do you need to hire, and what do you need them to do?

For example, you may need to hire any or all of the following:

* Structural engineer: to draft blueprints for permit approval, and to determine exactly what is structurally possible to install in your attic

* General contractor or homebuilder: to raise rooflines, to build dormers, or to install flooring, insulation, and drywall
* Electrician: to install lighting fixtures and outlets; to reconfigure or upgrade your house's main switchboard
* Heating, ventilation, and air-conditioning (HVAC) specialist
* Plumber: to install a sink, toilet, or full bath
* Window supplier/installer: to install windows, particularly dormer windows

TIP: On a remodel, when thinking about the work you can do yourself, remember: just because you can't do everything on a certain job—such as installing new lighting fixtures and outlets—doesn't mean you can't do some of the work yourself. For instance, you may not wish to do the electrical work, but it's worth asking the sparky if you can help out in other areas—pulling cables, nailing in boxes, and so on— to keep your costs down. This is also a great opportunity to watch and learn.

4
Plan your calendar and schedule the subcontrac-tors. Jobs need to be completed in a particular order (see "Remodel the Attic," page 216). The subbies will love ya if you coordinate a project well, staggering the jobs to prevent multiple trades-people from working in the same location at the same time. If a site is clean and free from other tradespeople, each trade will be in and out before you know it.

5
Apply for and acquire any necessary building permits. Your local building inspector's office can tell you exactly what is required in your area. Don't skip this step—permits are important. Not having them could affect the sale of your house in the future, or result in fines, removal, and stop-work orders (see "Permit, Please! Make Your Efforts an Asset, Not a Liability," page 214).

6
Coordinate with your family about how everyone will work around any disruptions in your home and living spaces. Will someone "lose" their bedroom and bunk with a sibling or sleep in the basement "rec" room so his or her room can become the

"staging area" for the attic above? Be prepared for the house's electricity and water supply to be shut off occasionally.

Remodel the Attic

What follows is a general outline of what happens first during a remodel. This outline will help you plan in what order to hire subbies; how much time to schedule per job (each contractor can give you estimates of how much time it will take him or her to complete the work); and when to purchase which materials, if you plan on supplying your own.

1 ....

Plan the flooring application. If there is no floor in your attic, consult with a flooring pro or experienced builder about installing a plywood subfloor (or do it yourself; see Project: Attic Storage, page 209) and a final surface finish. Wall-to-wall carpeting is a very economical choice, and, combined with the padding underneath, it provides a sound barrier for the people on the floor below. Hardwood also can be installed in an attic.

2 ....

Install any necessary HVAC systems. Particular attention must be paid to insulation, ventilation, heating, and cooling attic rooms because they can get hot.

3 ....

Install plumbing, if necessary. Have a plumber relocate existing services and rough in a bathroom, kitchenette, or wet bar plumbing so he can come back later to install fixtures. "Rough in" means installing or laying in necessary wires and pipes that can be connected to fixtures later.

4 ....

Do the electrical work. All electrical work must be done according to the National Electrical Code (NEC). Don't skimp on electrical systems. Make a list of what you intend to use in the room (light fixtures, outlets) so the electrician can calculate the required loads and make sure you have enough

power to draw from. The electrician can rough in wiring for eventual ceiling or wall fixtures at this time and come back to install the fixtures when the drywall or dropped ceiling has been installed. Think ahead. Make sure you can access the main electrical panel or the telephone or cable TV termination points if they are located in the attic. Ask the electrician to install conduits through which additional wires can be added at a later date.

5 ....

After the plumbing and electrical work have been roughed in, an inspection needs to takes place. Welcome the inspector at this stage, as you will not have access to these areas once they are covered up. Make sure it's done right while you can!

6 ....

Install cable and phone lines. You can save a lot of money if you do it yourself. Even if you just run the cables, you'll save money; then call your service companies and schedule a time for them to connect the new telephone and cable or Internet wiring in the basement or attic.

7 ....

Install new or additional dormer windows, skylights, and doors, if applicable.

8 ....

Build out and insulate the walls. You can install 2x4 studs if they do not already exist; after that there are many insulation materials, from traditional soft batting to rigid foil-faced insulation, to choose from. An insulation representative will be able to advise you on what is recommended for your region and application.

9 ....

Install walls. You can choose drywall or paneling. I prefer drywall over prefab paneling because it gives you the most flexibility. You can apply bead board wainscoting, traditional raised paneling, or other treatments over drywall at a later date.

10 ....

Install the ceiling. Again, I prefer drywall ceilings, but acoustical ceiling tiles have come a long way. They now come in a variety of styles, from bead board to decorative embossed styles that look like old-fashioned tin ceilings. The advantage of installing a dropped ceiling is that it creates an accessible tray for ductwork and wiring, and if one tile gets damaged, it's easy to replace. Always buy what's appropriately called "attic stock"—that is, get 10 percent more than you need. The disadvantage of a dropped ceiling is that it lowers the ceiling height.

11 ....

Install the floor. Assuming there is good insulation, hardwood flooring, engineered hardwood, laminate, and carpet tiles all work well in attics.

12 ....

Install baseboards and all trim pieces.

13 ....

Install doors and hardware.

14 ....

Install final fixtures. Call back the plumber and electrician to install permanent fixtures, such as lighting, outlets, smoke alarms, and any plumbing features.

15 ....

Prime and paint ceilings, walls, doors, baseboards, and trim.

16 ....

Move on in. You have almost doubled your space and added tremendous value to your home.

CREATE A BUDGET BOOK

Establishing a realistic budget and sticking to it is a crucial part of being a successful owner builder. The best way to keep the bottom line in sight is to keep track of out-of-pocket expenses and labor and material costs as you go. Sure, you can use your computer to keep track of expenses on a spreadsheet. Programs such as QuickBooks and Mint.com can help you do that. But when you're on site, working with subbies, there's nothing like a notebook and clipboard to note progress, capture changes to work schedules, keep track of materials and receipts, and write down change orders or ideas that may occur. Receipts can be organized in a file—but during a project it might be easier to keep everything in a sleeve in a spiral notebook and sort them out later. (Keeping receipts is very important for tax reasons if you sell your house.) Create a subcontractor checklist that includes seven columns with the following information:

+ What needs to be done (use the outline in this chapter)

+ Who is going to do what (including names and contact info)

+ Start and estimated end dates of task

+ Actual start and completion dates

+ Estimates of labor and materials cost

+ Insurance details for both you (the homeowner) and all subbies

+ Actual cost (determined after each task is completed)

REMODEL A BASEMENT

REMODEL A BASEMENT

Basements are, for so many homeowners, the last frontier in their homes. Don't let unfinished concrete walls and floor or old seventies carpet and cheesy paneling obscure the potential. It's an ideal space for a luxurious "man cave" replete with 57-inch plasma screen TV, leather chairs, pool table, and bar. Or create in-law and guest suites. Or make recreation spaces big enough to play kick ball in on a rainy day. Basements can be all these things—and more.

This project is organized like the Project: Attic Remodel as an "Owner Builder" (page 213): it describes how to approach renovating your basement as an "owner builder," in which you act as the general contractor, doing some work yourself and hiring subcontractors for the rest. All of the advice in the attic remodel project applies here, plus there are a few wrinkles that are particular to basements.

Don't forget about other projects in this book that are suitable for basements. These include wall niches, closets, raised-floor platforms, shelving, and cabinets. A basement renovation is your golden opportunity to take advantage of all these great space-saving ideas!

TIME:

Depends on the remodel; anticipate spending a few hours daily for the project duration.

DIFFICULTY:

ㅜㅜㅜㅜ

TOOLS:

Budget with estimates and actual columns to keep track of costs (see "Create a Budget Book," page 217)

25-foot-long blade tape measure

Calendar

Folder for keeping notes

Clipboard and pen

Cell phone

Digital camera

Patience and understanding

MATERIALS:

Depends on the remodel

MAKE THAT SPACE HAPPEN

Before you start!

Before you begin your renovation, there is one DIY job you can do—find and fill (with caulk and spray insulation foam) every gap between existing framing and masonry. Also fill around any pipes or wires that penetrate the rim joist or exterior walls. Sealing potential air leaks will save you money in the long run.

Plan the Basement Remodel

1..

Decide how you want to use the space. If you simply want to finish the space to make it livable for occasional use (say, for family Ping-Pong tournaments), you may be able to put up the drywall and lay carpeting or laminate flooring on your own if you have good carpentry skills. However, you still have to consider the following issues when making a basement plan.

TIP: If your basement redo includes adding a bedroom and bath, a bar, a kitchen, a fireplace, or other unique features, it is best to hire an architect or designer who can help you plan the best use of space. Contractors, even good ones, may not be as well-versed in design and aesthetics, so having a designer on board will ensure your basement looks and works as well as it can.

2..

Moisture: Is your basement dry or damp? Solve any moisture problems first and then seal masonry walls to avoid future moisture problems. Damp walls first need to be diagnosed (why is it happening?) and then treated appropriately. If your walls are damp, one way to determine if the moisture is from exterior water seeping in or simply from condensation of humid interior air is to tape a 2-inch-square sheet of plastic to an exterior masonry wall. If moisture collects on the front of the plastic, the moisture is from humidity in the room. Humidity is solved by venting the room (adding or expanding the windows helps) and then either using a portable dehumidifier or installing a more permanent system.

If moisture collects on the backside of the plastic, you have water wicking in from the outside. If you notice regular seepage or water puddles

(or flooding) after rainstorms or from melting snow (even if this happens only occasionally), the problem must be solved before any work begins. Not doing so will result in water damage and dangerous mold growth. Consult a professional contractor experienced with basements. You may need to reroute downspouts, which is relatively simple and inexpensive, or you may need to regrade the ground around your basement so that it slopes away from foundation walls. This is a more expensive endeavor. If flooding is or has been a problem, you may need to have a professional install a sump pump somewhere in the basement at its lowest level—this does not preclude finishing off the space, but it does require some maintenance.

An application of a water-resistant sealer to the interior masonry is a good idea no matter what kind of basement you have.

3..

Framing: Most basements aren't perfect rectangles and rarely are their corners perfect 90-degree angles. Many basements also have obstructions like posts (which can become neat architectural features when boxed with wood and trim molding), heating ducts, and pipes. Some have water heaters and boilers that must be safely sectioned off in a utility room or closet. Basement stairs are often centrally located. This under-stair area can be left open or framed and turned into a storage closet or shelving (those would be my picks).

4..

Access to services: You need to maintain easy access to valves, cleanouts, sewage pipes, electrical panels, and any other utilities located in the basement. If utilities are consolidated in one area, you might section off the area and frame a utility room off the living area. If you do this around any appliance (such as a water heater), it is a good idea to consult the product's manufacturer for space and ventilation requirements to avoid causing problems like overheating and so on.

5 ....

Measure and design your space. Once you've dealt with any moisture issues, decided how you want to frame out the space, and figured out how to create access points for your home's mechanical systems, measure the area you want to finish. Go back to your handy grid paper and draw the area to scale using your measurements (see "Make an Accurate Floor Plan," page 15). This drawing becomes the "plan" that you will submit to your local building inspector. Include wall dimensions of the proposed finished area and utility areas, window and door sizes, ceiling heights, bulkheads that will cover low-hanging ductwork or pipes, and special features such as a wood-burning stove, whirlpool or hot tub, or darkroom. Check with your building inspector to find out how detailed the plan needs to be.

6 ....

Get the proper permits. Yes, that's right: even a basement job needs to be built to code and inspected, especially if you plan on adding more plumbing or more electrical lights and receptacles to the space.

If you plan on doing your own electrical work, draw up a plan for where outlets, lighting fixtures, cable, and other electrical features will go and submit that with your general plan. When the inspector examines your plans, he or she will doubtless have questions for you, and you'll also find out if you need to make changes to bring it in line with local code (many communities follow international code). For instance, if you are adding a bedroom, you may need to install egress windows for fire safety. Once a permit is issued, it will detail when and what kinds of inspections are required. A new project may result in the inspector requesting you to update other areas of your house, such as handrails, and so on.

7 ....

Decide what work you can do yourself and hire subcontractors to get the rest of the job done. I always encourage homeowners to do as much as they can themselves, as all of these projects are great challenges and learning opportunities for you! However, as with Project: Attic Remodel as an "Owner Builder" (page 213), you may need to hire subs to make your basement space happen.

Remodel the Basement

1 ....

If any windows need to be enlarged, replaced, or added, this should happen first.

2 ....

Whether or not you're doing the reno yourself, framing the walls happens next. If you're doing it yourself, you will lay "bottom plates" along the wall and perhaps into the room itself (depending on your plan) on the floor where you plan to finish the space. You, or your contractor, should use pressure-treated lumber for the floor plates, since they come in direct contact with the concrete floor.

3 ....

Next, create a plan for stud placement. Normally, this starts in a corner; then, with a tape measure on the floor, every 16 inches is marked on the floor plate. This mark represents the center of each stud. Make another mark ¾-inch back from the center line. This mark represents the edge of each stud. Measurement continues around the area you plan to frame. If the opposing corners of the room do not end up with 16 inches, it's okay, as long as the measurements started out with 16 inches.

4 ....

Once the measuring is done, install a top plate between the first-floor joists (your basement's ceiling). See Project: Wall Construction—Make One Room into Two (page 195) for useful tips and illustrations. Use a plumb bob to ensure the top plate lines up perfectly with the bottom plate. This is important! Then the studs go up, starting at the first corner that was measured. Studs should fit snugly but not so tightly that they bow. The studs are attached by toe nailing them with nails hammered in at a 45-degree angle, so the nail goes through both the stud and the bottom plate. Always plumb studs with a 4-foot level before toe nailing them at the top. Once the first stud is in, it's a good idea to check the marks you made by hooking your tape measure to the plumb stud you installed and re-marking the others (if necessary).

continued

5

If your plan includes interior basement walls or partitions—say, in the case of a bedroom, bath, and living area—those walls are built next and then installed. Measure floor to ceiling at several spots where you plan for the wall(s) to go to find the shortest measurement and then use shims as necessary (this is a lot easier than making cuts after the fact). Before standing the wall framing up, you need a chalk line on the floor to mark the location of the wall(s). I like to use what's called the 3-4-5 Method (see Tip, below) to ensure that the interior wall is perpendicular with the exterior wall.

TIP: A challenge of creating corners is getting them square. Not many rooms are perfectly square, but they should be as close to it as possible. If not, any tile, carpet, or ceiling tiles will look—not to mention be—off square, and this will bother you and everyone in the house for years to come. The 3-4-5 Method is a simple way that is commonly used to square corners: Measure 3 feet out from a corner in one direction, and 4 feet out in the other direction. The line between the two points should be 5 feet. If it measures more than 5 feet, your corner is more than 90 degrees. If it's less than that, the corner's not square either. In either case, adjust the position of your interior wall (since you can't move the exterior wall) to bring it into square.

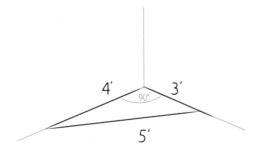

6

Any plumbing is roughed in at this point—including for toilets, tubs or showers, and sinks.

7

Unfinished basements generally don't have as many electrical outlets as you'd like, so before drywall goes up, plan where you'd like to locate outlets, including those for cable and phone. Existing outlets may have to be moved because they should be secured to the framing studs. Even if you're doing this project yourself, I recommend you call in a licensed electrician at this point to run wires and cable and to install junction boxes and outlets properly and to code. Don't forget to install hard-wired smoke alarms.

8

The ceiling is next—many people install dropped ceilings, but I feel they scream "BASEMENT!" and are not terribly attractive. Plus, they lower the height of already low ceilings. I recommend drywalling the ceiling.

9

Now is the time to install the necessary housings for recessed lights, wall fixtures, and ceiling fans. Choose insulation contact, or IC-rated housings. These allow insulation to be placed directly against them. Otherwise, insulation in contact with non-IC-rated housings can get very hot!

10

Wall and ceiling insulation and drywall go up next.

11

The next step is the flooring. I do not recommend laying hardwood floors in a basement, nor do I really like carpeting, which can retain odors and become moldy in a humid space. I like floating floors, made from laminated wood or another engineered product. Tile is also a good choice.

12

Doors, door trim, and baseboard molding are installed next, then plumbing jobs are completed. All electrical fixtures are installed, and priming and painting of the ceilings and walls are completed.

11

OUT OF THIN AIR

I've been converting two-story rooms into, well, two stories for years. Call in the pros and add a mezzanine, which can add a fully functional 100 or 200 square feet around the perimeter of your great room. Adding an entire floor—enough to fit a bed and bath, or a den and an office—is the most complex and costly but is still about 50 percent less expensive than adding a conventional addition or second story to a home.

Both of the projects in this chapter require the highest level of homebuilding experience to complete. In both, it's likely that you will need to hire a general contractor to complete them. However, if you feel confident, you can also act as an "owner builder" and manage the job yourself as the general contractor. This will keep your costs down and allow you the most involvement in the project, but it definitely requires more time on your part to manage the project. For more advice on being an owner builder, see Project: Attic Remodel as an "Owner Builder," page 213.

PROJECT:
ADD A MEZZANINE

ADD A MEZZANINE

Very large great rooms—those that have a large expanse of floor space, meaning 600 square feet or more—may be candidates for a mezzanine around some or all of the room's perimeter. Such a feature is useful as a library space (line it with book shelves), a home office (get away from it all), or a gallery (great if you're a collector!). You need to be able to stand upright on the mezzanine if you want to actually use it. A fairly rectangular (or square) room that doesn't have too many odd corners makes the build easier—the more corners and angles, the more expensive and time-consuming the project. A mezzanine also adds a tremendous amount of value and architectural presence.

This is a major construction job for the pros, so I am going to walk you through what needs to happen to make a mezzanine a reality as I did with attic and basement remodels (see pages 213 and 218). There is enough information for you to determine if this is a good solution for your space—and you'll also know what to expect when the architect, contractor, and tradespeople show up at your door. An architectural feature this complex can cost several to many thousands of dollars, meaning it's the kind of project you want to get at least three bids for from both architects/designers and builders (for tips, see "Best Bets for Bids," page 226). Just like finishing off an attic or basement, expect to spend one to several hours a day dealing with some aspect of the project while it's in progress if you plan to act as owner builder—whether this time is spent checking in on tradespeople, maintaining a clean worksite, inspecting work, paying bills, or troubleshooting.

If you have the time and you feel you can tackle this on your own—go for it!

TIME:

One month or more, depending on intricacy

DIFFICULTY:

↑↑↑↑

TOOLS:

Budget with estimates and actual columns to keep track of costs (see "Create a Budget Book," page 217)

25-foot-long blade tape measure

Calendar

Folder for keeping notes

Clipboard and pen

Cell phone

Digital camera

Patience and understanding

MATERIALS:

The contractor/installer will supply a materials list

TIP: On complex projects like this, I suggest that you come up with a running list of materials with your architect and contractor. This way, you can keep track of materials and their cost as you go, especially if the contractor is going to do the buying.

BEST BETS FOR BIDS

It always surprises people that bids for the same job can vary so much from contractor to contractor. Sometimes they come in fairly similar; other times, the difference in price is shocking, from high to low. Likewise, contracts can be pages long and filled with every detail imaginable, while some are one-pagers with minimal information. Here are some tips to make the bidding process go smoothly:

+ Skepticism pays. I always tell people to be suspicious of a very low bid. A low bid can be the result of an inexperienced contractor, one whose work is not up to par, or one who plans on adding costs later simply because he wanted the job and "low-balled" the bid to get it. Likewise, an astronomical bid (one that's 30 percent more or higher than the other bids) can signal trouble, too. Ask why the bid is high—maybe the fellow just needs the money: beware of destitute contractors!

+ See the work. Ask for recent references, pictures of work, and tours of completed jobs. Previous customers are valuable assets, so be specific when talking to them, and don't waste their time. Ask explicit questions that require more than a "Yes" or "No" answer, such as these: "What was the time schedule for the job, and were the budget and schedule met or how did they change?" "What were your biggest frustrations?" And, "Were there surprises not anticipated by the contractor?"

+ Be up front. Tell the contractor what you expect to happen, and let him or her know whether you would like to keep costs down by putting in some sweat equity or buying materials. Many contractors are willing—and even enjoy—a homeowner's participation. Agree on what you "bring to the table" and detail it in the contract. For instance, you agree to demo a room in preparation for work or you will do clean up and junk removal and supply all building materials.

+ Think before you sign. Anything you sign or initial, even a piece of paper from a scratch pad, may legally constitute a contract. Don't put your John Hancock on anything until you've read it and are sure you agree with the provisions. Also make sure that the contract document includes the business name, street address (not just a post office box), and local telephone number (not just a toll-free number) for the contractor, as well as license number, insurance details, detailed description of all work to be done, a detailed materials list, estimated timeline, payment schedule, and any warranties.

+ Verify. Always check with your local licensing board to ensure the contractor's license is up to date and active. Check the Better Business Bureau and respected opinion Web sites to make sure the contractor does not have serious complaints lodged against him or her.

MAKE THAT SPACE HAPPEN

Plan for the Mezzanine

1 ....

Determine your budget. Every decision you make will flow from there—from how much to spend on flooring to how fancy you want your lighting fixtures to be.

2 ....

Hire an architect or a designer and a structural engineer. A licensed architect can help you determine what style makes the most sense in terms of your existing room. She or he can also make suggestions that save construction money and that use the space most effectively and efficiently. For instance, the support structure might include columns and arches that will add interest to the space beneath the mezzanine. Or the architect can suggest the latest materials for a modern and light look, such as acrylic panels instead of balustrades, mesh screening, and industrial-style staircases.

Then that person can design it to code, provide detailed plans to you or your builder, and make him- or herself available to answer questions and make any adjustments. The architect's design should include structural plans, as well as placement of access stairs or doors, built-ins and closets, electrical outlets, plugs and switches, and any additional ceiling lights.

A licensed structural engineer is a must for this kind of project. Your architect may also be able to fulfill this role—or he [or she] can recommend people with whom he has worked successfully in the past. The structural engineer can tell you what kind of support system you need for the project and what amount of weight the mezzanine can bear once it is built.

3 ....

If you aren't running this project as an owner builder, select and hire a licensed general contractor who is verifiably experienced in mezzanine installation. As with any major construction project, building a mezzanine requires attention to detail and meticulous workmanship—perhaps more so because it is a raised area that depends on a series of structural and safety elements, including railings, stairs, supports, and floor joists. With a set of plans that leaves nothing to question and a builder who understands the intricacies of these unique projects, the actual construction can proceed relatively quickly and smoothly.

4 ....

Apply for and acquire permits if you are acting as owner builder; if you hire a general contractor or architect, he or she should do this on your behalf. Your local building inspector's office can tell you exactly what is required in your area for an internal renovation job. Permits are important for your own safety—you want another set of experienced eyes checking the work to make sure it's to code. It's also important for a future sale—prospective buyers will want to know that the house is safe and sound. Besides, not having permits could result in an unpleasant visit from the county, fines, removal, and stop-work orders.

5 ....

Once you have a design, an approval to build, and a contractor in place, you have to clear the space. If it's problematic to empty the entire room, consult with your contractor to determine if perimeter furnishings can be moved to the middle of the area and covered with a tarp. Also plan with your family how you will deal with the disruptions that construction involves in terms of living space.

continued

Build the Mezzanine

1 ....

Work commences with the building of the framing and basic structure. The contractor will build a scaffolding system to access the space.

2 ....

After the framing is complete, the subfloor and flooring is installed.

3 ....

The railing system goes in next and then the staircase(s). Access to the mezzanine needs to be safe, and sturdy, and take up minimal floor space. Prefabricated and spiral staircase kits are one option; traditional staircases are another. However, spiral staircases take up the least amount of floor space and come in a wide variety of styles, from traditional to contemporary.

4 ....

Electrical rough in comes next, and this will likely need to be inspected with the framing. Since there were likely no outlets or switches installed 8 or 9 feet up your wall, you'll need to add some if you want the space to be fully functional. Provide the electrician with a list of fixtures, outlets, and switches (your general contractor may do this if he is hiring the subbies), so together you can calculate the required loads and make sure you have enough power to add additional circuits. He or she can rough in wiring for eventual ceiling or wall fixtures at this time and come back to install the fixtures when the drywall or dropped ceiling has been installed and painted.

TIP: Have the electrician install conduits through which additional wires can be added at a later date if desired.

5 ....

Install cable and phone lines. You might want to try doing this on your own, as it can be expensive to hire out and it's relatively easy. Simply running cable and having the service company add new telephone, cable, or Internet wiring in the basement or attic will save money.

6 ....

Install flooring.

7 ....

Install any built-ins, such as shelving, cabinetry, desks, daybeds, and so on. Install baseboards and all trim pieces, doors, hardware, and final fixtures.

8 ....

Prime and paint ceilings, walls, doors, baseboards, and trim if applicable.

9 ....

Furnish the space. If you plan on placing bulky furnishings, such as a couch or club chairs, ask your contractor to keep some scaffolding and help hoist up the pieces.

PROJECT:

ADD A SECOND FLOOR
ABOVE A GREAT ROOM

ADD A SECOND FLOOR ABOVE A GREAT ROOM

It is possible to add a second full floor in a high-ceilinged great room if the space meets certain requirements. While not as disruptive and expensive (about 50 percent less) as raising a roof and adding an entirely new second floor or building out and adding an extension, building a second floor within the footprint of a room has several important structural issues that must be addressed. For example, second-story living space requires access via a staircase—a loft ladder or spiral staircase may not be adequate or even permissible under local building codes.

An architect and/or interior designer is a must in designing the new floor so that it meets code requirements and blends in seamlessly (to look as if it was always there) with the rest of your home. Moreover, the architect or designer can specify placement of extra windows, as well as provide a detailed electrical plan (including how the additional wiring will be tied into the existing electrical panel box). You also need to heat and cool the new room—which means designing a plan for running ductwork into the new space, or installing baseboards or radiant-heat flooring. A structural engineer has to assist in determining that the new floor is designed to be strong enough (and safe enough)

for furniture, people, and activity. If you're up for it and you need the space, this project adds genuine value to your home, since nowadays a majority of people are more interested in usable as opposed to visual space—particularly since you are already paying property taxes for this useless air space! It's square footage, and it counts.

This is a disruptive project, so I recommend seeking advice and clarification from both architect and builder on whether you can live—and function—in the house while the project is underway. If you have a secondary living area, such as a basement family room or a formal living room that can double as the old great room, great. Chances are that you can stay put. If not, you may want to consider moving out for the duration of construction—and that expense has to be part of your overall budget.

TIP: I am passionate about advising people to give their architect or designer a firm budget and have them stay under it, as many designs and egos can go way beyond! Also, don't let someone go designing something that you are not 100 percent happy with, as it will be your space at the end of the day! Try to visualize the end result and know up front what you expect from this space. This is super important and will make the planning process go more quickly and smoothly.

TIME:
2 months or more, depending on intricacy

DIFFICULTY:
ᴛ ᴛ ᴛ ᴛ ᴛ

TOOLS:
Budget with estimates and actual columns to keep track of costs (see "Create a Budget Book," page 217)

Calendar

Folder or diary for keeping notes

Clipboard and pen

25-foot-long blade tape measure

Cell phone

Digital camera

Patience and understanding

MATERIALS:
Depends on project; consult with architect and contractor and keep a running list

MAKE THAT SPACE HAPPEN

Plan for the Second Floor

1
Hire an architect and a structural engineer.

TIP: If you want to add another bathroom, the septic system, if applicable, must also be checked for capacity to see if it can handle sewage output from additional plumbing fixtures.

2
The structural design of the new floor depends on the kind of reinforcements that are needed to support it. The first thing the structural engineer will do is examine the footings beneath the walls of your great room and any other area that will be impacted by the second floor to determine the type of reinforcement needed, whether it is additional joists, concrete footings, or metal beams. This is important because the additional weight of a second floor can cause structural damage to the great room's walls. Any structural or decorative beams will have to be either redesigned or removed (if they are decorative only).

TIP: If you are sure of your own design and the outlook of your project, you can skip the architect and use the structural engineer to create the drawings for the permit. This can save you money.

3
If you choose to hire a general contractor, put out a call for bids (see "Best Bets for Bids," page 226). If you want to do this job yourself as an owner builder, see Project: Attic Remodel as an "Owner Builder," page 213, for more advice on what that entails.

4
Once you have a structurally sound design in place, apply for the necessary permits from the local building office. Once the permits are pulled for the job, you are set to go.

5
Clear the room to the bare walls. (It will be unlivable during the construction process.) Low-hanging ceiling fixtures such as chandeliers and fans need to be removed as well. Make sure the contractor (or you) seals off the room while work is going on. Plastic sheeting taped over the entry to the room will keep the dust and debris getting into other areas of the house to a minimum.

TIP: A great room generally contains a lot of furnishings and personal belongings that, when cleared out of the room, will make clutter in other rooms of the house. Consider renting an external storage container to store your stuff in for the duration of the build, such as from 1-800-Pack-Rat (www.1800packrat .com). This will enable you to start with a clean slate, work in a safer environment, and still have access to your belongings. Not to sound like a broken record, but when it's time to move back into the new space, try to eliminate as much of your stuff as you can.

Build the Second Floor

1
The contractor will likely begin by installing the structural components required for your new floor.

2
A staircase connecting the great room to the new floor will be built next. (Unless there is an entrance from another room.) There are many options available, depending on your new floor design. A spiral staircase, if permissible under your local building code, saves the most space. Traditional tread-and-riser stairs can be attached to one wall of the great room and lead straight up to a hall or second-floor "foyer" that leads to the new room. If you have more space, a staircase that runs alongside a wall and turns 90 degrees into the new room by way of a landing is graceful and attractive. Keep in mind that staircases are an important aesthetic element of any build—they are always more inviting if they face or open out into the great room.

continued

3 ....

The subfloor will be installed next, followed by any new walls and entryways.

4 ....

All wiring and any plumbing will be roughed in, and additional permanent lighting fixtures will be installed. An inspection will likely occur after this.

5 ....

Once the basic structure of the room has been completed, windows are added or modified, if necessary.

6 ....

Drywall is applied to ceilings and walls.

7 ....

Flooring, trim molding, and baseboards are installed next.

8 ....

Finish work, such as painting or the construction of any built-ins, is completed next. Then a final "fit out," or punch list, for all the trades should be checked and completed, such as finishing touches or tasks related to plumbing and electrical (installing faucets, fixtures and switch plates, etc.).

9 ....

A final walk-through inspection will likely happen on completion.

10 ....

Now just picture this and go for it!

STAIR FLAIR

In my house, I used 12x6 laminated structural parallel strand lumber (PSL) beams, normally enclosed within a floor, to make what we think is a beautiful, modern, up-to-code staircase. The steps never squeak or bow, and they require less labor to install than a conventional tread-and-riser stairway. Cut the lumber to your desired width and then use a belt sander to sand them smooth. Add your favorite stain and finish, such as polyurethane, place the step on your cut stringer, and you have a riser and tread in one. They cost approx $13 per lineal foot—I know it seems expensive, but installation and labor is quicker and cheaper in the long run, as you do not need to line the stairs and risers or treads with finished wood, tile, carpet, and so on.

12
THE GREAT OUTDOORS

Your garage, sheds, and decking provide much usable space for both storage and living. Think about it: a two-car garage is 500 square feet—as big as many urban apartments. And a single-car garage is about 300 square feet. Cars rarely take up the available space in a garage, so there's generally plenty left over to work with for workshop and hobby space, pantry and food storage, or an office, gymnasium, or extra living space. More good news: If you have a small garden shed— say, 80 square feet or more—it can, with a few adjustments, become a personal retreat, guest quarters, or a playhouse. The under part of a deck can safely and neatly store all sorts of equipment, while the top can sport built-in storage benches. Even a balcony of a city apartment can expand exterior space.

PROJECT:

EXPAND GARAGE STORAGE SPACE

EXPAND GARAGE STORAGE SPACE

Anyone who has a garage knows that it often becomes a dumping ground. I've met more than a few homeowners who were unable to put the car in the garage because it was so overstuffed with boxes, equipment, tools, and miscellaneous household items (clutter!). That's a shame, because the garage offers so many opportunities for organized storage, function, and even entertaining. The garage is a large part of your home's footprint—reclaim this valuable real estate to create a more efficient lifestyle and expand your home. If you have an organized garage workshop, you can find that screwdriver straight away, complete projects in short order, and save hours and weeks each year that you might otherwise use just trying to find things.

CLEAN OUT THE GARAGE AND REFINISH THE FLOOR

It's tough to get a garage really organized unless you start with a clean slate. Then, if you are going to go to the trouble of hanging tools and equipment (which I highly recommend), organizing a workshop area, and stowing bikes and other sporting goods neatly, you may as well complete the picture with a clean floor instead of a stained, oily concrete slab. A clean, smooth floor does give you more options for using the space. A nice garage can be transformed into an indoor/outdoor party space. It can also easily become an attractive and safe play space for kids (think cabin fever meets rainy day).

There are many types of floor systems on the market today. In this project, I describe three that I recommend.

TIME:

1 weekend

DIFFICULTY:

TOOLS:

Work gloves

Safety glasses

Knee pads

Mop, sponges, and bucket

Tape measure

Tools to apply floor covering (depends on floor choice)

MATERIALS:

¼-inch graph paper and pencil

Floor covering (see Step 5 for options)

MAKE THAT SPACE HAPPEN

1..

Declutter your garage (and/or shed, if applicable), using the process described in Chapter 1, "A Clean Slate" (beginning on page 10). In other words, approach the garage as you would any room in your house: take everything out and winnow your belongings to only what you really need and want.

2..

Determine your storage and workspace needs. If you're not sure where to begin, review Chapter 2, "Dreams vs. Reality" (beginning on page 14). Make lists of what you would like to store in the garage and what you want to use it for (workshop, tinkering with cars and other machinery, extra pantry space, and so on). Then "do a 360" (see page 15), draw up a simple floor plan on ¼-inch graph paper, and determine what can go where—including your vehicle.

3..

And then get cleaning. Wash the walls, and particularly the floors, to prepare for refinishing them.

4..

Repair the walls and floor as needed. Once the space is empty, it's easy to see what needs fixing—from a moisture issue (an oft-neglected feature of many garages) and broken screen windows to cracked concrete or damaged wallboard.

5..

Next, refinish the floor. While adding a new coat of paint is the easiest and fastest approach, it is also the least durable. Instead, consider one of the following three systems (beginning with the easiest to install):

Cover the garage floor with snap-together plastic floor tiles. This system is great, as it floats on your existing slab. It hides imperfections in concrete and is easy to clean or hose off. It is easy to install, and offers many colors to choose from. Gladiatorgw.com has a good product line.

A DIY-friendly epoxy floor covering is an inexpensive way to go and is also very easy to install. However, your current concrete slab needs to be in good shape to take the application. Epoxy resists oil stains, beads water, and easily wipes clean. Applying an epoxy coat is more complicated than painting, but it's still a DIY job—the materials (floor-etching solution, epoxy paint, color flakes, and top-coat hardener) are all available at the local hardware store or home center and can be—must be, in fact—completed in a couple of hours because epoxy dries quickly. Simply follow the manufacturer's directions for application.

Finally, the most attractive, but also the most expensive and work-intensive option, is to lay non-slip porcelain tiles. The process is similar to the tile instructions in Project: Storage Island (page 62). Tile is the best choice if you plan to use the garage as a partial or occasional living space or play area. If you can match the existing tiles within your house, the garage will feel like an extension of your home.

REORGANIZE THE GARAGE AND ADD STORAGE

Now that you have a plan in hand and a clean slate to work with, implement your ideas. Obviously, how long this takes and what you need are up to you. So, what follows are my storage and organization suggestions for items most commonly stored in the garage.

TIME:

1 weekend

DIFFICULTY:

⚒⚒

TOOLS:

Vary for individual projects, but most likely include the following:

Tape measure

Handsaw or circular saw

Drill/driver with bits

Hammer

4-foot level

Pencil

Work gloves

Safety glasses

Ear protection

MATERIALS:

Vary for individual projects, but most likely include the following:

Ready-made storage or drawer systems

HARDWARE:

Screws

Nails

Wall anchors

Hooks

Brackets

MAKE THAT SPACE HAPPEN

1 . . . .

Organize your carpentry or workshop area. Smaller tools like screwdrivers, drill bits, and tape measures are easy to misplace yet so essential to most DIY jobs. It is useful to keep a tool chest under the kitchen sink or in the hall closet for quick fixes, but the bulk of your tools should be kept organized in one place where you can get to them easily.

Ready-made units with multiple drawers and compartments are a wise investment, since making a chest of tiny drawers is labor intensive and really not worth the time unless you are an avid carpentry hobbyist. Look for chests with deep drawers and a variety of compartments that will fit larger items, such as hammers, mallets, power and hand tools, as well as sections for smaller items, such as socket sets, screwdrivers, and screws.

Hand and power tools can be hung on the wall using various hooks and brackets. These are superior as you can move the hooks and brackets around, particularly if they are part of a pegboard panel or (my favorite) modular slat wall system. This enables you to create zones as well as make adjustments to your storage for the changing seasons! Some wall systems enable you to lock brackets and hooks into place so your gear does not drop onto your car. A sheet of pegboard screwed into the studs is an inexpensive way to go. With accessories such as pegboard hooks, cups, and bins, you can create a custom storage system that lets you see and grab everything you need quickly and easily.

TIP: If you're working within a limited budget, go for a mix of ready-made organizational units that allow you to add on over time. Combine those pieces with DIY projects, such as niche shelving, to reduce costs but not storage space.

2 . . . .

Floor space does not restrict your garage's storage capability. The walls and ceiling are generally wasted space and can sometimes support 100 percent of your gear. You can find hooks and brackets specifically made for holding bicycles, lawn tools such as rakes and shovels, and skis and other sports gear.

3 . . . .

If you want to add pantry storage, plan this very carefully. The most frequent point of entry into a home for mice and other pests is an attached garage. The presence of food makes the space even more enticing to critters.

A fridge and/or freezer can be quite convenient to have in a garage. This is often a great idea and luxury, as it takes the weight off your kitchen fridge. However, I don't recommend placing an old conventional refrigerator in the garage. Choose a refrigerator that has been specifically designed to withstand the extreme changeable temperatures and humidity of the garage; otherwise you will find a costly energy bill, as standard appliances have to run overtime to accommodate extreme temperatures.

For nonperishable food items, you will need secure storage cabinets or shelving. You can stow unopened jars, cans, and bottles in the garage if they are protected from changes in temperature. Dry goods such as bags of flour, pasta, cereal, crackers, and candy should ideally be kept inside, unless you can place them in tamper-proof food-safe bins and buckets. A heavy-duty steel cabinet made for food pantry storage will keep items free of dust and ready for consumption. Niche shelves can hold bulky items, such as paper products and cleaning supplies.

SAFETY ALERT: Never place food storage components or shelving near gasoline, cleaning products, fuel oil, pesticides, or lawn or other chemicals. These chemicals are sometimes stored in a type of plastic that is porous, making it possible for the contents to leach into food. Keep all hazardous liquids and materials locked in a safe place away from consumable items and away from where pets and children can access them. Keep all cabinets fastened to the walls and use only waterproof materials for durability.

EASY DECK STORAGE BENCHES

EASY DECK STORAGE BENCHES

One or more storage benches arranged strategically around the perimeter of your outdoor space have a dual function of providing seating and storage. This version is particularly easy—it's a good project for a budding carpenter and will build confidence. It's similar to building a rectangular box. We start off by building an exterior-grade plywood box and then attach 1x6 facing lumber to the outside of it.

This enables the fasteners to be secretly hidden as they are screwed on from inside the box. The three boards that make up the sides provide the right height for seating. I used casters as legs to lift the bench off the ground, making it mobile and giving it a more refined appearance. This also allows the bottom to dry out more easily if it gets wet.

TIME:

4 to 6 hours

DIFFICULTY:

⫪⫪ to ⫪⫪⫪

TOOLS:

Tape measure

Circular saw

Framing square

Paintbrushes, roller, and tray

Drill/driver with bits

Screwdrivers

2 Quick-Grip clamps

Miter saw (optional)

Hammer or nail gun (optional)

4-foot level

Safety glasses

Ear protection

MATERIALS:

WOOD:

All facing lumber should be the same (you can use pressure-treated pine, cedar, redwood, teak, Ipe, Mangaris, or mahogany)

1x6 boards (finished size is typically ¾ by 5½ inches), 4 cut to 8-foot lengths and 3 cut to 10-foot lengths

1 sheet ½- or ⅝-inch exterior grade plywood

HARDWARE:

1 box 1¼-inch galvanized wood screws for pressure-treated lumber, or stainless-steel screws for cedar, redwood, teak, or mahogany (galvanized screws can stain fine woods)

1 box 2-inch nails

1 box 2½-inch galvanized screws

4 casters

Brass hinges (optional)

Lid closer support (optional)

1 square foot of rust-proof screen mesh

FINISHING SUPPLIES:

Sandpaper, 220-grit

Wood glue

Deck sealer appropriate for the wood you are using (or primer and paint)

MAKE THAT SPACE HAPPEN

Make your storage bench to suit your own storage needs. The dimensions below are a suitable size for storage, seating, and appearance.

1

Using a circular saw and your safety gear, make the following cuts to your sheet of plywood:
Two 48-by-13-inch long sides
Two 20¾-by-13-inch short sides
One 48-by-19¼-inch base
One 48-by-20¼-inch lid

2

Using wood glue and 2-inch nails, build your five-sided box. Connect the four sides first. The short sides are placed inside the long sides. Then insert the base inside the four sides. The base will ensure the box is square. Use your framing square to ensure this! When the box is nailed and formed, screw all around, using 2½-inch galvanized wood screws, spacing screws approximately 6 inches apart for added strength. (The lid is added later.)

Optional: You may wish to paint the plywood with a dark exterior grade paint or stain at this point to help protect it from the elements and to give a nice shadow line between the board spacings.

3

Fasten the casters to the base of your box using 2½-inch galvanized screws. I recommend placing the casters approximately 2 inches in from each corner.

4

Cut and attach your 1x6 lumber all around. If your plywood lid is ⅝ inch, attach the first boards so the top is ⅝ inch above the plywood sides. Remember to fasten the boards from inside the box using the 1¼-inch screws that will not penetrate the surface after the screws are flush. I recommend you try to miter the ends as this gives your storage bench a much more professional look. When cutting the length, don't forget to take into account the thickness of both side boards! Add this to your length. The plywood box is square, so all miters will be a 45-degree cut. If you do not have a miter saw, butt joints are AOK.

5

Attach the second and third boards with a small gap (approximately ¼ inch) between each one. This allows for expansion and contraction of the lumber.

continued

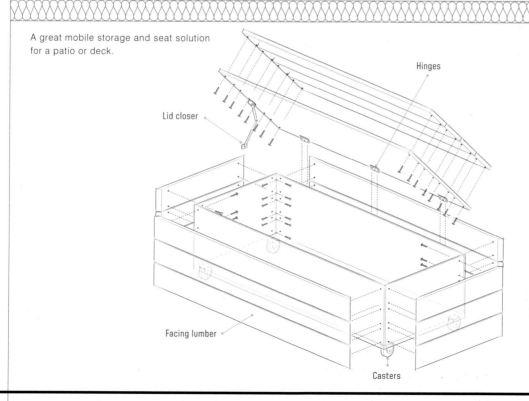

A great mobile storage and seat solution for a patio or deck.

Hinges

Lid closer

Facing lumber

Casters

The third board or bottom piece should be above the floor to enable your casters to roll smoothly. If you wish to have a larger gap at the base you can add an additional piece of plywood between the caster and the base of the plywood box.

6
Cut four 1x6 boards for the lid. Measure and cut them an inch or two longer than the sides so to create an overhang. This also enables you to easily lift off the lid.

7
Using 1¼-inch galvanized wood screws, attach the four 1x6 boards to the plywood lid. Space them ¼ inch apart and fasten them from the underside with the rear board flush with the long side. This enables you to place the unit hard against a wall and use a set of hinges if desired. The best way to fasten the boards is to have the plywood placed evenly on top of the boards. Use clamps to help you fasten each board.

8
Drill four ¾-inch holes in the base of the unit to enable water to escape. Add a small piece of screen mesh over the holes so our eight-legged friends do not come for a visit.

9
Place the lid on top, and you are pretty much done. You can add rustproof hinges. You might also add a soft lid closer, both for convenience and for the protection of little fingers.

10
Lightly sand the corners and apply a final coat of sealer. Then stand back and admire what you have just created!

EXPAND A TINY BALCONY

If the idea of building a storage bench for your deck seems impossible, because, well, you don't have a deck, don't despair. For those of you who have a balcony or terrace, take heart. A sliver of outdoor space can become a slice of solitude and sun. Here are some ideas:

+ Whatever is on the balcony should look good when you're inside your home. A garden sculpture or Japanese garden lantern can be left out all year, doesn't need watering, and tricks the eye by expanding the space of your living room.

+ A similar-colored exterior floor covering that matches the internal floor can help visually expand the appearance.

+ Floating shelves (see page 78) placed at side-table height can hold a drink and free up floor space.

+ Sturdy plant hooks anchored into the ceiling can hold small plants without taking up floor space.

+ Lighting is important—install clear strip or string lighting along the railing and along the ceiling. If possible, install an outdoor overhead fixture to make the space even more usable on warm evenings.

+ Miniature evergreens planted in small decorative frost-proof pots provide a bit of color through the seasons.

+ One or two metal folding café chairs with weatherproof cushions provide seating that can be stored flat when necessary. (Caution: lightweight patio furniture can often go airborne in high winds!)

+ A surrounding ledge used as a planter or as a display for potted plants can serve two purposes. When you entertain, this ledge will also act as a seating area.

NOTE: Never position your storage bench near a guard railing as a small child may climb on top of it!

UNDER-DECK STORAGE RACK

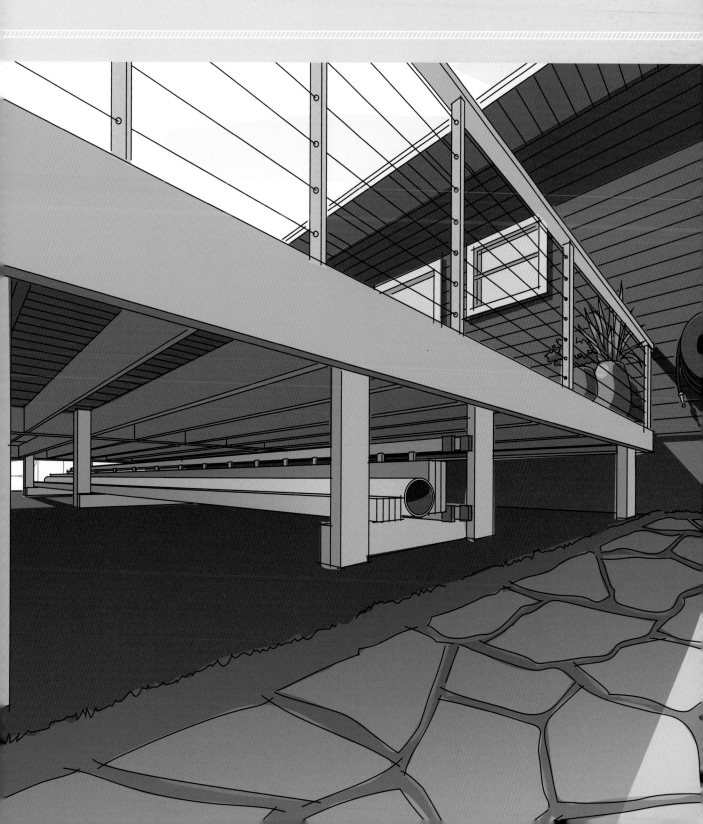

UNDER-DECK STORAGE RACK

If you have a wood deck with an open underside, that space is just too valuable not to take advantage of! But it is never a good idea just to throw your stuff on the ground under a deck: everything will pile up, making it difficult to pull out the bottom item, and it will also be subject to trapped moisture.

So a suspended rack or two is the way to go. This simple-yet-practical project provides a great way to store many odd-shaped items, from ladders and lumber to shovels and rakes, and so on. In the process, you'll free up garage space, yard space, and decks.

TIME:
1.5 hours

DIFFICULTY:

TOOLS:
Tape measure

Circular saw

Hammer

Framing square

Drill/driver with ⅜-inch drill bit

Wrench

2 quick grip clamps

4-foot level

Pencil

Safety glasses

Ear protection

MATERIALS:
3 to 4 pieces 2x4 lumber (either pressure-treated pine, or redwood or cedar cut to 8-foot lengths)

HARDWARE:
1 box 3⅜-inch galvanized bolts, nuts, and washers

1 box 3-inch galvanized nails

MAKE THAT SPACE HAPPEN

1 . . . .
Measure the length of what you want to store. As a rule of thumb, if the longest item is 5 feet or so, you need only two U-shaped frames; if it's heavy and longer than 6 feet, consider adding a third U-shaped frame to support the middle. If you have shorter items to store as well, you could add planks between the U-frames to make a platform.

2 . . . .
Measure under your deck: What is the clearance between the ground and the deck? Also, what is the distance between deck joists that most nearly matches how wide you need the suspended rack to be? Using these measurements, figure the U-frame's width (so that it aligns with two joists) and height (so that it is raised at least a foot off the ground).

3 . . . .
Using a circular saw, cut the 2x4 so that each U-frame has two same-size "legs" (that match the desired height) and one bottom (that matches the desired width).

4 . . . .
To construct each U-frame, lay the three pieces on their sides on a flat surface in a U shape. Use a framing square to square each side.

5 . . . .
Use a drill with a ⅜-inch bit to drill two diagonal holes in each corner. With a wrench, add two bolts, washers, and nuts.

6 . . . .
Lift up each U-frame to the underside of your deck area. Use a level to mark the position of the frame legs on the joists, so the U-frames will hang square and level, individually and relative to each other. Ideally, position one end of the underside rack near the end or edge of the deck, to make access easier. Ensure the U-frames are in line and the same height. Use your clamps to hold the frames in position while drilling two holes diagonally through the tops of the U-frame legs and joists. With a wrench add two bolts, washers, and nuts to each leg.

7 . . . .
Time to stash your outdoor stuff!

Exploded view of simple storage rack construction.

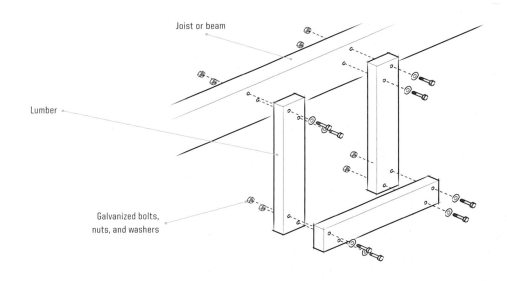

Joist or beam

Lumber

Galvanized bolts,
nuts, and washers

PROJECT:

A SHED BECOMES A
GUEST HOUSE

A SHED BECOMES A GUEST HOUSE

Ready-made sheds are available at many larger garden centers and home stores across the country. They are delivered to a level spot on your property and are ready to use. Often sided with a wood product called T1-11, and sometimes cedar shakes, these sheds come with small shuttered windows and doors. They come in many sizes. A small shed has enough space to house a desk, a chair, and bookshelves for a writer's retreat, or a single bed and dresser ample enough for an overnight visitor. First, however, you have to make a barebones shed livable. This is not difficult, but it does involve some skill. A permit may be required; check with your community before beginning.

TIP: Order a standard door with lights (glass) instead of a barn door opening to make the shed more inviting and practical as a living space. Also consider placing the shed close to a doorway of your home; then, you can later add a connecting roof to keep dry during inclement weather.

TIME:

A weekend to a week, depending on projects

DIFFICULTY:

⇑⇑ TO ⇑⇑⇑⇑

depending on projects

TOOLS:

Depends on project, but at minimum:

Tape measure

Staple gun

Nail gun

Drill/driver with bits

Drywall saw

Utility knife

4-foot level

Paintbrushes, rollers, and trays

Pencil

Face mask

Work gloves

Hammer

Safety glasses

MATERIALS:

Depends on project, but at minimum:

Drywall

Insulation

Staples

Drywall screws

Drywall tape, compound, and topping compound

Primer and paint

MAKE THAT SPACE HAPPEN

1...
Light and heat (or air-conditioning) are important features of a comfortable shed. A licensed electrician can run electricity to the shed. You can save money by purchasing all the necessary supplies: wire to the code in your state, an additional circuit breaker for your home's main box, outlets, wall switches, sconce or overhead light fixtures, and/or a fan fixture. You may also want to run cable for television or the Internet (if your wireless service does not reach to the location of your shed).

2...
Insulate and finish the walls. Most sheds come with open studs, so closing them up with drywall will make the space seem more like a real room (see Project: Wall Construction—Make One Room into Two, page 195). Leave some of the studs open for shelving. You can also add baseboard trim to really finish the "house" and give it a genuinely habitable look.

3...
Standard sheds have floors made of marine-grade plywood—the easiest floor option is to paint it and then cover it with a rug. Nicer options are to install pine wood plank flooring sealed with tung oil for a natural look. Tile or slate is another durable option (see Project: Storage Island, page 62, for help with tiling); this could be the perfect opportunity to develop your tiling skills. Another easy option is indoor/outdoor carpet tile. The Flor Company (Flor.com) makes several styles.

4...
A freestanding quartz infrared heater can be plugged into a socket and will keep the shed very toasty in the cooler months for very little cost. These small heaters are extremely efficient, do not get dangerously hot (as many conventional space heaters do), and, at just 14 inches high and wide, take up minimal floor space. EdenPURE is a good source (Edenpure.com). Likewise, a portable air-conditioner could be helpful, but, in such a small space, a ceiling or window fan may be just as successful at keeping you cool.

5...
Then, just furnish the room—and move in!

RESOURCES & SUPPLIERS

ARCHITECTURAL FITTINGS

Salter Spiral Stair
Complete spiral staircase kits in a variety of styles
Web site: Salterspiralstair.com
Available internationally

Simpson Door Company
A full line of ready-made doors and custom options
Web site: Simpsondoor.com
Available in North America

VELUX
Highly efficient windows, leak-free skylights, sun tunnels, and shades
Web site: Velux.com
Available internationally

Werner
A line of pull-down attic ladders for new and existing homes
Web site: Wernerladder.com
Available internationally

CABINETRY, FLOORING, AND FIXTURES

Kohler
Kitchen and bath products, engines and power generation systems, cabinetry, tile, and home interiors
Web site: Kohler.com
Available internationally

PORCELANOSA
A complete line of stone, wood, and ceramic flooring, as well as kitchen and bath fixtures and cabinets
Web site: Porcelanosa.com
Available internationally

THOMASVILLE CABINETRY
Cabinets for the entire home.
Web site: Thomasvillecabinetry.com
Available internationally

FURNITURE AND APPLIANCES

DirectBuy

Membership club offering a full line of furniture, appliances, and home decorating materials
Web site: DirectBuy.com
Available in North America

Modern Line Furniture

Movable furniture including sectional sofas, chairs, tables, beds, and night stands
Web site: Modernlinefurniture.com
Available in North America

HARDWARE

Blum

Hidden hinges, drawer systems, assembly hardware, specialty items including pocket door hardware and leg levelers, organizational aids, and knobs and pulls
Web site: Blum.com
Available internationally

C. R. Laurence Co., Inc.

Large selection of railing systems, glazing, and architectural hardware
Web site: Crlaurence.com
Available internationally

Häfele

Furniture fixtures, architectural hardware
Web site: Hafele.com
Available internationally

Emtek

Complete line of high-end door hardware
Web site: Emtek.com
Available in North America

MATERIALS

Benjamin Moore

Full line of paints, primers, and stains, including low- and no-VOC paints
Web site: Benjaminmoore.com
Available internationally

LATICRETE

Full line of green adhesives and other installation products for tile and stone
Web site: Laticrete.com
Available internationally

Leviton Manufacturing

Electrical and wiring solutions for lighting, home entertainment, home networking systems, and more
Web site: Leviton.com
Available internationally

OFF- AND ON-SITE STORAGE OPTIONS

1-800-Pack-Rat

Portable storage units and moving services
Web site: 1800packrat.com
Available in the United States

SALVAGE AND REUSE CENTERS

For information about European and international salvage and reuse centers, check RREUSE at http://rreuse.org/t3/. RREUSE is a European umbrella for social enterprises with activities in reuse, repair, and recycling. RREUSE's members are national and regional social economy networks that combine both social and environmental objectives and give them equal emphasis. The following is a short list of reuse centers in the United States.

Build It Green! NYC

Sells reclaimed architectural items, kitchens, appliances, and tools
Web site: Bignyc.org
Store in New York

Green Demolitions

Collects and redistributes cabinets, fixtures, lighting, and architectural elements
Web site: Greendemolitions.org
Stores in Connecticut, New Jersey, New York, and Pennsylvania

Habitat for Humanity ReStore

Collects and sells salvage, including entire kitchens
Web site: Habitat.org/cd/env/restore.aspx
Stores throughout the United States

Murco Recycling Enterprises, Inc.

A mid-western demolition company that holds sales and auctions

Web site: Murco.net

Auctions primarily held in Illinois

Silverlake Architectural Salvage

Buys and sells a variety of items, from vintage molding to built-in Victorian cabinets

Web site: Silverlakearchitecturalsalvage.net

Store in California

SHEDS

Arrow Group Industries

Complete line of vinyl-coated steel, resin, wood, and steel sheds, garages, carports, patio covers, greenhouses, shelving, and accessories

Web site: Arrowsheds.com

Available internationally

Sheds USA

Vinyl, cedar, pine, and engineered sheds in a variety of styles and sizes

Web site: Shedsusa.com

Available in the Eastern United States

STORAGE SYSTEMS

Gladiator GarageWorks by Whirlpool Corporation

Innovative products to improve your garage—modular storage items including flooring and appliances built to handle harsh garage environments

Web site: Gladiatorgw.com

Available in North America

IKEA

DIY flat-pack storage units, shelving, and cabinetry

Web site: Ikea.com

Available internationally

Rev.a.shelf

Complete line of closet, drawer, and shelf storage systems; baskets; bars; bins; and built-ins

Web site: Rev-a-shelf.com

Available in North America

TOOLS

The following quality manufacturers offer a full line of cordless and plug-in power tools, spring tools, and other useful items including saws, nailers, hammers, sanders, grinders, drills, and table tools.

3M

Safety and DIY gear such as drop cloths, tape, masks, and goggles or safety glasses

Web site: 3m.com

Available internationally

Bosch Tools

Full line of power and table tools

Web site: Boschtools.com

Available internationally

Craftsman Tools

Full line of power and hand tools, tool accessories, and equipment, including top-quality garden equipment

Web site: Craftsman.com

Available internationally

Hitachi Koki U.S.A.

Full line of power tools

Web site: Hitachipowertools.com

Available internationally

Little Giant Ladder Company

Well-made household and professional-grade ladders

Web site: Littlegiantladder.com

Available in North America

Pacific Laser Systems

Levels, including my favorite, PLS 5 self-leveling tool

Web site: Plslaser.com

Available internationally through certified dealers

Rockwell

Full line of power tools

Web site: Rockwelltools.com

Available internationally

Spring Tools By Noxon

Spring-loaded tools, including nail sets

Web site: Springtools.com

Available internationally

ACKNOWLEDGMENTS

This book would not be a reality without the hard work, dedication, and support of the following people and organizations:

My beautiful mother, Patricia, for sitting me down at a young age and explaining to me that there is a bigger world outside of my suburban hometown of Dundas Valley near Sydney, Australia. I have never forgotten that conversation, and as a result, I have never stopped seeking out new adventures.

My old man, Stanley, for just being plain cool with whatever I wanted to do.

The support of my entire family back home in Australia. I love you all.

Karen Kelly, my angel, who helped me compile all of my knowledge and get it into words. Without you this book would have little color. It has been a dream to work with you!

Everyone at Chronicle Books has also been a dream to work with, especially Jodi Warshaw, Laura Lee Mattingly, Molly Jones, Michelle Clair, Jennifer Tolo Pierce, and Andrew Schapiro. You guys have made this experience a pleasure with great direction, patience, and advice.

Arthur Mount, for your great illustrations.

My agent Laura Nolan, for channeling me to Chronicle Books and Karen Kelly.

A big thanks to all of my fans and viewers, as it is your many questions that encouraged me to write this book, and made me aware of the need for this information.

Lastly and most importantly, thanks to my patient wife, Diane, and precious little boy, Kai, who have both had to endure the experience of living in our garage while I wrote this book right in the middle of building our house. You guys have been amazing and so uncomplaining. Many families would not have survived this ordeal. Diane, wasn't it your idea to move to the U.S.? Look what you made me do.

INDEX